Eleanor Robson played many important roles, in *Romeo and Juliet, In a Balcony, She Stoops To Conquer.* Her greatest popular success was in Israel Zangwill's *Merely Mary Ann.* When George Bernard Shaw saw her act in London, friendship followed. She tells of her last visit with him shortly before his death. Among many other letters included in this book is a generous number of hitherto unpublished letters from G.B.S. to her, some of them discussing *Major Barbara* which he wrote for her, but which, due to various complications, she never played.

After her success as Glad in *The Dawn of a Tomorrow,* a dramatization of Frances Hodgson Burnett's novel, she married Mr. Belmont. There followed a life of a completely different character: horses (it was she who christened Man o' War and his dam, Mahubah), polo, aviation, the development of her many activities in civic affairs and organizations to which she has devoted herself since her husband's death in 1924.

The fabric of Mrs. Belmont's memory is rich; its threads are sometimes somber but more often glowing with her own special kind of brightness which communicates itself to the reader in a book that is important for its fresh approach to historical happenings and warm in its constant awareness of the human beings that motivate them.

THE FABRIC OF MEMORY

ELEANOR ROBSON BELMONT

THE

FABRIC

OF

MEMORY

FARRAR, STRAUS AND CUDAHY

NEW YORK

ACKNOWLEDGMENTS

The core of this book lies in the letters it contains which are published here for the first time. Innumerable people in thought and deed have participated in its production. To all, my thanks are genuine but it will not be possible to mention the entire list.

Undoubtedly acknowledgment should go to G. Bernard Shaw whose letters and advice when I went to see him in Ayot St. Lawrence the year before he died started this record on its inky way.

To John Farrar I am deeply indebted for his friendly encouragement, professional guidance, and his unfailing patience, without which the present volume would never have appeared. A special note of gratitude is due to Margaret Farrar whose careful reading of the manuscript helped to correct or confirm many a wavering fact. I am also indebted to Diane Amussen for her constructive assistance in the early assembling of this material. To John Mason Brown who first and always insisted that the G. B. S. letters regarding *Major Barbara* should be published.

I should like to acknowledge with particular appreciation the permission granted by M. Elizabeth Barber, secretary of The

v

Society of Authors (London) to use the letters of G. B. Shaw and thank Archibald Henderson for identifying and granting permission to use the quotation from G. B. Shaw which appears at the opening of Part VIII of this book. My thanks are due to the National City Bank, Ltd. (Dublin) for permission to reprint a letter from Charlotte Frances (Mrs. G. B.) Shaw. I gratefully acknowledge the permission given by G. d'Andelot Belin and H. Bundy to use the letters and verses of Amy Lowell, and thanks are due to Samuel Foster Damon for permission to use that section of a letter by Miss Lowell to me that appears in his book, *Amy Lowell: A Chronicle;* to Mrs. Vivian Burnett for permission to use the letters of her mother-in-law, Frances Hodgson Burnett; to Katherine Garrison Chapin for permission to use her poem "Immortality" from her book *Outside of the World;* to Mrs. W. Murray Crane for permission to use a letter of her sister, Mabel Boardman; to Mrs. Richard Derby and William Cruikshank for permission to use the letters of Theodore Roosevelt.

I am indebted to Mrs. Winthrop Ames for permission to use the letters of her husband; to Lawrence H. Houston for permission to use the letters of his father, The Honorable D. Franklin Houston; Olivia James for permission to use the letters of The Hon. Lady Lindsay; to Hope Davis Kehrig for permission to use the letters and telegram of her father, Richard Harding Davis; to The Honorable Henry Cabot Lodge, Jr. for permission to use the letter of his grandfather, Senator Henry Cabot Lodge; Mrs. Leah H. Moses and Richard W. Fitch for permission to use the letters of Clyde Fitch; to Corinne Robinson Cole for permitting the use of her mother's verse about Ethel Barrymore; to Oliver Zangwill for permission to use the letters and cablegram of his father, Israel Zangwill. My thanks are extended to Dr. Bruno Walter; to Kirsten Flagstad; St. John Ervine; John William Rogers, and to the Dowager Marchioness of Reading, for permission to use their letters; to Irving Kolodin for permission to use the selection from his book *The Story of the Metropolitan Opera* and to Elizabeth Gilman for the passage from *Toscanini and Great Music* by her husband Lawrence Gilman.

This record is dedicated with admiration and gratitude to the devoted workers I have known, both professional and volunteer, in the field of social service and in the arts.

PART ONE

I count myself in nothing else so happy
As in a soul remembering my good friends . . .
—*Richard II*, Act II, Scene 3

BECAUSE SHE LOOKED BACK, we have been told, Lot's wife was turned into a pillar of salt. Probably she mingled too much regret with the long look over her shoulder. Yet it has always seemed to me that mortals should turn their thoughts backward. How else can we evaluate the past or hope to profit by individual or collective experience? That we do not look back often enough may explain why human beings seldom benefit from the experiences of others and learn little from their own mistakes.

Events move so rapidly these days that, just as in Wonderland, "it takes all the running you can do, to keep in the same place." Yet I like to remember what James M. Barrie said in an address to St. Andrews University: ". . . God gave us memory so that we might have roses in December."

Those whose lives have spanned the period from the late nineties to the middle fifties of the present century have seen an era of incredible achievement. They have also seen the universe descend to great depths of misery, due to what might be called the vast collective folly of mankind. They have witnessed a revolution in living, as well as a revolution of ideas. The survivors cannot treat casually either the misery involved in the change or the miracles of accomplishment.

One cold, foggy day many years ago, my mother left London and arrived in Wigan, Lancashire, to spend a few days with her mother, who was playing there in an English provincial company. My mother was expecting a baby in three or four weeks' time, and she had looked forward eagerly to this event. To her discomfiture and the inconvenience of everyone, the babe decided to see the world before the date; and so it happened that I was born in Wigan on the thirteenth of December. My father, who died during my infancy, was a musician, the conductor of a small orchestra. Several years later, Mother, who had married again, decided to try her fortune in this country. After a year's trial, it was my stepfather who returned to fetch me to America at the tender age of seven. I remember the sultry September heat, my new high button boots, *and* the swarming, hungry mosquitoes.

One day, after I had spent nearly six years in a convent school, a friend who was lunching with my mother asked, "When do you expect to graduate?"

"I finish school next month," I replied.

He looked at me gravely and said, "Education really begins, my dear, when you leave school." It was a startling thought. Mother had assured me he was a clever man; obviously he didn't know how much I knew.

That summer I traveled to San Francisco to join Mother, who was playing with the Frawley Stock Company, known from coast to coast as an outstanding group. My heart always goes out to youngsters in their teens who must earn a living, yet are uncertain of the road to take as they swing a groping antenna before them. Mother had persuaded Daniel Frawley to give me a chance, which offered at least an immediate objective. Fifteen dollars a week.

I crossed the continent in charge of the conductors, never before having seen the inside of a sleeping car. Railroad stations usually mean adventure to the young; the world expands as they watch humanity dashing off in every direction like sparks from a Catherine wheel.

Mother's friends took me to the train and explained the mystery of modest dressing in a lower berth. Then, looking about, they discovered that all the other occupants of this Pullman car were men, except for an elderly lady destined for Chicago. Anxiously they drew me into a platform conference, the burden of which was: "Be very careful, dear; it can be dangerous for young girls to talk to strange men, especially old ones."

The first night I was tortured with fear, shut in behind closed curtains. The train rushed so fast it seemed impossible that it could stay on the tracks. However, Pullman car procedure of dressing and undressing in one's berth became easier as time passed. Fear of my surroundings lifted as interest grew.

After the kind lady left at Chicago, the male occupants took over and showered the teen-ager with attention. A solicitous gray-haired gentleman frequently offered his services: Did I eat chocolates? "I have some candy." Magazines? "Thanks, I have books to read." Would I like a walk at the station? Every offer was politely but firmly declined. A backward look reveals that this gentleman was almost clerical in appearance, probably fifty-five, but at the time he seemed definitely in the "old" group.

Another passenger, however, I welcomed as a savior in the situation. This one was probably in his middle thirties. His approach was entirely different. Enthusiastically he described the beauty of California, the mountains covered with blue lupine and poppies, the steep hills of San Francisco, fish that swam in the waters near by and appeared in restaurants as tempting food; all were strange tales and fascinating. When he proposed that we get some air at the next train stop, I confidently paced up and down the platform by his side.

Shortly after my arrival in San Francisco, two of Mother's friends, Mr. and Mrs. S——, invited us to luncheon at the Baldwin Hotel. Suddenly I saw my friend of the train and darted across the lobby to greet him. Mother followed to express her appreciation for "your kindness to my little girl." As we returned, Mr. S—— said, "How in the world do you happen to know that man?" Mother explained the circumstances and asked what was wrong. "Nothing, really," was the reply, "only he is the most notorious gambler on the West Coast." As they talked on, I reflected that anyway he couldn't be too dangerous—he wasn't old.

The theatre at that time had no real interest for me, although my background might have indicated that this should be the profession to follow. My grandmother and mother were both of the theatre, and my stepfather, Augustus Cook, was an exceptionally fine character actor. Only one thing seemed to indicate any personal connection with the stage. We were told the Italian actress Eleonora Duse, whose accomplishments stirred me deeply, had turned gray when young in life, and at seventeen a definite gray streak was noticeable in my own chestnut-brown curls. Lifting the lock from my temple one day, I said dramatically, "Me and Duse."

Mother replied, without a smile, "That gives you plenty of room to grow, dear."

My hair went up in time for a first interview with the press. I have had an affection for people in this walk of life ever since, because of that "girl reporter's" kind treatment. Zona Gale was several years older than I, and she was trying her wings with a San Francisco newspaper. When we met again, she had become a most successful writer. Her Pulitzer prize story *Miss Lulu Bett* brought her fame and thousands of friends among readers, and later among theatregoers when she dramatized it. She was often referred to as birdlike, which probably irritated her considerably. She was small, quick in movement and speech, with a sparkle in her eyes; she was modest and unaffected, yet had a special kind of charm that swept you along with her mood.

It was presumed that I would have only small parts, ladies in waiting and the like. However, my first performance was in a play by David Belasco and Henry C. de Mille, *Men and Women*. The role allotted, Marjery Knox, was unusually important for a beginner, with a charming little love scene in the last act. One day at rehearsal William Lewers, the juvenile who played the scene with me, and I were on our knees facing each other, groping for a key or something dropped on the floor. The stage directions read: *Quickly he seizes both her hands and kisses her.* Mr. Lewers caught my hands, then drew back and said, "Miss

Robson, where would you like me to kiss you?" As I was always overready with a blush, this question produced a deep purple. Seeing my embarrassment, he added in a matter-of-fact tone, "You know, we might crack our skulls together if we don't settle this kissing business here and now." With dignity I indicated that my right ear would suffice.

On September 13, 1897, my opening night, Mother watched from the wings transfixed with fright, while on stage I apparently accepted the situation with complete calm and an expanding sense of pleasure in the friendly response of the audience. Mr. Frawley told her, "Don't worry; why, she's an old stager." Truth to tell, the old stager was blissfully unaware of the responsibilities involved, and so had relatively few qualms. These came with the years.

The friends in New York in whose care Mother had put me for holidays and after my graduation from the convent had been convinced that the stage trial would end in failure, therefore they agreed to tell no one of the attempt. Their story would be that I had gone away to visit my mother. Their dismal anticipation was based on my exceptional shyness, and the fact that my voice, as they expressed it, was sweet but low and unlikely to be heard in the theatre.

Mother had refused to allow me to take elocution lessons in school, partly for reasons of economy, also because she had a theory that such instructors only teach students to elocute.

Fortunately, the reviewers said that my assets were naturalness and sincerity, and that the voice was well placed and the English diction gave it carrying power.

2

DIFFERENCES in audience reaction have always fascinated me. Just how far can one go to produce laughter or tears before the former becomes burlesque and the latter maudlin buncombe? The line between laughter and tears is very slender indeed, and some situations are so delicate that overemphasis may turn what is intended to be tender emotion into a ribald snicker or outright laughter. Musicians have a measure of detachment: the individual instrument, piano, voice, or violin is the medium through which they operate. With actors the approach is direct. The audience, their instrument, resembles an organ having many stops to be played upon, and each performance presents a new instrument. Only by unceasing experiments can one measure accurately how to expand or contract a scene without changing a word. Some audiences are cold and need "warming up," while others are too impulsively responsive and require restraining. To control a laugh till just the right moment for it to break into spontaneous enjoyment, or to hold it off completely when the situation requires seriousness, takes skill.

An actor must communicate his author's given message— comedy, tragedy, serio-comedy; then comes his unique moment, as he is confronted by the looked-for, yet at times unexpected, reaction of the audience. This split second is his; he is in command of his medium; the effect vanishes into thin air; but that moment has a power all its own and, like power in any form, is stimulating and alluring.

The actor becomes involved without being responsible for a character. Naturally he doesn't have to be a murderer to interpret one who commits murder. An actor rides in a bus or railroad train; he sees a movement and applies it to a new role. A woman in agony of spirit *might* turn her head just so; a man in deep humiliation probably would wring his hands in such a way. From straws like these, drawn from completely different sources, the fabric of a character may be built. The whole garment in which the actor hides himself is made of small externals of observation fitted to his conception of a role.

It is shocking the way people force an actual love affair on a poet's life, frequently without any grounds for its existence, because he or she has had the gift to understand the human soul and its emotions under given circumstances. But so much of what poets write is "of imagination all compact"; the ability to picture what's in the mind's eye makes them different from the rest of us. The actor too can play with imagination and understanding roles that may be the antithesis of his own character.

3

ABOUT A MONTH after my arrival in San Francisco the leading ingenue, a tiny, exquisitely beautiful and clever actress, Gladys Wallis, lost her temper in an argument with Daniel Frawley, the actor-manager of the company, about being on time for rehearsals. She resigned in a huff as the company was about to sail for Honolulu, where a repertory of thirteen performances including matinees was planned over a period of three weeks. Another ingenue was hurriedly found by Blanche Bates, our leading lady, who starred in *Madame Butterfly* and *The Girl of the Golden West* when David Belasco produced them for the theatre.

The ocean, at first poetically impressive, speedily became enemy number one. Why anyone ever called it the Pacific Ocean has always remained a mystery. My eighteenth birthday was spent in utter wretchedness as the ship dipped and rolled dizzily about on a bad-tempered sea. After the company landed, the new ingenue, as a result of the unusually bad crossing and other complications, became seriously ill, with the result that parts which should have belonged to an experienced actress were thrust upon me, as obviously no agency for ingenues was available in Honolulu. Gladys Wallis, whose burst of temper thus provided my first real opportunity, was married a year or so later to Samuel Insull of Chicago. His career, alas, was a typhoid-fever chart of heights and depths.

Princess Kaiulani, niece of the deposed Queen Liliuokalani, was on the steamer going to Honolulu. The Princess, recently engaged to be married, was returning to her native land from school in England. Charming parties were arranged to welcome her, to which members of the Frawley company were invited.

Tall hibiscus hedges in gay pink-and-white bloom lined the roads and huge flowering trees decorated the lawns on this enchanting island. At night the trees, festooned with innumerable candle-lighted lanterns and aided by Hawaiian moonlight, resembled fairyland. Beautiful dark faces of the natives, crowned with gay multicolored bandannas, were framed in every window, smiling as they watched their beloved Princess and the rest of us dancing until dawn and after.

One beautiful cloudless day when I longed to be surf bathing on the then unspoiled beach at Waikiki, I stood, instead, while Mother and a seamstress hurriedly put together the dresses which I was to wear three nights later in William Gillette's famous Civil War play, *Held by the Enemy.* As they cut, pinned, and fitted five dresses, I studied, manuscript in hand, the part of the beguiling rebel, Susan. No less than sixty pages had to be memorized, with a Southern accent for good measure.

The company presented a different play every other night for three weeks. All but two of them held parts for me. Mother said I seemed not to study but to absorb the lines—in any case they pronounced me letter perfect when the engagement ended in Hawaii. Memories of the kindness and the beauty found there linger; they have outlived the fatigue and the grueling hard work of those early days in the theatre.

On the return to San Francisco, Mr. Frawley, with compliments on my work in Honolulu, engaged me as ingenue of the company, with a salary raised from $15 to the glittering height of $35 a week. This was an accolade, indeed.

We traveled from San Francisco to British Columbia, with its magnificent scenery, then back down the coast and east to Memphis, where, because of a flood, our train crawled over submerged tracks held in place by crossed logs and sand bags. The trees looked like shrubs and the telephone wires swayed coquettishly just above the water level. The tour ended in New Orleans during Mardi Gras. Looking back over those first seven months, I realized that education had begun in earnest—it even seemed to gallop apace.

4

THEN FOLLOWED two years in Milwaukee. The stock company's season there was fifty-two weeks. My schedule ran fifty weeks, only two out of the cast, with parts ranging from six lines, to

Fanchon, the Cricket, and other leading roles: eighty parts in two years. A marvelous training for a serious student bound up in ten performances a week, including three matinees—Wednesday, Saturday, and Sunday. My salary, still $35 a week, had to cover living expenses plus dresses for all except costume parts, which the company provided. Naturally, there were not many costume plays scheduled.

The first season, when Mother had not heard for some weeks, she anxiously asked a friend to look in on me in Milwaukee as casually as possible. She reported, "The company likes her; the public likes her. Your child is really doing very well—at least as well as could be expected on tea and toast for three meals a day, three weeks at a time." Mother immediately drew on her own slim resources to change the calorie balance. Somewhere I had read that Benjamin Franklin said, "Rather to go to bed supperless than to rise in debt." And it struck me as a good idea. Altogether it was a happy time. Discipline is good for the young.

During the second year in Milwaukee more important roles were assigned to me, of which Jane Eyre was one. At the end of an act when Jane and the hero, Rochester, confront each other in a dramatic clash of wills, she faints. I decided it would be a novelty to fall flat on my back as if felled by a stone. It was unbelievably effective from the audience's viewpoint, but for a matter of minutes I could not move to take curtain calls, even with assistance. After a time, the pain temporarily left me. The following year, when it became apparent that I had injured myself and needed surgery, Mother, who was playing in a stock company in Chicago, made arrangements for me to enter the Streeter Hospital, considered the best in the Midwest. This episode was the beginning of a rare friendship with Dr. John W. Streeter, who had established the hospital, and his family. One day about two weeks after the operation he came to my room to see me, still flat on my back. He and his younger daughter, Marjorie, about my age, were going to the races. He asked if I had read *Checkers—A Hard Luck Story*, a most popular tale by Henry M. Blossom, Jr. Checkers wins a fabulous sum at the races as the result of a long shot and is happy ever after—at least as far toward forever as the story goes.

Dr. Streeter invited me to join him in a gamble that day. If he found a long shot (twenty or thirty to one), *if* we bet $10 on the race, and *if* the horse won, it would wipe out my hospital bill! Suspecting that he realized it would take a long time for Mother and me to pay for the operation, I consented—provided that I paid my share in advance and provided that the newspapers showed a long shot had *won* a race that day. Strangely enough there was a long shot; stranger still, the long shot (thirty to one) romped in ahead. The net result—my bill after the operation and nearly three weeks in the hospital was $26 for medical supplies. The long shot took care of all the rest.

My friendship lasted beyond the lives of dear Dr. and Mrs. Streeter, and I gladly call their children and their children's children my friends.

If the young will take advice, mine would be: Never be afraid to meet to the hilt the demand of either work or friendship—two of life's major assets. Consider all friendship as a precious investment. Like life itself, it resembles a bank account. With some banks you get just what you have put in, some provide a modest percentage above capital deposited; occasionally you lose everything, and once in a rare while you find someone whose friendship provides an endowment for life. If you are fortunate enough to find such, "grapple them to thy soul with hoops of steel" and thank God on your knees fasting for the security that is yours.

5

CLYDE FITCH, David Belasco, and Henry C. de Mille, to mention a few Americans, held sway in our theatres at the time that Augustus Thomas was on his way to dramatizing every state in the Union. *Arizona* was produced under the management of Kirke La Shelle and Fred Hamlin of Chicago.

In August I was playing in stock at Elitch Gardens when La Shelle and Hamlin's office telegraphed that they needed

someone to succeed Olive May, who was leaving the cast of
Arizona after a successful initial run in Chicago. The part of
Bonita was gay, with serious moments that made for acting
contrasts. I accepted at once. It was an excellent company in-
cluding Theodore Roberts, Vincent Serrano, Lionel Barrymore,
Edgar Selwyn. Lionel took a hand in my education by intro-
ducing me to the works of Rudyard Kipling. He read aloud the
Jungle Books. As we jolted along, on one-night stands, we for-
got the uncomfortable road and reveled in the adventures of
Rikki-Tikki-Tavi, the song of the Bandar-log, and loved Wee
Willie Winkie with his "parkle crown."

When the engagement in Chicago ended, *Arizona* toured the
country until spring, with New York scheduled for the following autumn. When I asked at the end of the season for even a
tiny increase in salary (then $75 a week), Kirke La Shelle re-
fused, saying a New York opening should be sufficient advance.

Minnie Dupree, a friend of Mother's and a popular comedi-
enne, wanted to introduce me to important Broadway managers
before the New York opening; she argued that La Shelle-Hamlin
were centered in Chicago and had only one play. Accordingly
she took me to two or three leading business offices—"Not looking for anything, just a courtesy call," as she expressed it. When
we got to Liebler & Company, George Tyler, the producer and
controlling factor in the firm, greeted us. He was a short man,
stockily built, with a jovial, round face and sparkling gray eyes.
He was well liked by theatre folk. He aimed high artistically
and was noted for unusual loyalty to his people. In season and
out of season, he fondly tried to place old favorites, at times
oblivious of the passing years and the changing conditions in
acting methods.

All producers are gamblers, and there are few things less pre-
dictable than public reaction to plays. Mr. Tyler was an exceptional gambler among gamblers; he made and lost several fortunes. Twice he went through bankruptcy.

When Miss Dupree introduced me, he beamed cordially; to
our surprise, he knew my work. It developed that he had been
in Chicago the previous autumn, and Augustus Thomas had

taken him to see *Arizona*. At once he wanted to know my future plans—without, of course, interfering with my existing commitments. After a brief business discussion, he offered a five-year contract to start when the New York run of *Arizona* should be over. The salary would be $150 a week for the first two seasons. Two excited women reported these arrangements to Mother; we all agreed it had been a lucky day—the future looked rosy and secure. The very air seemed solid under my feet.

Arizona opened in September and was an immediate success. Mother and I rented an apartment and looked forward to a long, happy winter in New York. At the end of the second week, Mr. La Shelle sent for me to come to his office. Surprised but pleased, I went, thinking that at last he intended to yield to my previous request. Friends said the second year and my success in the part warranted a salary increase. Mr. La Shelle had no such idea.

He had heard a rumor that I had signed a contract with Liebler & Company for the following year. Was it true? I replied that it was no secret. He had previously told me he had nothing but the part of Bonita in *Arizona* when the play left Broadway. I said that I was young and could not learn my profession by continuing to play one part for three years. Bitterly angry, he stated that it was essential to have the New York cast when the play went on tour, and forthwith he gave me two weeks' notice and engaged someone to replace me.

This seemed not only unfair—it was tragic—mid-October with an apartment on my hands and the next engagement a year away. The company was up in arms; some members urged me to sue. Wiser ones advised that to sue a manager would only arouse antagonism among other managers, particularly if I won the suit. Besides, I had not the money to pay for a good lawyer.

Mother had a favorite proverb that she trotted out from time to time to impress me when I was rebellious about something. "Be grateful, dear, for the blessings that fly over your head," she would say.

This statement lacked conviction to youthful ears. "But if it is a blessing, why should I be grateful when it passes me by?"

To illustrate, she gave this example. Once it was imperative for her to keep an important theatre engagement in Scotland. It meant livelihood (a blessing even youth could understand) and she had a ticket on the crack express from Edinburgh. She missed it by seconds and stood weeping on the station platform as the train slipped away without her.

Everyone on the Scottish express was lost that night when the Tay Bridge collapsed in one of the worst train wrecks in British history.

Perhaps age alone can make us accept and be grateful for the blessings that fly over us, *when* they fly. At the time I couldn't reconcile myself to my abrupt dismissal, yet in retrospect it was indeed a flying blessing.

When informed of Mr. La Shelle's action, George Tyler promptly redated our contract to begin at once. Although he had nothing at the moment, shortly afterward he cast me as Flossie Williams in Judge Robert Grant's play *Unleavened Bread*, which was going into rehearsal.

There was a saying in the theatre, "Some parts are so good they are actor-proof; and some are bullet-proof." The part of Flossie Williams was bullet-proof. Two short scenes were all, but in each she scored a triumph over the star part of Selma, played by Elizabeth (Bessie) Tyree. The second scene, a thrilling battle of words between the two women, provided the only time in my career when a scene call came my way. The audience wouldn't let the act continue until they had registered their approval. Artistically, scene calls interrupt the action of a play; to an actor, they are peaches and cream.

6

ADA DWYER, a favorite daughter of Salt Lake City, Utah, was a skillful actress, but above all, a marvelous human being who had a definite influence on my life. Sixteen or seventeen years my senior, she had been a friend of Mother's from the time I was eight years old.

Our paths in the theatre and our friendship were coupled

when Mr. Tyler, my new manager, decided to produce Browning's *In a Balcony*. From that moment until I left the stage, Ada Dwyer was always at my side, on stage and in reality—a guide, philosopher, and friend. Her devotion held in it some portion of the tenderness she longed to shower upon the little daughter she idolized, but could not have with her. A player's life being the roving existence that it is, Ada's daughter Lorna Russell lived with her grandparents and her mother's sisters in the family home Ada maintained for them all in Salt Lake City, until the child went to school in England in her teens.

Ada's father, James Dwyer, had taken his sweet-natured young bride across the continent in a covered wagon to Salt Lake City, where Brigham Young had just started his trail-blazing Mormon experiment. Ada's pithy stories about this parent left the impression that although definitely born Irish, with a pronounced brogue to show for it, he might easily have been the spiritual twin of Clarence Day's father or Cyril Maude's artistic interpretation of Grumpy.

He established Dwyer's Book Store, the first bookstore in the West. Ada remembered buying trips to Boston with him, which began when she was eight years old. She would perch on a chair, dangling her legs, reading books by the hour while her father made his selection from offerings of eastern publishers. Love of books began at an early age. Her knowledge of the finest works in the English language made her an educational force in the truest sense of the word. But unquestionably her greatest asset was a warm, radiant love of people which she distributed generously, as a philanthropist pours out his accepted form of wealth.

7

IN THOSE DAYS, Sarah Cowell Le Moyne was the greatest exponent of Robert Browning; her beautiful interpretative readings drew large audiences of the intelligentsia. Mr. Tyler, a man with royal aspirations to produce the best in the theatre, decided to transplant this unique lecture-platform specialist to stardom on the stage. Her choice was *In a Balcony*. Mrs. Le Moyne naturally was cast as the Queen, Otis Skinner, Norbert; Julia Marlowe was selected as Constance. When the play came to rehearsal, Miss Marlowe was unavailable, and Constance unexpectedly fell to my lot. This poetic drama only plays about ninety minutes, so William Butler Yeats's *Land of Heart's Desire* was used as a curtain raiser, in which Mabel Talliaferro was the exquisite fairy and Ada Dwyer played the Irish peasant woman. That spring the company had a triumphal artistic tour from New York to the West Coast.

When we returned to New York shortly after a summer holiday, my business manager asked if Mother and I would listen to a play which interested him. It was a dramatization by an unknown author, Anne Crawford Flexner, of the book *Mrs. Wiggs of the Cabbage Patch*. Mr. Tyler hesitated to produce it because the social plays of Pinero and Clyde Fitch and others were the vogue, while this heroine, Mrs. Wiggs, was a *middle-aged* woman, and her companion characters were people on the *other* side of the railroad track. He read the play. We laughed; we cried; and with enthusiasm we prophesied that as a money-maker, it would be another *David Harum*. Mother joyfully accepted the title role and was acclaimed all over the United States and in England, where glowing notices were accorded her. For example, *The London Times* reported: "Curtain fell on a volley of cheering. Mrs. Cook is nothing short of perfection; she plays Mrs. Wiggs with exquisite art. Humor and pathos come equally easy to her."

The London *Daily Mail:* "Madge Carr Cook's acting was brilliant, an evening of sheer delight . . . audience went mad over her."

Mrs. Wiggs ran and ran, and revived, *ran* again, on stage and screen, making a fortune for her producer and, of course, a tidy compensation for both Alice Hegan Rice, her creator, and the dramatist, who was the wife of Abraham Flexner, a distinguished educator. I can hear Mother's sweet voice, soft with sympathy, yet gay with good cheer, as she consoled her mournful and ever-complaining neighbor, "Now, now, Miss Hazy, don't take on so. Ain't yer *glad* yer haven't got a harelip?"

8

A FINE PROFILE is indubitably a great asset to an actor. Kyrle Bellew presented his to admiring audiences and to dispassionate cameras with genuine success. On stage he carried himself so skillfully that inches were added to his rather short, slender figure; as a further asset, he fenced with the skill and grace of a professional. He was a natural choice for *A Gentleman of France,* in which Ada and I played with him for more than a year. The staircase scene, where he rescued Mademoiselle (myself) and her duenna (Ada Dwyer) with a lunge here, a parry there of his flashing sword, fighting off ten, a dozen—or was it twenty men?—was always stirring, although we saw it eight times a week. How the audiences loved it!

One of Mr. Tyler's grand old actors played Henry of Navarre. Poor soul, he had had a new set of upper dentures installed recently, and they didn't fit. Only affectionate respect kept us from laughing in his kingly face as he clucked his way through difficult speeches. One night the teeth made a desperate effort to escape; he gulped wildly and clutched at his mouth. His next line was addressed haughtily over my head to the Gentleman of France: "Am I an intruder at an assignation, sir?" Any one must admit this is not an easy line to speak, with or without false teeth. The audience saw the rebellious dentures and together we all laughed heartily as the curtain came down. The last lines of the scene were not heard that night.

Kyrle Bellew strutted somewhat, and intoned his lines even years later when he played Raffles with great success, for he made a most beautiful burglar. He was a conservative, gentle human being, unfailingly kind to me, a beginner; yet, true to human pattern, he had his dislikes. One of them was Beerbohm Tree, who frequently was pompous. Like most leading actors, Tree yearned to, and finally did, play Hamlet. From all accounts, no one in England wished to remember the fact, except the actor himself.

Autograph albums were very fashionable in those days. Stars whose names appeared in bright lights signed them automatically as they flowed by. In one such treasure book the erstwhile Hamlet had written with a flourish, *"This is I, Hamlet the Dane"* —*Beerbohm Tree.* The same album was later presented to Bellew for his signature. He told me, with evident relish, that he ignored the fresh page allotted to him and wrote under Tree's quotation: *" 'Tis true 'tis pity; and pity 'tis 'tis true."—Kyrle Bellew.*

This gallant gentleman cherished a lifelong devotion to Cora Urquhart Potter, and wrote poems by the score extolling her charms. One anniversary, K.B. produced a beautifully bound book. The poems were handwritten on vellum; a golden chalice illuminated the flyleaf (her initials were CUP); the next page carried the dedication: "In thy dear friendship all God gives I know." Ada Dwyer was his confidante and counselor for these poetic effusions, as she, in years to come, became the counselor and literary executor for Amy Lowell.

The next season came *Audrey,* a dramatization by Harriet Ford of Mary Johnston's popular book. Now for the first time my name went into the program in larger letters than those of the rest of the cast; in other words, Eleanor Robson was "featured." *Audrey* was not a good play, but it brought into my life a charming friend, Mary Johnston. To look at her it seemed impossible that this delicate Virginian, this wide-eyed ethereal creature could have written bold, heroic stories like *To Have and to Hold* and *Audrey.* We corresponded and occasionally visited as long as she lived.

I remember *Audrey's* opening night; it was in Richmond, where Mary Johnston lived. She sat in a box like someone in a trance, enthralled to see her visionary brain creations take life and appear flesh and blood before her. My dressing room, as is customary in the theatre on opening nights, was festooned with telegrams and good luck messages. The peak of joyous excitement was caused by a telegram from Eleonora Duse, whose magnificent acting in D'Annunzio's plays left imperishable memories for those who saw them.

NOV 17/02

UNION STATION   BALTIMORE   MD
I MIGLIORI AUGURI PER IL SUO SUCCESSO STASERA.

ELEONORA DUSE

Audrey went on tour in the Deep South through threatening floods, where to my horror and the distress of everyone, I came down with a severe case of mumps on both sides of my throat. It was the winter of *my* discontent. The company had to lay off for ten days. Sarah, our sturdy wardrobe mistress, tramped through miles of mud from farm to farm trying to secure fresh eggs, because a friend had written that as I couldn't eat, I must swallow twelve eggs a day to keep up my strength. Fortunately twelve eggs a day were never available.

The hero of the play had a line, "Audrey of the eyes, Audrey of the hair, Audrey of the full, brown throat." I was very slender, had plenty of hair and large blue eyes. On my return to the cast after the mumps, it was the first time that the salutation of the "full, brown throat" was justified. When the leading man saw those extensive lumps on either side of my naturally square jaw, he choked as if a crumb had gone the wrong way.

Ada Dwyer faithfully rubbed and massaged those swollen glands until they returned to normal. When one is grown up, mumps can be both painful and embarrassing.

Mr. Tyler declared that I was the despair of every press agent he assigned to cover these tours. As it is to many other women, personal publicity aside from performances was distasteful to me. One agent with a highly developed imagination, after making a racing yachtsman of Kyrle Bellew, produced a story which presented me as a passionate duck hunter who sought the marshes whenever possible and never missed the mark.

Indignantly I insisted on a retraction, stating that I had never shot a duck in my life and was opposed to the practice. "You'll never make a star," Mr. Tyler said gloomily.

"I'll never make a duck hunter, either," I predicted, thus limiting both fields of operation. The truth, stripped of fancy, was undramatic and lacked news value.

9

THAT WINTER our manager decided upon an all-star cast of *Romeo and Juliet* for Kyrle Bellew and myself. The spring tour was to consist of three weeks in New York followed by three weeks of one or two nights in the big eastern cities. I had never even seen the play, so a fine Shakespearian actor, Eben Plymton, joined the company in Texas to travel with us for two weeks to coach me in the part. He played Mercutio and was the best in my memory.

What an ordeal that experience was! We closed *Audrey* in New Orleans, traveled to New York where the rest of the cast were already working. Two weeks of rehearsal and fitting clothes faced me before the opening.

Each star, realizing my inexperience, undertook to advise me what was traditional; how Neilson always did this at a certain point, Cora Potter did thus and so, and Julia Marlowe that. My first magazine article bore the title "Hang Up Tradition"; sadly I told Ada Dwyer (our Lady Capulet) that, in the words of Romeo, I longed to "shake the yoke of inauspicious stars from this world-wearied flesh."

The youngest actress to essay the role in America, I stubbornly insisted on playing scene 2 Act III, usually cut to conserve the artist's strength.

For me the "Gallop apace" scene held the key to the potion scene, and poetry that was a joy past joy to say.

The *Audrey* tour through the Deep South, mumps, the long hours of rehearsing Juliet by day and acting *Audrey* at night, proved too great a strain. The doctor insisted, after the New York engagement, on a two weeks' rest before we went on tour for the final three weeks of *Romeo and Juliet*. As to the performance—people were kind and Mr. Tyler thought he had found a successor to Julia Marlowe in Shakespearian roles.

Mary Johnston wrote:

THE HOMESTEAD
HOT SPRINGS, VA.

My dear and veritable Dream Child

I have been very ill—ill through all your New York sojourn—or I also should have added my pipe of praise. And they say that you also have been ill! Now for a moment imagine me thy nurse and listen to me daughter of the Capulets! Be reasonable. Hist in thy ear!—He's not worth it. ('Peter! some aqua-vita!') Better marry Mercutio. Don't you know you have no business to work so hard when you've very little more physique than I have who, when I'm not up to mark, airily toss aside contracts, publishers, serials, editors and the public, and stroll, unincumbered (*sic*), down to the Bahamas or up to the Hot [Springs]? Dear child; rest now, and come back to us refreshed, elastic, as dewy as a rose in morn. Take care of yourself in that hurly-burly of a life which you lead, keeping a backwater still and deep, for yourself, for the great genius which gave you of His own, and for old friends. Am I taking a liberty? I am afraid that I am, and I hope that I am not. But you see, I believe with Keats in sheer love for sheer beauty: and besides, knowing as I do how the writing of one book tells inevitably upon the character of the author, so I know that through your almost a year of *thought-out* work upon *Audrey* I have touched you, influenced your nature somewhere, in some slight degree . . .

I have been here some days spent largely in the company of my nurse, my maid and the dentist (that strikes me like a *partie carrée* out of Alice). . .

June   *I can't think of the date.*

The whole appearance of this letter revealed how seriously ill she had been and the effort it was to write.

10

THE THEATRE is the playground of the world, and the majority of authors are usually keen to write plays. Either they will create a part to the measure of an actor's talent, or they will seek an outstanding actor as one appointed by the gods to interpret a character already in the mind's eye. For one reason or another they have always found their way to the doorstep of successful actors, whose lives are thus immeasurably enriched.

During the London vacation in the summer of 1903, Israel Zangwill came to see me. He had recently written a beautiful, though financially unsuccessful, play called *Children of the Ghetto*. It had been produced in the United States by George Tyler. Not long afterward Zangwill invited me to visit the London ghetto with him. I engaged a hansom cab for the excursion, but he begged me to dismiss it, saying there would be a horrified stampede if he arrived at the ghetto in a hansom cab. As we jogged through the narrow streets of the East End on top of a bus, he inquired whether I had read his story about a London slavey. He quickly added, "Of course, you might not have seen it in America. It is only a small shilling book called *Merely Mary Ann*. I will send you a copy. Let me know if you think it would make a good play."

This remarkable man was notoriously absent-minded. He told me that one night before he was married, when he had bachelor rooms in the Inner Temple, he set out for an important dinner. Suddenly, as he walked along concentrating on ideas for a new play, he became aware that a group was following him, the boys jeering as they danced along the street. A bewildering realization that something was wrong came to the author, who thought himself unusually well turned out, for he wore white tie, tailcoat, and high silk hat. Unquestionably he was in fine attire, except for one quaint detail—he had on a pair of bright red flannel slippers.

He laughingly confided that until he married he never knew the meaning of a little loop of tape on the neck of a white dress shirt, which accounted for the fact that ties never stayed in place, but continually climbed in an adventuresome way over the top of his collar.

Zangwill is reported to have said of Bernard Shaw, "It is fine that he had such an exalted opinion of himself in this atheistic age when so few people believe in any God at all."

An outstanding author, Jerome K. Jerome, also ambled into my life about this time. I was on tour, where he followed me by appointment. A man of talent, eager to write plays, he had an idea for one that he wanted to develop for me. "Robina's Webb" was the title of the scenario, but later it became *Susan in Search of a Husband*. At the moment he was truly discouraged, and his depression increased when I gleefully proclaimed my enthusiasm for *Three Men in a Boat* "to say nothing of the dog." Poor man, he said he regretted that he had ever written that gloriously hilarious tale, because as a result "No one, positively no one, takes me seriously." As we sat at a six o'clock supper before my theatre performance, he presented a bedraggled appearance. His sandy blond hair, streaked with gray, had a moth-eaten look. Suffering from swollen granulated eyelids, he blinked and appeared to weep into his soup as he mourned the limits of serious public appreciation.

Zangwill, who had become a friend, listened attentively when I described the disillusionment that overwhelmed me after this first meeting with Jerome. To my explanation that I had been eager to meet him, as undoubtedly he was a man of genius, Zangwill looked quizzically through his heavy eyeglasses and said, "My dear, never want to meet geniuses. You will find the best of them in their books; when you meet them, they have such *unexpected* noses and mouths." Nature, in a mischievous mood, created Zangwill with a decidedly ugly exterior and placed therein a truly fine mind, subtle wit, and a great heart.

That autumn Mr. Tyler had two plays in the offing for me. Contracts had been signed, one by a Frenchman, Henry Bataille, author of *The Resurrection*. The other, *Agatha*, was a new play by Mrs. Humphry Ward. Mrs. Ward's books were very popular, and her famous stories were widely read, but she was keenly anxious to write a successful play. To embroider and develop the outline of "Agatha," she invited me to lunch and spend the afternoon at her lovely home, Stocks, in Tring. With me came Louis N. Parker, author of *Pomander Walk, Disraeli,* and other successes; he was to guide Mrs. Ward's footsteps in this particular drama adventure.

Mrs. Ward was busy when we arrived; her daughter Dorothy showed us around the garden, and I saw for the first time a ha-ha, a sunken boundary that prevents animals on the other side from crossing one's path, a common sight today in a modern zoo. Beyond this deep ditch were many cows and sheep grazing on a lush meadow, a beautiful sight. I had seen them in picture books, but never before in my own front yard. As we talked about changes that apparently would have to be made in the draft script, Dorothy kept repeating, "But remember, Mother has the final word," until it resembled an ominously uncomfortable litany.

Mrs. Ward herself was typically Victorian in appearance, tall and stately, with a genuinely pleasant, although somewhat overwhelming, personality. We were far from being inspired by *Agatha;* however, we were impressed by Mrs. Ward. When I inquired with interest how she wrote her books—did she wait for inspiration and then take up the pen—she replied, "Not at all. My family, of course, comes first. I give the household orders for the day; at nine-thirty I retire to my study, put my knees under the table, and stay there until time for lunch. Sometimes thoughts flow easily. Sometimes only a paragraph will be the morning's work."

The phrase *Mother has the final word* kept echoing in my mind.

As we left Tring behind, Louis Parker dispelled the awesome atmosphere when he christened our hostess "Ma-Hump." However, nothing satisfactory emerged from our several talks with Mrs. Ward or from Henry Bataille, who unfortunately was too ill to deliver a manuscript at this juncture.

I sent Mr. Tyler the booklet which Zangwill had given me and shyly urged that the author be commissioned to dramatize his story of the little London slavey. Zangwill was cabled; incredibly, within four weeks the manuscript arrived and was put into rehearsal. Three acts were comparatively perfect; only minor changes were made. The last act, unfortunately, was never satisfactory. Authors are usually reluctant to make changes, yet occasionally even the great ones accept a suggestion. As everyone knows there is an old saying in the theatre, "Plays are not written; they are rewritten."

> 5, ELM TREE ROAD,
> ST JOHN'S WOOD, N.W.
> September 1 1903.

Miss E. Robson.

Dear Miss Robson,

I found your letter on my return from the Zionist Congress and have carefully considered it. There are several reasons why the end of Act II in the play has to be different from the scene in the book. One is, the book gives a lot of soliloquy which is dramatically bad. It being therefore difficult to explain that Lancelot is not a mere vulgar corrupter of Mary Ann, it is necessary that she in her innocence should wish to follow him when he leaves, and this tempts him. Otherwise he would lose the audience's sympathy and they would not be so eager for him to marry her in Act IV. Also the entrance is mere misery, not the suppressed sobbing of Act III. Nevertheless, I find one valuable idea in your criticism and it probably is really the main thing that was in your mind, namely, that Mary Ann shall learn on the stage instead of off that he is going. A tiny alteration produces this great difference, as follows:—End of Lancelot's speech.

LANCE: Did I give her that too?

M.A.   (Brightly) Yessir.

LANCE: (Laughing on) How funny! for I did give her notice.

M.A.   (Tragically) Notice! You are going!

LANCE: Yes, thank God, etc. etc.

This change enables you to come on, as you wish, unconsciously instead of miserably, while your tragic acceptance of Lancelot's laughing news makes the acting opportunity you suggest. The rest of the scene is really much more theatrically touching than it is in the book. I am notifying Tyler of this change which I owe to you. I told him to tell you that your Act III had undergone considerable changes and I venture to think that you will find that without adding a word to your part of the climax, I have yet by a new idea worked it up much more tellingly for you. I am very glad to hear that you are getting fat for I have every confidence that your acting ability will produce an underfed impression. The fat will only be in your lines. My people join in kind regards to yourself and mother, and best wishes for the success of "Mary Ann" and "Mrs. Wiggs."

Yours sincerely,
I. Zangwill

P.S. You should get a copy of the final version of the play from Mr. Tyler at once as it differs slightly in a good many places. I am really obliged to you for your last suggestion, which we all feel is an improvement. As regards your playing it should be something classical which you play half-unconsciously as you talk to Lord Valentine. Really, it would be a piece of Lancelot's music, so you can make it up if you feel equal to it.

11

WHILE WAITING, Micawber-like, for something to turn up, Mr. Tyler, with a perennial fondness for bringing together a galaxy of stars, put on an all-star production of Sheridan's famous comedy, *She Stoops to Conquer*. Kyrle Bellew, well schooled in the classics, played Charles, while I was cast for Kate Hardcastle. Critics and audiences declared it a delightful production, and we all thoroughly enjoyed doing it.

In later years, when he had brought Ellis Jeffreys to New York, Mr. Tyler produced this comedy for her. She wrote saying,

"I have seen your pictures as Kate and I like the way you did your hair. Where did you get your curls?"

I answered, "God made mine, but they say that Oscar Bernner, the wig-maker, is very good."

Miss Jeffreys promptly replied, "Thanks for the address. God made a failure of mine, so I'll try Bernner."

Mary Ann, after due progress of time between Act III and Act IV, was transformed from a lodginghouse slavey into a cultivated young hostess at a dinner party. Elsie de Wolfe, in later years Lady Mendl, a friend of some years' standing and always an authority on smart clothes, chose Lucille, "The Lanvin of London," as the dressmaker above all others to make my evening dress. Lucille was Lady Duff-Gordon outside her office, a sister of Elinor Glyn, whose book *Three Weeks* later caused a ground swell on both sides of the Atlantic. Lucille turned out an enchanting creation—tier after tier of dainty pink chiffon ruffles, edged with a slightly deeper shade of narrow ribbon, that was a dream of simplicity and charm, all stitching hand done, as was the custom with every first-class couturière in those days.

12

ZANGWILL, in Avignon at work on a new play, *The Serio-Comic Governess,* resisted all appeals to rewrite the last act of *Mary Ann.*

AVIGNON
Dec 15/03

My dear Miss Robson,

I trust this will arrive before your New York triumph, & find you thoroughly content with the new fragment of your role. I really think your "entrance" (or sudden popping up)* will produce an electric effect, especially as you will handle it. I can't believe Mary Ann didn't from the first pop up like that—it seems so natural she should stand rebukingly aloof from "the smart set"—& the transition from

* From the piano.

the little slavey crying over her canary to the towering mistress of her own mansion is splendidly dramatic. I take it she would have been brooding miserably over the song, and would only gradually awaken to the conversation.

I am living in confident expectation of reading the same delightful things about you in the New York papers, as in all the others, & rejoice to learn you are to come to London & that I am to make Mary Ann's acquaintance after all. . . . Well, it seems superfluous to repeat my belief that Mary Ann (alias Miss Robson) will soon have New York at her feet. Don't be more nervous than your artistic temperament can help—human nature is the same even on Fifth Avenue, & there doesn't seem any human nature that can resist you. So with anticipatory congratulations & cordial gratitude for your hard work and good ideas, believe me to be— what I find from all the papers I am,

> Yours,
> Merely I Zangwill

P.S. This may even be in time to wish you a merry Christmas—not to mention a happy New Year.

After a brief tryout on the road, for *Mary Ann's* first performance in New York at the Madison Square Theatre, Zangwill cabled:

BACK OF CURTAIN   GIRL UNCERTAIN   CURTAIN RISES   SHE SURPRISES   CURTAIN FALLS   LONG RECALLS   CURTAIN DOWN   TALK OF TOWN

Our author's friendly doggerel describes the opening. The audience, at first chilly, waxed enthusiastic. Critics forgot to be critical and became poetical, using phrases such as: "The character of the naïve little London slavey is as delicate as the perfume of clover fields in spring."

Of his creation, Zangwill said: "To paint a beautiful, simple loyal soul as a slavey doesn't mean that every slavey is a Mary Ann. A beautiful soul is as exceptional in slaveys as in swells. Personally I never use my imagination to create impossible persons, merely to get inside the souls of real persons." In any case, *Mary Ann* flowered overnight and was taken into the hearts of a theatre-loving public.

13

OFTEN in memory's house, "there are many mansions." Usually the doors are closed. Some may even appear to be hermetically sealed by the passage of time, when suddenly an event, a sound, a glance, performs some abracadabra; doors mysteriously fly open and treasures of memory emerge, making wistful rainbows of light which illuminate the recesses of the past and draw them into the present. Once again past and present become a connected whole.

The news of Bernard Shaw's accident, a broken hip, in 1950, followed by his death some weeks later, evoked from his friends and acquaintances memories that had been shut away, presumably buried in the past. My own mind went back many years; to be exact, to the autumn of 1904, when a young actress arrived in London from the United States to present a play based on a simple story. The title page of the book and the billboards on the Duke of York's Theatre announced, *Merely Mary Ann* by Israel Zangwill.

The cast was exceptionally fine; even for those days of all-round good performances, when trained actors were plentiful. Henry Ainley, London's outstanding leading man, poetically handsome, resembling Lord Byron in appearance, played the struggling musician, Lancelot; Gerald du Maurier, the popular comedian, son of George du Maurier, deftly illuminated a small comedy part, Peter, with skill and indescribable charm. Ada Dwyer was the cockney lodginghouse keeper. We two were the only Americans in the London cast.

One night, shortly before our opening, the Henry Dickens *
family had taken Ada and me to see a new play by Henry Arthur Jones. It was thoroughly disappointing; no one cared for it and the gallery gods showed their disapproval by sustained

* Next to youngest son of Charles Dickens.

booing between the acts, a mournfully insulting sound. When the author, in response to calls from first night friends in the stalls, appeared before the curtain, the gallery again booed vigorously and at length. It suggested a terrifying experience if one had to face it.

Mr. Tyler had just arrived from the continent for last rehearsals and the opening of *Mary Ann*. Ada and I went to tea with him at Morley's Hotel on Trafalgar Square, in front of which stands the famous Admiral Nelson statue with four lions to guard him. Thoroughly frightened at the mere possibility of a booing reception if they didn't like our play, I made a plea that the opening be abandoned and that I be permitted to sail for home. In the midst of this agitating discussion, as they were endeavoring to reassure me, a waiter announced, "Mr. Shaw is calling to see you, sir."

Startled at the untimely interruption, Mr. Tyler answered, "Shaw, what Shaw?" The brilliant Irishman was not unknown to my manager, who had already produced *You Never Can Tell* for Arnold Daly, and special matinees of *Candida*.

As the two men chatted, any idea of returning immediately to the United States left my mind. A play by Barrie had been one of my dreams for some time. However, there was only a slim possibility of this coming to fruition. Charles Frohman had first call on every Barrie script for his lovely and deservedly popular stars, Maude Adams and Ethel Barrymore. Thought of a play by Shaw intrigued me. After this brief unexpected encounter, my hope grew apace and my courage zoomed back where it belonged.

Others met Shaw unexpectedly. William Archer, the distinguished critic and dramatist, first met Shaw, so they say, in the British Museum, where the brilliant Irishman confronted him with the score of *Lohengrin* in one hand and a sandwich in the other. Mr. Archer told me of one occasion when he met Shaw in a Turkish bath. To his amazement, Shaw had a complete and novel theory about the bath, which he said was the exact reverse of how any presumably well-regulated Turkish bath would be run. There must have been some reason why he didn't tell me Shaw's theory; in any case, I don't remember and I can't imagine what it might have been!

14

CONSTANCE FLETCHER had rented me her charming wee house on King Street. I called it a "Ha'penny Stamp to Kensington Square." Fashionable Kensington Square itself was spangled with celebrities. Several of these "ha'penny" houses lined part of King Street with their narrow, dark-green doors, each dotted with a polished brass knocker. Rumor had it that they had been used by the ladies in waiting when Queen Victoria and Prince Albert were in residence and held Court at Kensington Palace. When Miss Fletcher bought the house she told me the walls were lined with marbleized paper. Once this paper was carefully scraped off, there, as she had believed, were the charming original paneled walls. Miss Fletcher being a woman of taste, the house was delightfully furnished, and with it came two perfect maids who, in the renting language of the day, "would do for you altogether."

Water for our baths came from a medium-sized boiler standing at attention beside the tub. It was well named a geyser, for an intermittent hot spring came chortling, sputtering with boiling water, when it worked; when it didn't, it looked with cold disdain on our efforts. No wonder Britishers talk about bathing. It isn't so much that they bathe more than the rest of us, but that they do it regardless of difficulties.

During that period London was enthusiastically applauding plays from the fertile pens of Arthur Pinero, James M. Barrie, Arthur E. Jones, and George Bernard Shaw. Popular acclaim and box-office returns accorded leading places to Pinero and Barrie. Any successful actor or actress at that moment, confronted with the perennial problem of where to find a new play, would turn to these authors for material after studying the press and billboards.

In the early years of 1900, the theatres of London annually presented plays by Barrie and Pinero. Yet Bernard Shaw, a fairly new figure as a dramatist, was attracting considerable attention. Shaw's plays were shown first at the Royal Court Theatre in Malvern, a suburb of London. J. E. Vedrenne and Harley Granville-Barker were partners in this distinguished intellectual venture, an experimental repertory theatre started in 1904. "Caviar to the general," some people described it, but the elite of London eagerly made the difficult trek out of town every time a new play was produced there. Masefield, Galsworthy, Granville-Barker, and Shaw were the outstanding authors.

The average run at the Court was usually confined to two weeks and a series of matinees, to be followed, if the play proved successful, by an indefinite, and usually brief, engagement at an undesignated London theatre.

Following the successful London opening of *Merely Mary Ann*, at the Duke of York's Theatre, our American business manager, Walton Bradford, sent an invitation to Mr. Shaw, stating that a box or seats would be available for any performance he might wish to attend. A prompt answer said that Mr. Shaw never accepted courtesies of this nature. On the chance that such acceptance might be misunderstood, he always paid for his own tickets. This information created a bristling atmosphere of managerial antagonism; furthermore, indirectly, it conveyed the impression that hope for a play from this quarter was slim, probably nonexistent.

Two weeks or more had passed without a sign of G.B.S. when a note arrived addressed *Miss Eleanor Robson, Duke of York Theatre, London, S.W. 1*. The letter, in Shaw's neat, legible, almost delicate handwriting, went straight to the point.

10, ADELPHI TERRACE. W.C.
1st December 1904

My dear Miss Robson,
    I have just seen Mary Anne (*sic*); and I am for ever yours devotedly. I take no interest in mere females; but I *love* all artists. They belong to me in the most sacred way; and you are an artist.

I am half tempted to ask Zangwill to let me rewrite that last act for you. You would not have to hurry it over then. And I should like also to steer the composer a little more delicately through the end of the third act. Had Zangwill seen you act the play before he wrote it, he would have risen to you.

We had your great baby of an impresario here today— alas! without his nurse. He talked the most naïve worldly wisdom to me until I felt inclined to put him in a cradle and rock him to sleep. But we liked him extremely; and I am glad your business is in his hands, because babies always succeed in business, the world being a great nursery. I scandalized him by asking him whether there was any chance of getting you to play in You Never Can Tell. He said that you had a great position now and could not be put into freak plays with that sort of crowd. And he meant it, too.

Will you come to lunch with us some day? Would Friday —not tomorrow, but the 9th December—suit you? My wife is enchanted with your playing, and will be greatly pleased if you will come.

> Yours sincerely,
> G. Bernard Shaw

The hour, one o'clock; the place, 10 Adelphi Terrace. At the moment, if anyone had asked, "Where is the center of the world?" the instinctive answer of Mary Ann's interpreter would have been, 10 Adelphi Terrace! The appointed hour found a shy visitor at the apartment door, half afraid to touch the highly polished brass knocker for fear the sound would shatter a dream that the warmly generous letter had created. Shaw himself opened the door. Tall, gay, and altogether charming, he drew me into the living room and introduced me to his wife. My first and lasting impression of Charlotte Shaw was that of a thoroughly poised gentlewoman, whose unaffected kindness was reassuring. She seemed to offer security to a sensitive girl. The other luncheon guest, H. G. Wells, arrived late. Meanwhile, our host cheerfully announced that while Wells knew nothing of

London's new, successful star, he had, nevertheless, a taste for the theatre, and before long he, too, would join the crowds flocking to see *Mary Ann*.

The outstanding impression this occasion left on my mind is that of sound—the sound of their voices: Shaw's gay Irish tones, musical, beautifully modulated, and the startling, surprisingly harsh falsetto of H. G. Wells. Mrs. Shaw spoke seldom, but gently and always to the point. For the most part she and I closely resembled silent partners at the feast.

Wells was amusing, almost frivolous, as Shaw led him on. Through all the badinage one had the feeling that he fancied himself quite a fellow. Strangely enough, there was a warmth about his personality that contradicted his voice, which grated on one's ear.

Through the mist of years comes again the table for four, the view of the Thames River from the window, the outline of fine etchings and other pictures on the walls, the perfection of the table appointments; rare old silver, Irish and English; fine china and linen. Everything about the Shaw apartment revealed exceptionally good taste and the habit of comfortable living.

Shortly after this visit came another message from Bernard Shaw, asking if he might come to tea. I promptly arranged an appointment, hoping he had a play in mind. However, that day he concentrated not upon the theatre, but entirely upon himself and a recent adventure. He had gone up in a balloon with a friend and had been exhilarated, he admitted, with the sensation of floating off into indefinite space. Suddenly something went wrong, and his companion began unwillingly to adjust ballast as they made a hurried descent, far from the expected destination. Finally, to their dismay, they landed in the center of a country gentleman's treasured greenhouse. The adventurers were unharmed, but understandably the effect on the greenhouse was catastrophic. The unfortunate owner was outraged. His excitedly repeated declaration that he would sue for damages drowned out their polite explanation that they accepted full responsibility, and would pay all costs of the necessary repairs.

"At last," Shaw gleefully said, "I ended the interview saying that it was impossible for me any longer to regret the accident. Miraculously we were safe; also he, the owner, wasn't hurt, which made it obvious that a glass greenhouse was the *perfect* landing place for an adventuring balloon, and the owner should be glad that *his* greenhouse had been selected for the experiment."

Shaw promptly followed this mad tea party by sending two snapshots of himself. On the back of one, which showed him, gay and debonair, leaning against a mantelpiece, he wrote, "This is how I looked before I met you." On the other, forlorn, dejected in expression, was written, "This is how I look now." Then came a succession of letters such as only Shaw could write when he was developing an idea for a play and really wanted a particular man or woman to bring his character to life on the stage. It must always be borne in mind that he truly loved "all artists."

10, ADELPHI TERRACE, W.C.
13th April 1905

To the Gifted, Beautiful & Beloved—Greeting.

My dear Miss Eleanor,

Fate has done its work. I have put you out of my mind and settled down hard to my business since you left England. After weary months of mere commercial affairs & rehearsals, I have begun another play—half finished it, indeed; and lo! there you are in the middle of it. I said I would write a play for you; but I did not mean in the least to keep my promise. I swear I never thought of you until you came up a trap in the middle of the stage & got into my heroine's empty clothes and said Thank you: *I* am the mother of that play. Though I am not sure that you are not its father; for you simply danced in here & captivated me & then deserted me & left me with my unborn play to bring into existence. I simply dare not count the number of months. Anyhow the heroine is so like you that I see nobody in the wide world who can play her except you.

And the play is wildly impossible, of course. You are a major in the Salvation Army & you do wonderful & mystical things in the most natural & prosaic way. It would run for a week. But what a week that would be! When are you coming over?

Yours ever & ever
G. Bernard Shaw

The next letter greeted me in Paris, where I had gone for a vacation.

10 ADELPHI TERRACE
LONDON W.C.

ADDRESS TELEGRAMS
TO "SOCIALIST LONDON"

21st June, 1905

My dear Miss Robson,

Miss Marbury tells me that you are going straight to Paris, and are due there tomorrow. This is a shattering blow to me: I had hoped you would pass through London, as I am leaving for Ireland about the 5th July. However, there is one consolation: nothing is ready for you yet in the shape of a play. I have been overwhelmed with rehearsals and business for months past; and my retreat to Ireland is a desperate measure to get a moments rest and then finish the Salvation play, of which only an act and a half (in the rough) is on paper. And I have no idea what it will be like from the practical business point of view when it is finished.

There is much distraction as to the ultimate destination of the play. The Court Theatre management has, of course, very strong claims on me: they say that if I insist on you (to which I always reply that I adore you) they will do what they humanly can to secure you; but their house holds only $800 (£160), and they fear they cannot afford you. Tyler offers me a blank contract, a book of blank cheques, anything & everything I please. Frederick Harrison of the Haymarket Theatre says that even if there is no money in the play he will cheerfully sacrifice his little all for its sake. How it will end, heaven perhaps knows—probably in my reading you the play some day, and then our parting in tears, you to play Miss Hardcastle or some such nonsense, and I to coach some deserving young female at fifty dollars a week or so in the part of the Salvation major. I can do nothing but sit tight and, when they ask me what I want for the play, what I demand from them, what my ultimatum is, reply Eleanor Robson, Eleanor Robson, Eleanor Robson. And she will probably be frightfully disappointed with the part & refuse to play it when the play is complete.

Meanwhile I contemplate Eleanor's photographs in the intervals of business & domestic earthquake—for we have to leave our countryhouse in Hertfordshire at the end of this month; and the horrors of moving are added to all the other horrors.

> In haste
> ever devoted
> G. Bernard Shaw

10, ADELPHI TERRACE. W.C.
4/7/05 [July]

My dear Miss Robson,

I dare not drag you to London to hear the wretched little act and a half—and only the preliminary draft of that—which is all I have on paper. It is not even good enough to serve as an excuse for going to Paris to see you. So I have heroically taken my berth for my passage to Ireland on Thursday night, and resolve not to see you again until I have the prompt copy ready for the first rehearsal.

Vedrenne, of the Court Theatre, will probably offer you an engagement of some sort, as I have made it clear that the way to secure the play is to secure you. Nevertheless I am not easy in my mind about the matter. It is true that Vedrenne has all the people that are almost indispensable to the cast, including the Shaw-Court-Theatre audience, and the Shavian prestige of his successes with John Bull and Man & Superman. But that he can do as much for you as a manager at an ordinary west end theatre with a play like Mary Ann doesn't seem possible. I should not bother much about that if I were sure that the part would do you any good. But I am going to exploit your reputation instead of making it. You have made it yourself already; and whereas I see the possibility of your mother the earl's daughter making a great comedy hit, and your father the millionaire cannon founder, wallowing in the golden spoils of war,

eclipsing all the big character-acting managers in London,
it seems to me that Major Barbara Undershaft, of the Salvation Army, will do nothing that was not at all events implicit in Mary Ann. She is a religious young pusson, who
has been a wonderful success in the Salvation Army, making converts in all directions, and, as to violent and brutal
roughs who beat women on the stage in the most melo-
dramatic manner, she stands them on their heads as if they
were naughty children. Her lover is a tremendously clever
young professor of Greek, a poet really, who has fallen in
love with her and joined the Army for her sake. She makes
him play the drum because he has a fine ear for metrical
quantities. But he is far too subtle for the Salvationist religion; and his one dread is that she will find out that he is in
the Army to worship her and not God. Her father, who is
fond of her (he meets her for the first time practically in
the first act) has a most terribly wicked religion of his own,
believing only in money and gunpowder; and he finally gets
her turned out of the Army as an enemy of religion in a
very subtle and very simple way. In the end he forces her
to recognize that her gift is not the result of any organized
religion, but a magic of her own which sets her as far apart
from the Salvation Army as from any other invention of
Man. He also shews her that this magic is akin to something
that makes the professor of Greek a poet, which is a great
relief to her, as she at first thought that her finding out the
Army would estrange him from her. The rest doesnt matter,
though it is all very interesting and ingenious, and full of
preaching. I cant connect Barbara with anyone but you;
and I am half tempted to take the play right up into the
skies at the end because there is a sort of desecration in
your marrying even your poet. However, that is not human;
so I daresay I will be able to get the marriage on to the
right plane by a twist of my finger if you will pray for me
often enough.

You see, the priest Keegan in John Bull was an immense
success (I mean inside myself, though he did very well on
the stage); and now I want to see whether I can make a
woman a saint too.

The part isn't solemn, by the way: it is full of fun.

I want Barker for the Greek professor: that is one reason why Vedrenne has got a grip of the play, Barker being his partner. Only, the play cannot get on without its father, whose name, strange to say, is Eleanor Robson, whilst its mother is an elderly gentleman named Shaw.

There will be so much mysticism in it that I think Tyler will simply die if he has it read to him. Still, Tyler has one great merit: he adores you, which really shews some insight in him. I can say no more—and no less—for myself.

Now I am sure I have told you enough to set you off imagining a far finer play than this will ever be in cold ink, though I assure you it will be a very fine play indeed in its way.

> Yours ever devotedly
> G. Bernard Shaw

Shaw told Louis Calvert, who had created the title role of *John Bull's Other Island* and was to play Barbara's father, Undershaft, the munitions manufacturer, that his speeches in this play were interminable, that he would probably go mad trying to memorize them, but "one thing is essential—that you should know how to play the trombone—it would add greatly to the effect if you played it prettily. By the way, trombone players never get cholera or consumption, never die until old age makes them incapable of working the slide."

On a postcard to me in Paris:

DERRY. ROSSCARBERY CO. CORK
21/7/05

Are you still in Paris? The Court manager has had an interview with G.T., who persuaded him that I could not have my Major Barbara for two years hence in London and that it was altogether uncertain whether I could have her in America. In fact that neither he nor Major B. had asked me to write anything; and it was like my impudence &c &c. Please tell G.T. that the play is to be announced as "A Discussion in Three Long Acts", and that it is going to be more wildly eccentric than anything that he could ever have imagined or dreaded. And tell *me* how the matter really stands. The Court Manager says he cannot get my Major and urges the transcendant talents of a Miss Annie Russell, of whom I have unluckily never heard. I want to give him a well-informed answer.

G.B.S.

CABLEGRAM

AUG 21 1905

JPBW31. ROSSCARBERY 26

ELEANOR ROBSON 1402 BROADWAY NEW YORK. ALL LOST SAVE AMERICA FORESEE THAT LOST ALSO CABLED TYLER NINETEENTH LAST DAY WAITED ELEVENTH HOUR HAYMARKET IMPOSSIBLE WRITING DESOLATE

—SHAW—

10 ADELPHI TERRACE
LONDON W.C.

ADDRESS TELEGRAMS
TO "SOCIALIST LONDON"

DERRY, ROSSCARBERY, CO. CORK
(UNTIL OCTOBER)
21st Aug 1905

My dear Miss Robson,

I really have nothing to say. What's the use?

It was my fault inasmuch as I left London and so allowed Tyler and Vedrenne to wreck the scheme to their own entire satisfaction. But Vedrenne is not to blame. He never saw you act; he was greatly interested in Miss Russell, whom, for the sake of the London opening and the Shaw part he can get much cheaper than you; he had heard the second act of the play and knew that Granville Barker (his partner) was absolutely indispensable in the cast; he had the Shaw theatre in his hands and the Shaw audience; and he had his houses guaranteed by the libraries on condition that the play was mine & the theatre the Court (the visits of the King & the Prince of Wales &c. have made the theatre fashionable when Shaw plays are on). Naturally he wanted to escape your salary. But I had made your engagement a condition of his getting the play; and Barker was prepared for a ruinous salary of $1250 a week for you if necessary. If Tyler had been serious in the matter nothing could have prevented an arrangement; and a failure would have been impossible. But Tyler, secure in his monopoly of you, and probably imagining that the Court was inferior to the Haymarket in standing, patronized Vedrenne; and Vedrenne, knowing the situation far better, and being only too glad to have difficulties raised for which I could not blame him, patronized Tyler; and so between them we were sacrificed.

Of course I retain the American rights still; but what am I do [*sic*] if Miss Russell—whom I have never seen—makes a great hit in the part, and then asks me whether I am going to throw her over in America? And suppose this does not happen, what sort of unspeakable mess will be made of it for you when you have not been at or in the London performance? I foresee that either the play will fail, in which case Tyler rightly enough will not touch it, or else it will succeed, and Miss Russell will be the heroine of the success, in which case I should not deserve to have anybody act for me if I denied her the refusal of the part in America.

The part is not a specially difficult one. To me there would be all the difference between you and anyone else in it because of a certain quality of yours that is a secret between you and the choice spirits of the earth. But to the public an actress such as you describe Miss Russell to be could do all that is necessary to make a mere acting success with Barbara. Now this is not the case with Barbara's lover, an exceedingly curious & difficult part. Nobody else except Barker could touch it or make the public accept it. There is Ainley, no doubt; and he wants to play at the Court in a play by me; but he could not touch Barker in the part because he does not know the original, a remarkable man who has just been travelling in the East with Barker. Then there is Calvert, who is engaged by Vedrenne. Tyler laughs at Calvert because C. wanted $500 a week in America (he would be quite worth it); but Calvert is a good actor and a manager whose time is worth money; and there is no use in laughing at him unless you can replace him. *I* was laughed at when I cast him for John Bull; but he made a huge success in it. In "Major Barbara" he could be replaced by

Eric Lewis or John Hare, just as you could be replaced by
a clever Pinero heroine; but the whole play would instantly
lose its freshness, and fail as if it were a bad attempt at a
Pinero play. Unfortunately I cannot get Tyler to see this?
His head is full of the fashionable fashions of five years
ago. *My* people are "outsiders" to him. When I propose a
25 dollar actor for a part and ask 40 dollars for him, George
feels as if I had asked him to buy a second hand hat and
carry a pinchbeck watch: what he wants is to pay 300 dollars to somebody whom Frohman engaged last season at
250. There is no getting over this by post and cable. No
doubt in five years or so, when he has seen my tactics succeed about fifty times (if they ever do), I shall be able to
paralyse him into doing what I tell him. But by that time
you will have married and left the stage. After all, he is devoted to your interests, and thinks nothing good enough for
you, which would be splendid if he only knew good from
bad in London.

You may ask why I did not wait until we had time to
straighten out the affair between us. The answer is that I
should have ruined Vedrenne & Barker, and in doing so dis-
credited my own authorship & destroyed the only conditions
in which so unusual a play could succeed. V & B are not
capitalists—not yet. They have got their position purely by
an artistic success; but nothing they have done has paid except my plays. By the help of my plays & the guarantee they
carry they are able to give matinees of good plays which
give the theatre its standing as the artistic & intellectual
London theatre; but these matinees barely pay expenses at
best; and without my support the enterprise must collapse,
and Granville Barker's career get a heavy set back at a
critical moment when one more successful season would
have brought him safe ashore.

I tell you all this so that you may see that the Court
scheme was really a very carefully planned and eligible
one—unfortunately so well planned that it was impossible
to drop it or defer it. Your great blundering baby has simply
made it a present to Miss Russell because his head is filled
with the east wind and he thinks he can do as he likes—
pick up a theatre here and a cast there, put you on the stage

and succeed anyhow. He may be right, provided he picks up the play also and does the ordinary thing right through; but to try to pluck me up by the roots and transplant me when I have only just made Major Barbara possible by a very delicate combination of circumstances & chances & interests is inconsiderateness gone mad.

I have not yet finished the play; and my inspiration, as far as the heroine is concerned, is gone. I shall finish it with my brains alone; and it will not now go right up into heaven. And I solemnly curse Tyler into the uttermost generation of his descendants.

I told him to get a Joan of Arc play for you from some real poet. No doubt he is in treaty with David Belasco for it.

Perhaps I may write another that "might suit you". But this was *your* play. I hope Harrison will find something good for you: he was very enthusiastic about you when he urged me some months ago to let him have Major Barbara for you; and he knows a good play from a bad one better than most managers.

I feel that I shall tear up all this unless I shut it up & post it suddenly: it rattles & grits like sand in the teeth; and I am furious.   G.B.S.

10 ADELPHI TERRACE
LONDON W.C.

ADDRESS TELEGRAMS
TO "SOCIALIST LONDON"

DERRY ROSSCARBERY. CO. CORK. (UNTIL OCTOBER)
14th September 1905

My dear Miss Robson,

Tyler is certainly a most audacious ruffian. That play was as much yours as ever it was mine; and the proof is that on losing you I handed it over without a word to an actress I have never seen and whose sole recommendation to me was your own description if (*sic*) her, and her reputation for having something of your style and feeling.

Vedrenne has no more hold legally over the play even now than Tyler or Harrison or anyone else. But all the cards were in Vedrenne's hands except one; and that one was in Tyler's, and was my demand for you in the title part. In-

stead of playing it, he set himself to snub Vedrenne, and
to rule out the possibility of your appearing at the Court
Theatre. Vedrenne of course desired nothing better: he was
playing for Miss Russell, not for you. I did what I could: I
held off Miss Russell until I had cabled to you and to Tyler.
Tyler stuck to his impossible condition about the Haymarket; and you confirmed him. I don't reproach you: I felt at
the time how little you would be able to grasp the situation.
But the very completeness of my own arrangements left me
no loophole for escape. There was my own cast, my own
theatre (so to speak), my own audience, all the conditions
I had demanded from Vedrenne all complied with and engaged on the strength of my word alone, without a scrap of
legal security. All that remained was to induce you to accept the part. Then came Tyler and said your appearance at
the Court was out of the question: he could only entertain
the proposition on condition that the play was produced at
the Haymarket, and even then not unless he were the principal in the matter, and Mr Harrison only allowed an interest of 50%.* My first impulse was to cable to you at once
to say that you must positively break with Tyler and come
over and play in spite of everything, for no salary at all and
in a barn, if necessary. But one does not do such things in
one's fiftieth year. Tyler can do more for you than I can;
and if he thinks the Court Theatre and my plays not good
enough for you, that is a fault on the right side so far as
you are concerned. So I simply warned you what was going
to happen; and I made poor Vedrenne wait until the very
last moment on the appointed day before engaging Miss
Russell so that you might have time to reply or change your
mind. But you only said that you had promised Harrison.
Then Vedrenne had his way; and the unfinished last act
came down out of the skies for ever.

I should not go over all this again but for the suggestion
that I was not in earnest about the part beimg (*sic*) yours.

As to writing you another, there can be no other so di-

* I knew Harrison and was in correspondence & in conversation with him
about the play; and I knew that he would not accept any such position in
the business even if there had been no other difficulty.

rectly inspired by yourself; for there are some things that do not occur twice in a lifetime; but I daresay I shall write lots of nice parts and that Tyler will turn up his unRoman nose at every one of them and leave them to Miss Russell and others; so that you will spend the rest of your life playing Miss Hardcastle.

When I said that WE were sacrificed, I forgot that I was to have my production, and my newspaper notices, and my celebrity, and my royalties, whilst you were to have nothing but your disappointment. And so I seem to have the better of the bargain. But I have had as much of all these nice things as I want, and a good deal to spare; whereas I have never before written a part for you and seen you play it. The disappointment is the only thing that matters; and we share that. And what a figure I shall cut before the public!— since you raise that point. Jilted for Mr Clyde Fitch, or Mr David Belasco, or Mr George Tyler. "Voila ce que l'on dit de moi dans les gazettes de l'hollande." I never thought of that before; and now I shall have to take care that the villain Tyler gets all the blame.

The success (as I understand) of Man & Superman in New York is probably the stimulus to a move of Charles Frohman's, who wants to acquire the American rights of Major Barbara. But I have refused to take any steps in the matter until the play has been tested by the Court production. And a nice deadlock I shall be in; for if Miss Russell covers herself with glory she will want to do it in New York; and if it fails it will not be done in New York at all. However, it wont exactly fail. There are four first rate parts in it: Barbara herself, Barbara's mother, Barbara's father, and Barbara's lover. Perhaps Miss Russell will get a London engagement on the strength of it, and refuse to go back to America. What is to be done in that case?

Why don't you play Nora in "John Bull's Other Island" by way of penance? My first Nora is gone: she was snapped up by a sick Colonel the moment it made her famous, and is now married & off the stage. But Tyler is bungling John Bull too—making difficulties about the casting. Why is he not crushed by you? Shall I tell him that unless you play Nora, John Bull goes to Frohman?   G.B.S.

My dream of creating a part in one of Shaw's plays was never to be realized. The reason—well, there were many reasons. In spite of his frank statement as to the doubtful importance of Major Barbara as a star part, letter by letter there had been built up a strong hope that a new tempting gold ring of achievement via a Shaw play was almost within grasp. My disappointment was profound.

The shattering of hope may be silent, but its splintering effect is far-reaching. I protested by letter, by telephone, with Mr. Tyler, I urged careful consideration; but I could not find any argument strong enough to meet his sensible reasons for not yielding to the blandishments of Shaw. When all was said and done, I was under contract, and being a fairly reasonable person, I finally agreed that the odds were against my departure from the escalator which apparently was carrying me upward in the American theatre.

Mr. Tyler reported in his book, *Whatever Goes Up:* *

> . . . when Miss Robson was out in San Francisco with *Merely Mary Ann*, half-way through a highly prosperous tour, there arrived a cable from G.B.S. It said that he had finished a play for Miss Robson—*Major Barbara*, by the way—which would be put on presently for two trial matinées in London, and would I please see that Miss Robson was in England in time for rehearsals? I could have the American rights, but the English rights went to Granville Barker. Somewhat flabbergasted, I answered that I couldn't very well chuck a highly profitable tour and throw a whole company out of their jobs just so Miss Robson could travel six thousand miles to play two matinées of a script that neither she nor I had ever seen. Which still strikes me as a reasonable attitude in the matter. Well, answered Shaw in effect, I'd be sorry. It was years before he got through sending me direct and indirect messages telling me just how much damage I'd done Miss Robson in particular and the theatre in general by being unreasonable.

* (Indianapolis, The Bobbs-Merrill Company, 1934), p. 173.

Meanwhile, according to English critics, the first performance of *Major Barbara* at the Court Theatre was not a success. They misunderstood Shaw's new production. In the letter which swiftly followed the first performance, the author spoke from the heart.

10 ADELPHI TERRACE,
LONDON W.C.
Edstaston, Wem, Shropshire. (for Xmas only)
24th December 1905

Eleanor, Eleanor, Eleanor,

At last a ray of comfort. A cutting from an American paper tells me that Tyler has at last done what I told him to do, and got you a play from Rostand. Is it Joan of Arc? For this be all his sins forgiven him!

I had to write a paragraph about him myself. The papers here sent me an interviewer with a statement from an American paper giving just the account the blasphemous rascals thought *you* would like about "Major Barbara". Mostly that my theatre was not good enough for you, and my salary not high enough for you, and it was like my impudence &c &c &c &c. I could not reply that you would have played *your* play for nothing in a barn; so I drank Tyler's blood in ten lines and then set you right as best I could by saying that you got Annie Russell the part.

That is what I must write to you about. I have had no luck since Barbara went wrong. I intended that you should play Barbara for me, and that thereafter no man in America would ever dare to misunderstand any play of mine; so that Daly could produce "Mrs. Warren's Profession" with impunity. But Daly was as bad as Tyler. By disregarding my instructions as to the cast, he made an utter failure of "John Bull", and then, in desperation at his loss, rushed at "Mrs. Warren's Profession", also in defiance of my warning that it was the wrong moment, with the result that I soon had reason to thank my stars that your skirts were well out of the way of the ocean of mud which was flung at me. Rostand will come to you with clean clothes and a young soul. At the same moment I had to fight a furious attack on

Barbara, which was denounced as blasphemous (because
Barbara says "My God: why hast thou forsaken me?") and
also a tremendous fuss about an article of mine on Irving
in a Viennese newspaper, which got stupidly misrepresented.
It was a perfect Gettysburg—good for me, I dare say; but
I really dont like fighting, especially with poor wretches who
cannot defend themselves when I drive my pen through
them.

But all this was a joke compared to the rehearsals of
Barbara. I was very nice, patient, considerate, did not turn
a hair externally; but I was inwardly furious, jealous, baffled,
revolted at first, and then resigned and ineffective. I could
only look on and do nothing. Miss Russell was all you said
she would be, and very patient under very trying circumstances; for the other principals could not master their parts.
At last she couldn't sleep and was panic stricken. At the first
matinée (we began with six matinées) she broke down after
the performance, thinking she had made a hideous failure.
Happily the press next day applauded her to the skies and
cursed me by its gods for inflicting on it a play that was no
play at all—that had not a dramatic moment in it. It lasted
from 2.30 to 5.55! Even my cleverest friends confessed that
the last act beat them; that their brains simply gave way
under it. We have now finished our six matinées. Every one
of them has been crowded to bursting; and hundreds of people have been turned away. Poor Candida is eclipsed—a
back number—people write frantic letters to me about Barbara. The audiences suffer horribly; they are pained, puz-
zled, bored in the last act to madness; but they sit there to
the bitter end and come again, & again. Oswald Yorke has
made a great success as the rough whom Barbara converts.
Granville Barker was extraordinarily good in a part which
nobody else could have touched. The enormously difficult
and heavy part of Barbara's father beats Calvert. He admits
it and is trying to get hold of it; but he has kept up appearances well enough to be enormously praised; and he may
yet master it. After a few performances I cut the last act
to make it easier for him and for Miss Russell. How she
plays you can imagine better than I can describe. All the
part that is within her range she plays excellently in a really

touching intimate way, with sincere feeling, very right and sympathetic. But she is hampered by the heavier, more tragic passages. She has not a strong voice, and has no idea of making rhetorical effects in long speeches. And the whole balance of the play is strange to her. To have to struggle for supremacy with the other parts; to be scored off and have the sympathy snatched from her, and her own sympathetic attitude suddenly shown in a fiercely ironical light; to know at moments that the interest has gone away from her and that the audience is in a scare (about their own souls): all that is a bother to her. But fortunately Yorke, who makes the most obvious success in the ordinary sense, is her husband; and she is apparently very fond of him. And she has had splendid notices, and feels that the occasion is an important one and a success; so I hope she is, on the whole, satisfied.

But oh! Eleanor, between ourselves, the play, especially in the last act, is a mere ghost; at least so it seems to me. This is no doubt your fault to some extent: I see you in the part; I love you in the part; I was inspired to write the part so that when the Word became Flesh (these old religious catchwords are the plainest common sense to me) the flesh should be yours. I cant let the play go to America now. When I said to Vedrenne one day that I did not see Miss Russell succeeding with Barbara in America, he replied promptly "She doesn't want to". I have strained the resources of the stage to breaking point: the acting requires three stars of the first magnitude. Once or twice at the early rehearsals I felt that I ought to kill you. You should have done it. You should have broken all your engagements—risen up in the middle of the night—come naked & hungry if no better might be. I could have waited two years, ten years, any number of years; but unless you saw the play you could not understand how impossible it was anywhere but at the Court Theatre. I don't know what is to be done now. Miss Russell cannot stay here all her life to play Barbara: it is hard enough on her that when it goes into the evening bill on New Years Day it is only for six weeks, when another Court play goes up in the course of the repertory system. Later on comes Brassbound with Ellen Terry.

Barbara will not come on again until the winter of 1906-7. Some day perhaps you will be free to play it for us by way of rehearsal and then go to America with the whole Court company. All dreams!

If Rostand does less than his greatest for you, may his name perish and all his plays be revised by Tyler!

How is that immeasurable blunderer? Had you to make him go to Rostand, or had he the saving grace to see that this was the only amends he could make you?

I am just recovering from a touch of exhaustion after Barbara. It was a fearful job: I did what I never have had to do before, threw the last act away and wrote it again. Brainwork comes natural to me; but this time I knew I was working—and now nobody understands. No matter: there is the thing done: there is your baby; for it is yours, though you have left Miss Russell to nurse it.

Man & Superman seems inexhaustible: even Tyler would gape at the houses in New York & London, full every night, and apparently always the same people. And Barbara's spirit homeless in America!

I will strive to get it into print soon so that you may read it. I wonder will you be horribly disappointed with it. Oh Eleanor, Eleanor, dearest Eleanor! Oh infamous Tyler! When shall we see you again in London?

G.B.S.

I have already mentioned that Mr. Tyler had produced for Arnold Daly *You Never Can Tell;* also, special matinees of *Candida.* Later, he presented *The Man of Destiny* and *How He Lied to Her Husband,* which Shaw wrote for Daly.

Ever practical, Shaw forgave Mr. Tyler, when, in 1914, the latter produced *Pygmalion* for Mrs. Patrick Campbell, one of his and her greatest successes.

15

DURING THE SEASON of *Mary Ann* in London, offers came along from other playwrights. Newly discovered personalities in the theatre draw a tide all their own. Among others who wished me to participate in their plays were Constance Fletcher and John Oliver Hobbes. In spite of her nom de plume, John Oliver Hobbes (Pearl Craigie) was a most feminine and gracious woman. Her lovely house on the Isle of Wight was exquisitely furnished and decorated with choice *bibelots*. It was perched on a hill at the edge of the sea; the view, especially at sunset, was beautiful. Nothing came of these play offerings but friendly associations.

Our London season closed December 15. Ada Dwyer and I left the next day with applause ringing in our ears, accompanied by scores of invitations to come back soon. We returned to the American cast in New York with a new leading man, who had joined us in London in order that we might rehearse on the voyage home. Alas, we saw him only once that late December crossing. The Atlantic was plagued with terrific storms and the *Deutschland* plunged about mercilessly. The ship arrived two days late and we were literally snatched from the customs officials and rushed from ship to stage for a rehearsal which lasted until sunrise.

The welcome-home matinee that day at the New Amsterdam Theatre was sold out and overflowing. The lobby was decorated with floral pieces—at least a dozen different cities were represented with huge offerings. With the crowd milling about both inside and outside, the theatre resembled a popular flower show. Ada and I, poor, miserable sailors, enjoyed no moment of the enthusiastic, tumultuous occasion. Every move across the stage seemed to reflect the rock, roll, and plunge of the tortured *Deutschland*. A letter of welcome was waiting from one of Ada's sisters in Salt Lake, who described the family Sunday dinner as we crossed the ocean. She wrote, "Father made us all stand to say grace, which was an unusually long one even for him. Then he added, 'And may God bless our beloved daughter, who is wandering on foreign shores in the middle of the Atlantic Ocean.'" The Lord must have been occupied elsewhere or He would have paid more attention to James Dwyer's prayer.

The company entrained that night for Toronto, Canada. After traveling some twenty hours, we arrived at night, nearly three hours late. The train diner had been taken off early in the day; the American-plan hotel dining room was firmly closed; even a delicatessen shop in the neighborhood was locked against us; but my faithful dresser, Sarah, finally found sandwiches and two bottles of soda. This unattractive combination at eleven o'clock was our Christmas Eve dinner. Next day when I entered the dressing room where one faint electric bulb, as Ada said, "only made the darkness visible," we saw that a huge mirror on my table had been smeared heavily with a frosting of soap on which was written, *"Merry Christmas to our beloved Mary Ann."*

Although we had arrived so late the night before and the scenery had to be set up, the stagehands had scoured the town, found a Christmas tree, and decorated it with the usual trimmings. The company put toys and poems around. Because I was overjoyed and touched by their friendship, the men packed the tree with all its bright baubles and set it up in the next town to pleasure me into the New Year.

The holiday season brought a letter from an old friend.

JEWISH TERRITORIAL ORGANIZATION.

15, ESSEX STREET,
  STRAND.   LONDON Dec 15 1905

Dear Miss Robson,
  Somebody has sent me an Australian Advertisement of "Merely Mary Ann" which may serve for a Christmas card to amuse you. I have been rather sorry for you, despite your enormous success, to think of you tied monotonously to "Mary Ann" for so many months, & so I thought I would tell you something that might comfort you even under the burden of future triumphs in the same rôle. You know the appalling position of the Russian Jews, how they live under the daily dread of massacre & pillage. Well, it is largely the wages of poor hardworking Mary Ann that have supported me & enabled me to put aside all other work but that of founding a new country for them under the British flag. If ever this new land arises, Mary Ann will have been its chief

servant, & the benefactress of generations to come. So wishing her & you the happiest of New Years, believe me,

Yours very sincerely,

Israel Zangwill

16

WHILE PLAYING in Detroit that winter, I was taken one afternoon by Alph Chittenden, an architect friend, to see the notable Charles L. Freer art collection on Ferry Street, then shown only by special permission. Whistler's pictures were becoming famous; also, Mr. Freer had recently imported from England, and installed in his home, the much talked of Whistler painted Peacock Room with its unusual placement of blue-and-white porcelains. Mr. Freer, an impressive personality with precise knowledge of his collection, took charge of the showing. The delightful experience of viewing the collection was that you saw each object, piece by piece. A remarkable butler-custodian brought out from concealed cupboards items of particular interest one by one as Mr. Freer called for them. Whistler's work, from earliest sketchbook glimpses of life in military service to the latest painting, was placed before us.

My enthusiasm for the exceptionally fine Japanese screens, *kakemonos* and prints called forth an invitation to come next day to Mr. Freer's home in Bloomfield Hills and at leisure view other Oriental masterpieces. Two performances on Saturday made acceptance impossible. Sunday, perhaps? Alas, I must leave Detroit about two-thirty for the next tour city, and the Freer country home was an hour's drive from Detroit. Undaunted, he kindly suggested that I come Sunday morning at the hour of my choice, see the collection, and lunch with him. Meanwhile, he would arrange to have the train flagged as it passed through the village station, not five minutes from his house. With alacrity I accepted for Mrs. Russell and myself, and we reveled in the feast presented while Mr. Freer told Arabian Night stories of how he had pursued and secured each object. Even during that delectable lunch he repeatedly sent for some precious item and we held the treasure in our hands and listened with rapt attention to its history.

Arriving at the station exactly on the split second as the train pulled to a halt, we found our company discussing with considerable agitation what could be done if we failed to appear. The Freer Gallery of Art now occupies a special wing of the Smithsonian in Washington, only seeing it could never be the same as on that Sunday when the personality and expert showmanship of Charles Freer brought it to life for the benefit of two wandering but appreciative players.

17

VACATIONING IN EUROPE the next summer I tried to see the Shaws, but fate was against me. It was impossible to fix a meeting, as I had to hurry away to join friends in France who had arranged a motor tour through the château country.

27 June 1906.
10 ADELPHI TERRACE, W.C.

My dear Miss Robson,

How delightful to hear you are in England! I want to see you again so very much. Unfortunately we are horribly full of engagements. Tomorrow & Saturday we are quite tied up, & we go out of town from Saturday to Monday. Can you come to luncheon on Friday at 1.30? The only drawback to that is that my husband will have to hurry away directly afterwards. On Tuesday we are quite free & would be so glad to have you then. But are you staying as long as that? If neither of these times suit you I must settle something else; only let me know. We would not miss you for anything! . . .

Yours sincerely
C. F. Shaw

18

JEROME K. JEROME finally delivered, after several revisions, his transformed play, now called *Susan in Search of a Husband*. It came into being when we produced it out of town. Only half alive, it soon faded away into silence without reaching New York. Again the public decided this was not the moment to take Jerome seriously. A few years later, when he wrote *The Passing of the Third Floor Back,* the public, in all earnestness, took that lovely play to their hearts.

After three years of phenomenal success with *Mary Ann,* we produced another Zangwill play, *Nurse Marjorie.* It was definitely a slender reed, due undoubtedly to the fact that his interest in the theatre had taken second or third place in his life, and Zionism, to which he gave more money than he could afford, had become a ruling passion. He dedicated the remaining years of his life to the Zionist movement, in which he believed profoundly and devotedly helped to create. Nevertheless, *Marjorie* filled a season, largely drawn along in the wake of *Mary Ann's* popularity.

The hazards of play production were considerable then, and unfortunately they have not changed with the times. Like Eliza crossing the ice, one is no sooner perched on a play that promises good floating possibilities than, perforce, the anxious search for the next and the next landing begins.

I first met Clyde Fitch when Mother took me to a rehearsal of his cleverly topical play, *The Climbers,* in which she was cast. A sensitive man with keen dramatic insight, he was an exceptionally good stage director. The subtleties of inflection and of gesture which he introduced enhanced each character from the written words he originally provided for the part. Once he stopped the rehearsal and said to a young actress, "No, Miss So and So, I suggest that it would be better if you played the scene this way," and he read her lines to demonstrate his meaning. "Be careful not to exaggerate; always remember the woman you are playing is not vulgar; she is just a little more of a lady than a lady."

This popular, witty, much sought-after author crossed my path again at a tea party given by Elsie de Wolfe and Elisabeth Marbury, in their enchanting old house on Irving Place, reported to have been the home of Washington Irving. Miss Marbury, a successful and somewhat aggressive play agent, held a leading position in that field and was Clyde Fitch's representative.

That winter, after seeing *Mary Ann,* he telegraphed, "THANK YOU, MERELY CLYDE FITCH."

Two years later he wrote *The Girl Who Has Everything* for me. He was a prolific writer; some sixty plays were reported to his credit at this time—many of them popular. Two outstanding successes for women stars were *Barbara Frietchie,* played by Julia Marlowe, and *Captain Jinks of the Horse Marines,* with Ethel Barrymore. It was a delight to work under his direction. From his chair at the footlights at rehearsals, he would start upstage with an idea as I moved down to suggest a detail along the same line. Finally he said, "We must not carry this enjoyment of subtle detail too far or *The Girl* will never reach the audience." Then he told us about James M. Barrie. If a member of his company laughed too quickly at rehearsal, he would say, "That line must be rewritten; it won't travel over the footlights."

We rehearsed as we went from town to town, the idea being to open in Cleveland, give the play a short spring tryout, then start the autumn of 1906 with *The Girl* first in a season of repertory, a hope of mine following three years of *Mary Ann.* Clyde Fitch dashed off frequent letters to me between visits.

<u>What an E pistle!</u>

113, EAST FORTIETH Sᵗ.

Dear Miss Robson,

    <u>Welcome to Indianapolis!</u>

Thanks for yʳ kind note. I am glad you are having such a good time! I am on a noisy hunt for furniture, ETC. "Liebler" I call the "Bogie Man"—he is too intangible & indeterminate a person for me! Tyler is in Phila: Liebler told me over the phone Morange * was making the "sofa" for Act 3—but Morange tells me later he has never heard of it—so he & I are now trying to find Presbrey † to whom I explained it all when Tyler was ill. I dont know why I

---

* Scenic designers of Gates & Morange.
† Stage director Eugene W. Presbrey.

dont just "let things go", but I suppose it's my self & my extreme liking of you! I find from her that my contract with "Liebler" for you has loco motor ataxia, Marbury having given in in several of my usual points. So it is more or less easy to not give me what I at other times have—I throw myself therefore on your mercy regarding a dress rehearsal. I have no idea I can get one any other way. And I feel it is so necessary to have one at least by Sunday night. So that we will have time to change before Thursday what is wrong. I never have less than two—generally three dress rehearsals, because I find actors till they are used to their new clothes are not easy or convincing, but I don't hope for more than one, tho' I should be grateful for two if after the first a 2ᵈ seems necessary. I am sorry that I am not able to do for YOU in yʳ rehearsals all I am accustomed to do, but I will do all I possibly can, it is "detail" that we will have to lack.

. . . Tuesday night I went to see "Cashel Byron's Profession." Have you heard about the lady who went to the box office & asked if it was the same profession as Mrs. Warren's & when told "no" took her money back! Tuesday night.—If Shaw had only done the play himself it might have been SPLENDID! But done as it is the play is silly & unconvincing, & BADLY played except by Corbet who is rather natural nice & boyish. There was a bad house however & I hardly think it will go. Ethel Barrymore on the other hand is crowding the Criterion. . . .

I met some Cleveland people at dinner the other night— who are to be back by Feb 1. & swear that you shall have a very smart audience for the premiere. I SOLD ALL THE SEATS I COULD! ! !

I am actually looking forward to Detroit & seeing you again in spite of all my disgruntions with Liebler & Co.! & I consider this week minus yʳ author you are only "The Girl who has nearly Everything."

Yours ever
Clyde Fitch

His underlining makes me think of Queen Victoria.

One episode after our Cleveland opening delighted us. The heroine in the first act talked to the doctor, who had been called in to prescribe for her sister's baby, the sister having just died, and he gives instructions for the baby's formula, temperature of bottle, etc. A few days later came a letter. Three pages were charming commendations; the fourth stated: *"By the way, I'm a doctor, and I advise you to tell the nurse to heat the milk to 98 degrees. Your present instructions, if carefully followed out, would boil the baby."*

Some time later a friend sent me a clipping from a newspaper which read: "A woman who attended classes at a school for mothers wrote out the following instructions for using a feeding-bottle: 'When the baby is done drinking, it must be unscrewed and laid in a cool place under the hydrant. If the baby does not thrive on fresh milk, it should be boiled.'"

Following the opening, we proceeded to Cincinnati, and thought we had a success. The author was confident.

113, EAST FORTIETH ST.

Dear Miss Robson,

I was delighted to hear from Cincinnati splendid things about you in the play, & that it was a[s] real a success as in Cleveland. Do you know what is the chiefest memory I have carried away with me, of it? The last quarter of Act 3. Your face & y^r voice at the fire place when Guy speaks to you. Your whole attitude & expressions in the corner of the sofa, & y^r "Ono! never again speech", & y^r virginal horror in his arms, & y^r close of the act! All that is my deepest & most definite memory. And I think you do something there that I have only seen Duse do.

I wish you would give two or three consecutive weeks of performances, (& then go back to y^r odd no of performances) but I am sure the several weeks of consecutive performances w^d give a something that nothing else could give. Of course if this is impossible, it is, but I hope it is not.

I have not seen Miss Closser, & I see she is to play in some new piece, but the more I think it over, the more I think her performance would be most valuable, & that in

<u>N.Y.</u> anyway it is the performance that counts. I hope you will cast the play for N.Y. this spring, or else next autumn you will <u>not</u> be <u>able</u> to get yʳ people. I am casting my new plays now. Would you be willing to try Mrs. Sheldon again? or who would you say for Aunt Fanny? Somebody soft, & sweet? & who do you want for Guy? I am off to Phila. I wish <u>you</u> were there! I sail March 1ˢᵗ.

Yʳˢ ever,
Clyde Fitch

When *The Girl Who Has Everything* opened in New York, one critic caustically remarked, "Everything but a good play." Some were kind; generally speaking, however, the play had a poor press. Even unboiling the baby in this case was of no avail, and *The Girl*, after close to three months of fostering, was abandoned, January 17, 1907.

Meanwhile, about December 1, Paul Armstrong had been practically locked up in a hotel suite by Mr. Tyler with a set of Bret Harte's stories and told not to come out without a play. Gallantly following instructions, he emerged in two weeks with *Salomy Jane*, based on "Salomy Jane's Kiss." Put into rehearsal promptly with a magnificent cast, this play was pronounced a success of the first order when it opened January 19 at the Liberty Theatre.

At the dress rehearsal, in the small hours of the morning, every member of our company was dazed with fatigue, including the two children. It is no easy matter to act one play at night and rehearse a heavy new production all day, but we went over the ending again and again, wearily twisting it this way and that; still no one liked the finale. Out in the auditorium the manager restlessly paced up and down; the author suggested first one thing then another between softly muttered oaths of strange extraction.

A "tag line" was needed to bring the curtain down on an effective finish. Salomy had saved the hero, a stranger, when he was accused of being a horse thief, and they have fallen deeply in love. Throughout the play he was referred to as "The Man."

Suddenly I called to the author, "Mr. Armstrong, what's The Man's name? I don't know yet."

Armstrong, a tall, broad-shouldered creature resembling the typical Texan, jumped to his feet, waving his arms wildly—"That's it! That's it. Bring the curtain down fast when Salomy drawls, 'Say, Man, what's yer name? I don' know yet.'"

The children in *Salomy Jane* were Donald Gallagher, eleven, and Ruth Wells, going on eight. He was a shy, intelligent child; she was precocious to a degree. We had a long wait together in Act I, so I always had picture books to entertain them. One night Ruth put her two hands on the open book and leaning across my lap, said coyly, "Donald, what are you going to do when you grow up—get married, I suppose?"

The boy blushed and drew back; I plunged into the awkward pause. "Of course he's going to marry; he's going to marry me, aren't you, Donald?"

"Yes," he answered, "if you'll wait for me."

Ruth ignored me entirely, and with the severity of her going on eight years, coldly answered, "Why, she'll be dead by then!"

19

THE AUTHOR of *Soldiers of Fortune* and the "Van Bibber" and "Gallegher" stories was a storybook character himself. To say that Richard Harding Davis was a man's man is to say only a part of the truth. Aside from a few critics, his popularity was extremely high with both sexes. Someone called him a "D'Artagnan brandishing a pencil instead of a sword." Parties at the Charles Dana Gibsons' with the Thomas Hastings, Finley Peter Dunne ("Mr. Dooley"), Oliver Herford, and Richard Harding Davis were highlights of the period.

Had R.H.D. written *Vera the Medium* as an all-out melodrama, and had it been frankly played as such, it might have succeeded, but only if someone else had played Vera. In any case, I was hopelessly miscast and I knew it, a dreadful feeling for an actor. The public did not like to see a star they had put on a pedestal portray a person with any stain on her character.

The attitude current was that you might accept bad behavior in private life from people you loved, but you did not have to pay to see it in the theatre.

The story was that of a girl who pretends to be a medium and with the use of an "illusion cabinet" brings voices from the past, table tappings and so forth. Imposed upon by crooks, she inadvertently becomes the villain until she discovers their plot and, sacrificing herself, denounces the criminals, at which point she and the hero join hands and lives.

Richard Harding Davis was a brilliant war correspondent and a generous friend; he tried to adjust his play to audience reaction and to my non-melodramatic methods. Never was a play so rewritten. Practically every time the company met we had a new version, at least a new scene or two. The manager was irritated to frenzy; the author discouraged. No understanding existed between them; neither could bear to speak to the other. I appeared to be the only means of communication, and nearly every message had to be tactfully redrafted before it could be delivered, a festering state of affairs, painful for all.

Finally Richard Davis decided to go to England. Before sailing, he gave every assurance that he would abandon the trip and try another and yet another rewrite of Vera if I said the word. However, a play surgeon had been called in (with the author's consent) to prune and to graft new ideas on the original stem. It seemed an unnecessary hardship to ask a sensitive author to watch another man hacking away at his play. Therefore I wrote something to the effect that although, like Martha of Biblical fame, I was "troubled about many things," I understood his need to get on with new work and wished him and his wife a happy trip. The note drew first a telegram, then a letter.

IS IT FAIR OF MARTHA TO WRITE A WONDERFUL LETTER WHEN SHE KNOWS IT WILL BE DELIVERED OUTSIDE OF SANDY-HOOK AND ONE CANNOT GET BACK A VERY GRATEFUL PERSON THANKS HER ESPECIALLY FOR THOSE THINGS SHE WILL NEVER KNOW SHE GAVE.

ON BOARD R.M.S. "ADRIATIC."
December 9th 1908

My Dear Miss Robson,

"I would be a coward, I would be ungrateful if I went away, and did not tell you how much you had helped me." Showing, that it is easier to write noble sentiments than to act up to them. I am very much ashamed. I hate being here at ease on a "floating palace", that with each turn of the screw, floats us nearer to London, and all that London means, while you, single handed, lead the forlorn hope among the uncharted seas of one night stands in the South. I know I am a deserter. And, what makes my base flight the more base, is that, as I said in my wire via the pilot, I have so much to thank you for. That is what chiefly hurts me. I gained so much during those days of rehearsal, of dress choosing, of rewriting by telephone, and of snatching at lunch at Sherry's, that, later "what happened to Vera" failed to move me. On your account it did affect me and I tried to make up to you for foisting that young person on your hands, by altering her, reshaping her, re"turning" her as often as you saw possibilities of reform. Certain dark and lonely Sundays in Hartford, and on the farm, should be counted to me for righteousness. For had anyone else than yourself tried to range that young person, I would have refused my feeble aid. But, now, when all is said and done, when the "illusion" is working, and the Wall Street edition of the end of the third act is on the street, and the amended amendments to "a bill to amend a bill", known as the fourth act, have passed both houses, and received the signature of the Governor, I find that what counts, is not hopes of royalties to come, or the shame of having done a piece of poor work, but that all I chiefly value, is having known you. I can hear you say, "That is very polite, Mr Davis, but, in the meantime—what are we going to do about your bad play?" I prefer to waive all that. At an immeasurable distance, even safe off your own Isle of Wight, "Vera" and her delinquencies cannot disturb me. I am secure in the recollection of benefits received that lift me far above the sordid cry of the box office receipts or the lack of them. I see your point of view. I see that to one existing by the grace of Texas hotels my indifference is aggravating. But, to be fair to me, remember that already I have been paid in full, that I have received my reward.

It has been a very great privilege to have worked with a great artist, who can take a poor line and as she wills, make people cry, or laugh; to see her turn gold out of Shaw; to hear her with a lifting note, hold her audience breathless, or drive it to applause. But, the greater privilege has been in knowing you. Had the courage, the patience the sweetness Eleanor Robson showed us during the bad days, been lost upon me, I would be poor indeed. They were not lost. I keep them as very rare and delightful assets. So, to me, "Vera" does not mean a failure, a waste of six months of work. Rather, it means the opportunity of knowing a very lovely and wonderful woman, to whom I am grateful for much help, much good. Some one wrote, "It is given to few men to carry a line to a sinking ship, or to plant a flag upon the walls of Lucknow." And, I feel, it is given to very few men to have known "a great and gracious lady" like Eleanor Robson.

I beg to sign myself, her very obedient servant

                              Richard Harding Davis

And to wish her a Merry Christmas and a Happy New Year.

20

THE SUMMER OF 1908 Ada Dwyer had gone to play *Mrs. Wiggs of the Cabbage Patch* in Australia. Mother and I for a second time had taken a house at Bonchurch on the Isle of Wight. London was full of attractive friends—the Gilbert Murrays, Mr. and Mrs. Henry Dickens and their charming daughters, also Lawrence Alma-Tadema, the artist, and Edith Craig, daughter of Ellen Terry. But it was imperative to get away. I was threatened with a nervous breakdown.

The Dickens family took a keen interest in my health, which warmed the heart of my worried mother. After considerable investigation, they sent me to a famous nerve specialist in Harley Street, London. He assured us a home rest-cure was useless, that my woefully underweight body of ninety-six pounds could not withstand the physical and emotional stress of hard work that was impending. Immediate professional care was essential in order to avoid a complete nervous collapse and the likelihood of an enforced vacation of two years or more. One of the best nursing homes in Europe was near Bonchurch, at Ventnor, and the specialist made arrangements with the Scotch director to take me at once.

Having crossed three thousand miles of ocean to a remote cottage on that tiny island in search of rest, it seemed a strange coincidence to find myself in a nursing institution which gave what they called the Weir Mitchell treatment. Dr. Mitchell's own famous clinic was in Philadelphia.

Worried, depressed, irresolute about my future course of action, I cried literally for three days and nights.

Naturally enough, matrimony had beckoned before on several occasions. Now, with the steadfast insistence of August Belmont, it confronted me like a fork in the road to destiny, and either route involved a serious sacrifice. This to be or not to be was not easy of solution, for my decision involved not only the two most concerned, but many individuals: my manager, who, by careful planning, had built up a career for his star, an investment of time and money from which he hoped to reap increasing financial benefit; an author involved in creating a new play; my mother; and an entire company, many of whom had been with me for years and for whom I felt affection and a sense of personal responsibility.

To take my mind off my dilemma and to supply a tangible reason for tears beyond physical and emotional weakness, I recited pages and pages of *In a Balcony* to myself and wept on into the night. No letter, no newspaper, no word from the outside world was permitted to reach me; even to sit up was forbidden. I was miserably lonely and unhappy. After a week, every fine day skillful nurses lifted me from the bed to a small cot that was then rolled on to my balcony, where an ocean view, which under other circumstances would have been an inspiration, brought a measure of peace.

At last abandoning the role of Niobe all tears, I settled down to the business of relaxing, toning of muscles and consistent feeding by the nurses. I was permitted to read books and papers and could recognize and understand the words before me. The Scotch doctor, with a fascinating accent that I imitated when alone, talked more of scientific developments in medicine and less about my symptoms.

Three weeks later I left this haven, rosy, at least physically, ready to face life's endless procession of decisions. To even the apparently insoluble question of matrimony I seemed to have found a clear and definite answer. The immediate problem concerned clothes—not usually important to me, and the approaching theatrical season. The recently acquired eighteen pounds took up more room than my existing wardrobe permitted.

Marion Crawford had a half-finished play that he was eager to discuss, so Mother and I traveled to Edinburgh to see him before returning to America. He was a gentleman of the old school, distinguished and cultivated; but in spite of his almost irresistible charm, I hesitated, and finally, from America, refused his play *The White Sister*. He was a remarkable storyteller. In the midst of one tale he used a completely unfamiliar word. Frankly I asked for a dictionary. He said the word probably wouldn't be found in the average book and from his desk took a small volume, which he praised highly, *Jenkins's Vest-Pocket Lexicon. An English Dictionary of All Except Familiar Words*. He inscribed it, "To Miss Eleanor Robson, With Best Wishes," and I have valued it ever since.

Early that summer, Mrs. Frances Hodgson Burnett had come to Bonchurch to discuss her scenario of a play based on *The Dawn of a Tomorrow*. When her book was published, a friendly dramatic critic, Burns Mantle, wrote suggesting that Glad was a personality which he thought could be developed for me. The slender story contained no structure of a play, only an idea and a novel character. New Thought had just appeared over the horizon. The old Biblical instruction, "Ask, and it shall be given you; seek, and ye shall find" appeared in a new and effective form.

When I first urged the dramatization, Mrs. Burnett had declined "to commercialize" *The Dawn;* as she expressed it. Her
book she felt had been written under the compulsion of religious
inspiration; however, it was agreed if she did it for anyone, it
would be for me. Finally, after a brief reflection, she agreed to
try her hand at a play assisted by Harriet Ford.

Mrs. Burnett was a sweet woman and an interesting character,
totally different from anyone that I had known or worked with
before. She was passionately devoted to her son, who had been
the Little Lord Fauntleroy of my girlhood. But all children appealed to her. She kept in her living room a large cabinet; when
the doors were opened a doll's house was revealed, with downstairs and upstairs; it was perfectly equipped with furniture and
alluring toy gadgets which she kept to entertain young visitors.

She was quite plump, rather a squatty little figure, with a
mop of red hair going gray. She had a habit of half-finishing a
sentence, skipping to the next and the next, then weaving back
to finish, at least partly, the original thought she had in mind.
One picked up her thoughts with careful concentration, as if
they were dropped stitches. My private nickname for her was
"the Crimson Rambler." It was a pleasure to learn that her sister
and intimate friends called her "Fluffy."

After she died, I joined a small committee of loyal friends, including her publisher, Frederick A. Stokes, to build a memorial
to her in Central Park in New York City; it is named after one
of her best-known stories, *The Secret Garden.*

Mrs. Burnett followed our rehearsals of *The Dawn* with keen
interest and took pride and intense satisfaction in its genuine
success. The difference between a literary development of character built up by degrees and the quick almost instantaneous
revelation of a dramatic interpretation in the theatre fascinated
her. When finally committed to the dramatization, she was
completely flexible: anything we wanted she was willing to try.
An infinite number of changes were made in the script, but once
her doubts about using her story for the theatre were resolved,
she co-operated eagerly. Words, as given to us by poets and

other authors, have an amazing power of survival; as John Masefield might say, ". . . outlasting clocks that outlast men." When almost insuperable problems present themselves, I still quote the philosophy of that courageous little cockney child of the slums, Glad, "There ain't nothin' as bad as ye think it is," and, "When things ain't cheerful, people's got ter be, to fight it out."

1909 Q STREET
WASHINGTON D. C.

My dear Miss Robson,
 Your letter was a pleasure to me. It told me things about you. Do you know you use the word which to me means *all* that makes work worth while. I am so glad it means the same thing to you. It is that word 'real.' Now I know we shall understand each other. My feeling about a dramatization of Glad is that nothing earthly would induce me to do it if the play could not be made to produce the effect of the story. If that could not be done, to dramatize it at all would be vulgar sacrilege. The effect of the story has been an extraordinary thing. The letters I receive & the things I hear have a tone of intensity beyond words. You can see what a mistake it would be to shock the people who so love the thing by destroying an ideal. The real thing might be achieved by two people who had the same point of view—an actress who could embody the thought itself as it was dreamed by the creator of it. Ever since I saw your Mary Ann I have felt that I should like to write something for you. I hope this may be the something. . . .

Yours Sincerely
Frances Hodgson Burnett

May 19 1908   SANDS POINT
PORT WASHINGTON
LONG ISLAND

Dear Miss Robson,
 I have written the scenes & made the changes we talked

of. The first scene between Glad and Sir Oliver—the one from which we felt it necessary to eliminate the dangerous speech—has evolved into something immensely better, I think. A certain astute philosophic sentiment Glad propounds is one which will I believe become a popular quotation. It is a simple but eternal truth & said with her half sly, ironic air of good cheer will carry across the footlights with great effect. Here is her exposition of it. It comes at the end of her explanation that she was 'born cheerfle'

Glad

Tell yer wot: Theres a lot o' things 'appens in this 'ere world. I aint eighteen but *Ive* seen abaht arf of 'em—*I* ave. But theres one thing I aint never come acrost yet.

Sir Oliver

What is that, pray.

Glad

—with sly upward sidewise glance of mischief—
—A thing as was bad as wot yer *thort* it was. There aint *nothin* as bad as that. That there aint been done to *none* of us yet.

I know you will like that. It is such a good thing to remind people of.

She refers to this three or four times & you might prefer to cut out the first time & the last—which could be done by merely drawing a pencil through the words. That can be as you feel it. I am happy to say that the more I work at the play the more interested I become & the more I see you in it. You are not old enough to have seen Joseph Jefferson when you were sufficiently mature to analyse his power & charm of subtlety. The wonder of him was that you saw each thought dawn and grow in his face & eyes before he uttered. One could not look away from him a moment. It was too absorbing to sit & *see* a man *think*. You will be like that in Glad. You know you have very wonderful eyes—thinking eyes—on the stage. This young savage is possessed each moment with strange dawning thoughts—vague wonders she must follow. She doubts, she hopes—she fears, she is awed and compelled—she disbelieves—she believes—she is passionately uplifted. . . . I hope you are rested.

Yours with regard
Frances Hodgson Burnett

CHAPMAN COTTAGE
BROADWAY—FLUSHING

Dear Miss Robson,

My sister and I are going to New Haven on Thursday morning so that I can be at the rehearsal in the afternoon. I suppose Miss Marbury has explained the reason for my absence from the last two days rehearsals. As there are no cabs at the station here one has to walk to the train & as the way there is a sheet of glassy ice it seemed wiser to remain at home until the worst was over. Miss Marbury telephoned yesterday that all was going perfectly & there was no actual need of my presence. Will you please see that Sir Oliver does not cause you to lose your climax in the last act by hurrying over the points which lead up to it. You remember we spoke of that at Norfolk. The final scene beginning 'Come here to the fire. I am not going to inquire &tc' must be done on his part, first with the suggestion of gradually awakening revelation. There must be a definite pause before that second 'Saved me'—a pause & then a slight start as he recalls his cry at the end of Act 1st— If he does not make his points *you* lose yours. You are leading him word by word—thought by thought to the absolute, solemn, profound conviction of his *'So do I. So do I.'* That last scene between you two is so far from being the ordinary 'clear-things-out-of-the-way' ending of a play. The audience must not have the power to *think* of moving until you utter your last rapturous cry.

. . . My certainty of your power to make my words mean what I *intended* them to mean is a happiness I could not express to you. It is a new experience to me. I have usually been very unhappy when I have produced a play. Your realization of this part has given me actual delight. I have not had to say to myself, 'Well, perhaps her audience will accept it.' I myself have accepted it—with acclamations. . . .

I am writing these things because we do not seem to have time to talk them over—& it is so difficult to recall the things one really wants to say—just when one has the hurried chance to say them <u>You are going to have a great success.</u>

With all good wishes
Frances Hodgson Burnett

Audiences loved *The Dawn of Tomorrow;* the response was extraordinary. Ministers preached sermons on the subject, urging their congregations to see it. People wrote hundreds of letters to me about Glad and her influence, as if they had been to a religious service for comfort or guidance and had found what they were seeking.

From Canada I wrote to August Belmont of one memorable audience.

Last night we had a funny experience; it was College Night and the house was crowded with University of Toronto students. Their President and the Mayor addressed them during the entr'actes and they sang college songs.

The Glee Club did the special singing and it was delightful, their tenor had one of the sweetest, purest voices I have ever heard. Well this was all right between the acts—but when the play started they were there for sport and had brought rice, shot, etc. with which to entertain themselves should entertainment not be forthcoming. They talked and made remarks through Sir Oliver's scene with which the play opens. Well in the next scene when the fog came on, it was joy to them, they cat-called, they talked, threw shot which caught in the fog gauze and then fell back with a clatter on the footlights. I was nervous, wondering what would happen later and I sat under my sacks shivering. But the blessed boys were as good as angels once I made my appearance. They seemed to like the play and at the end of each act tried to make me make a speech. They rah-rah-rahed so they almost shook the roof. Of course I didn't make one but it was amusing and I loved them for pocketing their desires for wild mirth and their shot and becoming

just a very appreciative audience. It is rather thrilling to
see so much of youth and backbone of the country massed
together.

Annapolis particularly with an audience of Navy students
always clutches my throat somehow. I respond to a college
yell as some people respond to a bugle and I quoted a line
from Arizona—"Maw ain't much on leather [cowboys], but
she loves gold braid."

That whole year 1909 was one of agonizing indecision, debating with myself whether to stay in the theatre or to abandon
the known world of interesting work and mounting achievement
for marriage and a new way of life. People in the theatre had a
claim on me. Mr. Tyler wrote from Europe that he had seen
Sardou. This famous author apparently was interested in the
report given by an enthusiastic manager, who saw no fault in
any of his stars. Sardou had consented to assign a new play
he was writing to me. Henry Bataille, who had been ill, was
supposed to be recovering, and had a novel story, better he
thought than *La Princesse Lointaine* by Rostand. "It has a tender
yet wonderfully heroic part, with a dramatic death scene in the
last act. You'll enjoy that," was Mr. Tyler's comment.

The New Theatre had just come into being. The handsome
edifice nearing completion was the gift of a small group of
public-spirited New Yorkers, among them Otto Kahn, William
K. Vanderbilt, Archer Huntington, Clarence Mackay, and August
Belmont. The initial contribution of each had been $50,000; the
purpose, to provide for New York a medium-sized opera house
comparable to the Opéra Comique and similar to buildings in
the major cities of Europe, where more intimate musical works
could be presented than at the Metropolitan. Important dramatic
productions were also contemplated. The managing director appointed to launch the project was Winthrop Ames. Thomas
Hastings, the architect, and Helen, his wife, good friends of
mine, invited me to inspect this last word in theatrical architecture. A little oversize for theatre, it seemed to me, yet from
cellar to garret, it was beautifully laid out, and the stage a

dream of technical equipment. I even mounted the scaffolding until I touched a rosette in the ceiling of the New Theatre, "just for luck," as Tommy Hastings said. Winthrop Ames on June 19 wrote that the first season would begin in November and probably run for thirty-two weeks.

> During the first year, we shall make twelve productions, and during the second season probably only eight or ten, carrying over the successes. Of the first twelve one-third are to be classics—Shakespeare and the Old Comedies—the remainder, modern plays of various types.

After telling me about the people in the company he wrote:

> . . . Miss Julia Marlowe will be with us, and . . . if you look favorably on our proposal, . . . you and Miss Marlowe will share the leads between you.
> As far as I now know or expect, there is but one play in which I shall ask you both to appear and that is "A Winter's Tale", in which you would play "Perdita" and Miss Marlowe, "Hermione", and I think it would puzzle the wisest to discover which of these two is the lead. . . .
> If the proposal "likes you", will you tell me what you will expect? I will try to meet you in any way I can, for as I have said in the beginning, we want to persuade you to come with all our hearts, and the only reason I did not ask before was that I inferred a refusal would be inevitable, on account of your previous arrangements.

Winthrop Ames was a delightful friend in the theatre and beyond its confines. And everyone who knew Maude Skinner, mother of Cornelia Otis Skinner, thought her one of those souls that poets write legends about. After an enchanting bit of whimsy on her part, Winthrop Ames's favorite comment was, "Only Barrie could have invented her." His own devoted wife, Lucy Ames, has a touch of this quality; and next to my mother she is the most loyal, the most unselfish person I have ever known.

Winthrop's delightful imagination illuminated every production. He was a perfectionist where detail was concerned; no item was too small to claim his attention. When he retired after thirty years of work lovingly performed in the theatre, the best of the theatre followed him to his home to have the pleasure of listening to his wise, witty conversation and to seek his counsel.

He believed that the theatre was four-dimensional—author, artist, producer, welding together the material and extracting the best from each. The audience was the fourth dimension, and played an exceedingly important part in the whole. His productions were in high favor; he was the pioneer and peer of the best in the theatre of his day.

By holding out a bait tempting to any actor—repertory in a first-class New York company—Winthrop Ames had unconsciously added to the mental turmoil of "Will you, won't you" which I was going through.

PART TWO

I said to a man who stood at the gate of the year, "Give me a light that I may tread safely into the unknown," and he replied, "Go out into the darkness and put your hand into the hand of God. That shall be to you better than a light and safer than a known way!"

—M. Louise Haskins

THE FOUNDING FATHERS considered the pursuit of happiness of so much importance that they wrote it into the Declaration of Independence. On February 26, 1910, newspapers announced that Eleanor Robson was married to August Belmont at her home, 302 West 77 Street, by the Right Reverend Monsignor Lavalle. In Brooklyn only two weeks before I had played my last performance of *The Dawn of Tomorrow,* surrounded by a weeping company. I had slipped quietly away from a life that had held my complete attention for thirteen years, into a new world and, as I then believed, into private life.

THE LAMBS
130 West 44 Street
New York

Dear Miss Robson,

Eight o'clock in the evening and I've just fully realized that I'm not to see "Glad" tonight. I remember that I could hardly speak to you on Saturday—I was too horribly choked —so will you please not regard my note as an impertinence? I presume to send it only to wish you all the happiness there is in the whole wide world.

Roy Fairchild

Roy Fairchild was a young actor who played a minor part in *The Dawn;* for some inexplicable reason his is almost the only letter I kept of the hundreds that came after the public announcement. Some were so poignant, almost funereal; they were frankly disturbing. Several hopefully prophesied my return—one specifically stated within five years. I told my husband, "If I stay as long as that, you may be sure I'll never go back."

In retrospect, the past seems not one existence with a continuous flow of years and events that follow each other in logical sequence, but a life periodically dividing into entirely separate compartments. Change of surroundings, interests, pursuits, has made it seem actually more like different incarnations.

The first, of course—the theatre—now ended. Then came a world of horses, polo, social events, new friends, civic interests and farming, with which I had never dreamed I would be involved and much of which I found fascinating. Each compartment had its joys, its pains, and its problems. In each I found myself engaged, absorbed, like a horse in blinkers, not seeing to right or left, but only concentrating upon the immediate objective ahead.

2

AFTER OUR MARRIAGE and a brief visit to his plantation in South Carolina, my husband chartered a yacht, the *Beryl,* that belonged to Lord Invercauld. It was to meet us in Europe. A motorcar was slung on board so that we could take to the land and explore selected spots of interest. We sailed that spring to Italy, Greece, and Sicily to see their marvelous temples of art. We visited Palermo, Tunis, Girgenti, Corinth, Athens, Corfu, Trieste, Venice.

We stopped at Naples to pick up Mrs. Frances Wolcott and Charles Coleman. They were old friends. He was an artist born in Buffalo who lived in a dream of a house on a hill in Capri. On his terrace by moonlight, Mr. Coleman, a slender, handsome old man, would dance the tarantella with verve and grace for a few delighted friends. He knew Italy and Greece intimately, both as an artist and tourist. Mrs. Wolcott was an extremely well-read traveler who had lived abroad for part of many years. We were fortunate to have them as traveling companions.

Mrs. Wolcott accused me of having a sticky fly-paper memory. Her own was amazing, at times photographic. She could describe exactly where she had seen a particular work of art, in which museum, on which side of which room, twenty years later. She had an intense curiosity about people and things, and a relish for gossip, true or false. She always managed to keep talent about her. In spite of being stout and plain of features, she wore her Worth dresses with an air. It was shortly after she had divorced Senator Wolcott of Colorado that I first met her, after the *Mary Ann* opening. Referring sadly to her lined and almost accordion-pleated skin, she said, "You have only to look at my face to know that a man has walked all over it."

Filled with zest to visit Greece again, Mrs. Wolcott overcame her apprehension as to yachting in early April. Someone had advised raw onions as a preventive measure for seasickness, and one day in a storm, although our rooms were far apart, I became miserably conscious that we seemed to have onions to the right of us, onions to the left of us. This courageous lady was trying the drastic remedy. After we reached port she told me that our steward, a Scot with a broad accent, called down to her: "Mrs. Wolcott, Mum, ye should be on deck, here's Stromboli coming up." At the moment, onion-ridden, she couldn't bear the thought of anything else coming up. So, reluctant as we were to miss Stromboli, neither of us saw the small island and its volcano which was smoldering picturesquely when the *Beryl* danced by. A horse we later named "Stromboli" in remembrance of that day gave a fine account of himself for many years. Yachting makes sightseeing easy, but it should never be recommended for a honeymoon unless both parties to the contract are good sailors.

Because I had read a book on Dalmatia, an area unfamiliar to most Americans at that time, we decided to explore the coast, going to places where the inhabitants had rarely, if ever, seen Americans.

One gray evening, moist with fog, the *Beryl* put in to Cattaro, the main harbor of Montenegro. My husband was genuinely cross because I refused to obey the ship doctor and take care of a cold in my comfortable stateroom. We decided not to use our motorcar but to hire one to take us up the perilous road that weaves its way back and forth along the steep mountainside to the capital, Cetinje, which is perched on the top.

Shrouded in fog, we could see nothing beyond a few feet ahead. My husband seated himself beside the chauffeur. In all my life I never saw such an angry back. However, the next morning revealed one of the most beautiful sights imaginable, mountainous scenery for miles and miles, with flourishing farms scattered like rugs of many colors in the valleys. The countryside was inhabited by sturdy women and the handsomest men we had ever seen outside the sculpture galleries of museums, all dressed in gay Merry Widow costumes. Many of the men had pistols stuck in either side of a broad silk girdle. They looked fiercely picturesque, yet they had kind faces wreathed in come-hither smiles. Mrs. Wolcott looking eagerly about sighed, "Oh, to be eighteen and live in Montenegro!"

Enthusiastically we walked about the streets. Suddenly, at ten o'clock, we were face to face with seven or eight ministers arriving for a conference with Prince (later that year, King) Nicholas of Montenegro. Dressed in black cutaway coats and wearing high silk hats—a strange contrast to the native costume—in that brilliant sunshine they resembled emperor penguins lost on a mountaintop.

By this time it was agreed that my reading had introduced us to a gem of a country. Everyone wanted more of Dalmatia—by land, however—and when we returned to the yacht we decided to take our car and drive along the coast, sending the *Beryl* ahead to meet us at Ragusa.

The road was not too good, but no one cared; it didn't roll around like a yacht and the views were superb. After some sixty miles or more we were confronted by a startling dilemma. The road ended in a small fishing village and directly in our path was a broad inlet with no visible road to circle round the jungle growth and no bridge or apparent means of getting across the expanse of water. To add to the difficulty, the several languages at the disposal of my husband and the others were useless as a means of communication. Even our courier-chauffeur spoke no tongue familiar in Hertzegovina.

Finally a bright-looking fellow, using the sign language of the first man Adam, signaled us to wait, and disappeared. To go back the way we came was useless, the yacht had gone on its watery road up the coast. So while the natives poked and patted the car, we waited as patiently as possible. Once again I was out of favor. Hadn't I read a book about Dalmatia? Had it said anything about this road failure? Definitely it had not. When the bright boy returned he brought with him a man who spoke broken but welcome English. It seemed he had worked for two years in Pittsburgh. An uncle died leaving him property so he came home, yet he longed for Pittsburgh, and welcomed us as blood brothers. He told us the road round the inlet could not be completed because they ran out of money, but next *year* it would be finished. This in no way solved our problem. Once he could make himself understood my husband was wonderful— he always was when confronted with a crisis. That day the strategy and fighting spirit of his grandfather Commodore Perry were clearly revealed.

With the aid of our friendly interpreter he secured sturdy boats and fairly soon the natives had constructed a pontoon for transporting automobile and chauffeur, while another boat took the rest of us, plus our local and most useful friend to engineer the return of the pontoon. Like Washington cautiously moving his army across the Delaware, my husband slowly but trium-phantly landed us on the other side amid cheers and hand-waving from the receding shore. We proceeded to Zara, explor-ing the coast; ultimately, after our pioneering trip, once more met the yacht at Ragusa. Leaving our friends and the *Beryl* at Venice, we motored back to France.

After nearly two months voyaging, we returned to America for the late spring, enthralled by all we had seen.

3

HOUSEKEEPING was the greatest difficulty that confronted me. I was transplanted from a little house which Mother and I owned and operated with one do-all, care-for-all Negro maid, to houses here and there: in Hempstead, Long Island; Nursery Farm in Babylon; a bungalow in Kentucky; The Surcingle, a cottage in Saratoga, set in the center of a small, private training track that adjoined Saratoga race course; a shooting place in South Carolina; houses like that in New York and By the Sea in Newport, with sixteen servants for indoor housekeeping and four men in the garage, three in the stable, and several gardeners. It was a new world. The innumerable details necessary to smooth administration in this department oppressed me. Other things, almost anything, could take my mind off housekeeping. Those agitating problems, while many and various, are now for several reasons over the hills and far away.

In the big houses of fashionable New York and Newport in the season, party followed party in rapid succession. I must say I enjoyed it thoroughly. To the wanderer from another planet, where protection from the outside world was a basic rule for stars in those days, people were unbelievably kind. But I found such an endless round of strangers and entertainment was frequently more exhausting than previous hard work had been.

Golf, the only sport I attempted, proved hopelessly baffling. My point of view was that of an anti-golfer who once queried, "What's the use of chasing a little ball round the field, *especially* when you have the ball to begin with?"

The lovely low-hung Victoria that had belonged to my mother-in-law, Caroline Perry Belmont, was used for afternoon drives and the inevitable round of calls and leaving of innumerable cards. This carriage, the whole turnout, was a thing of beauty, but I preferred seeing the sunset on the renowned ocean drive at Newport with Maude Wetmore, daughter of Senator Wetmore of Rhode Island, in her small self-driven automobile.

My husband liked to drive four-in-hand, and we frequently sallied forth in this picturesque coach with four prancing horses, which he controlled skillfully.

At my earnest request, perhaps prompted by a now restrained dramatic instinct, a coaching party was set in motion that first summer in Newport. Five or six coaches assembled in our driveway one afternoon and then, as the footmen on each coach blew repeatedly on the horns, we drove out of the gate and down Bellevue Avenue in formal parade. William Woodward led off with Colonel William Jay, a renowned whip (who was visiting his daughter, Mrs. Arthur Burden) on the box beside him. Other coaches, driven by Frank Sturgis, William Goadby Loew, Victor Loew, turned out, and F. Ambrose Clark, also a visitor, borrowed a coach for the occasion. We drove down the avenue, circling the ocean drive to the golf club; there we were greeted by a group of summer folk who thoroughly enjoyed the show. After tea was served, we remounted, and amid more horn blowing and a great deal of fanfare, we returned at a spanking pace to By the Sea, "the observed of all observers." To my knowledge, it was the last coaching parade in Newport, the home of many coaches in the picturesque age of graceful living.

I remember one Newport party at the home of Mr. and Mrs. Stuyvesant Fish. Mrs. Fish was an indefatigable hostess with a flair for providing the unusual in entertainment. She had a habit of making witty, occasionally caustic, remarks that provided her less accomplished neighbors with stories that lasted all summer, and all winter, too.

Stuyvesant Fish, a large-framed, reserved man, admired his wife enormously and was entertained by her. Mrs. Fish had a fine figure, but lacked beauty of face. Blessed with a nimble mind and a dominant personality, she expressed her opinions forcefully and gave the impression, "Wherever MacDonald sits, there is the head of the table," with herself cast as MacDonald. This particular day she had hurriedly arranged a luncheon in honor of Bishop Brent, who had arrived unexpectedly in Newport from the Philippines, where he was administering a spectacularly fine diplomatic and missonary job. As we went in to lunch, our hostess murmured a warning to me that the neighbor on my right might need to be coaxed to good humor. Ambassador George Bakhmeteff, married to an American, was a clever, crusty old diplomat, abrupt of speech and a stickler for protocol. He always liked a bottle of claret to himself so that he would not have to wait for the butler to refill his glass. Whenever he lunched or dined out, a carafe of claret was set beside his glass. Mrs. Fish had provided him with her choicest wine, *but* she had placed Bishop Brent on her right and the Ambassador of all the Russias on her left. Needless to say, the going during luncheon was difficult; the aura of his displeasure was evident.

After the ladies left the dining room, Mrs. Fish whispered to me that at table the Ambassador had questioned her seating arrangements, saying, "Mrs. Fish, please explain; I do not understand. Is it customary in America to put an ambassador on your left and a bishop on your right?"

Mrs. Fish swallowed hard before she replied, "Oh no, Your Excellency, I assure you it is *not* customary. It just depends on which you put first, God or the Czar."

Two parties that we ourselves gave in Newport come to mind, the first a dinner of forty-eight and the second a lawn party with Houdini, the great magician, as star performer.

The dinner, I remember, did not come off well. Perry Belmont had recently sold the old family place to my husband. After it was thoroughly renovated we decided to give a house warming. My one criticism of the parties where we had been generously entertained was that either the older generation dined *or* the younger set; generally it was a case of "never the twain shall meet." I proposed to have our dinner half and half—to allow an older man the pleasure of a younger woman on one side at least, she to have a young man on the other side and so on round the long table.

That first year—unfamiliar with the ancient or modern feuds of Newport—my mistakes were many and varied. One couple, who hadn't been invited to By the Sea for years by the senior Mrs. Belmont, accepted my invitation with alacrity. I placed lovely modern-minded Elsie Clews next to the formal, old-school chairman of Bailey's Beach, not knowing that he had re-fused to speak to her after she went in bathing there without stockings, in spite of the committee ruling in the summer of 1910 that long stockings were required articles for ladies at this beach. This was typical of the times. They assure me that the wording which was tacked on the wall of each of the ladies' bathhouses at Northeast Harbor swimming pool when it was opened in 1898 was: "Ladies in bathing suits are requested not to lounge in the sun, as it may cause just criticism."

After that dinner Newport buzzed with gossip for days. My husband laughed it off, and said it was all part of experience. About this time I confided to him that I should like to write a book to be entitled, "The Outlaws and In-laws of Society."

He objected to this flight of imagination. "If you don't tell the truth, there would be no point in it—if you told the truth, the points would make you and everyone else uncomfortable." And he quoted a saying attributed to Mark Twain, "A little truth is a dangerous thing; a great deal is fatal."

The second party went smoothly. Houdini was at the height of his fame. My husband, a veritable Peter Pan in youth of mind, fell completely under his spell. Indeed, so did everyone. In front of his tent on our lawn his paraphernalia—a screen, trunk, life-sized milk can, handcuffs, sacks in which he would be tied—were spread out by his assistant to be examined.

The *Scout* was anchored not far off shore and, as a final demonstration of the magician's ability, my husband took him in the launch out to the yacht. They were accompanied by several of our guests, who were to watch every move. Houdini was bound with ropes, handcuffed, then placed in a huge box that was roped securely and slowly lowered over the side of the *Scout* into the water.

The rest of us stood on shore watching breathlessly to see if and when he would appear. What if he couldn't get out? Thank goodness he came to the surface—Houdini always did—and was towed by the launch to shore.

The party was declared a great success, the day divine, and our lawn sweeping down from the house to the ocean drive made a perfect setting.

4

SEVERAL TIMES that first winter we went sleigh riding in Central Park, a pleasure that quickly disappeared from city life with the rapid advance of a motor age and changing climate. Sleighing had style: the coachman and footman on the box in their smart liveries with cockades in their hats, their big fur capes; the open sleigh lined with buffalo robes; fur boots for ladies' feet and sealskin rugs for two; Central Park beautifully wrapped in sparkling white; the spirited horses; the gliding motion of the sleigh. It had poetic glamour.

The luxury of dinners and balls in the great houses in New York in 1910 was impressive. Footmen frequently lined the hall and stairway, standing motionless in full livery, like a guard of honor, as you passed, dressed in your best, to the drawing room or ballroom.

Everyone fortunate enough to be invited went to the Harry Whitney parties. You enjoyed the people you met there; great artists played and sang for them with warm appreciation for the cordial reception they received. Enrico Caruso was a frequent guest, and we reveled in his incomparable voice. Anna Pavlova and Mikhail Mordkin danced on one occasion, I remember.

As a stockholder, my husband owned a box at the Metropolitan Opera. That first winter Mr. and Mrs. Joseph H. Choate dined with us and then went to a performance. Ambassador Choate, a noted raconteur, was in the midst of a delightful tale when the curtain rose following an intermission. Unconscious of the fact, Mr. Choate went on with his story. Suddenly we were startled; someone was shushing. I whispered that the curtain was up. Mr. Choate whispered back, "Do you like opera?"

"Yes," I murmured. "Don't you?"

"No," he said softly, "I think it is just an interruption to good conversation."

Box No. 4 offered a perfect vantage point from which to watch the orchestra and its leaders. My attention was riveted upon Maestro Arturo Toscanini much of the time when he was in the pit. The scoreless desk before him, his beautiful head, his baton that commanded and restrained with superb musicianship, his left hand, palm upward, that quivered tremulously over his heart when he desired an artist to give out more feeling— these were spellbinding. One saw a powerful magician at work, a benevolent Svengali who evoked whatever mood and tone he wished from singers and orchestra alike.

In box No. 2, close to the proscenium, sat Augustus Juilliard, an opera lover, who attended more performances than anyone in the famous Horseshoe. On the other side was the William K. Vanderbilt box, No. 6. One night the performance had been *Aïda*, sung by Emmy Destinn, Louise Homer, Pasquale Amato, and Caruso, with Toscanini conducting—a glorious memory. After the third act Nile scene, when the audience was spellbound, I became aware that Mrs. Vanderbilt was preparing to leave. "You're not going?" I asked incredulously.

"Yes," she answered; "when you have heard perfection, why wait?"

The winter of 1911 was an exceptional season. Engelbert Humperdinck arrived for the premiere of *Die Königskinder* with Geraldine Farrar as the Goose Girl, Louise Homer, the witch. Giacomo Puccini was here also, for the world premiere of his latest work, *The Girl of the Golden West*, with Destinn and Caruso in leading roles. The William K. Vanderbilts gave a dinner for these two distinguished composers.

Short and tubby of build, with a gentle nearsighted smile on his Germanic countenance, Humperdinck was strangely gnomelike in appearance. His close association with witches and fairy tales such as *Hänsel und Gretel* seemed to have left a mark on him, as he left his artistic stamp on them. Somewhat elusive, he made you feel that at any moment he might disappear from sight.

Puccini, on the contrary, was very much a man of the world, good-looking, a vibrant personality, and completely at ease with all comers. The two men could hardly have been more unlike —yet each had a personal success that night.

In addition to the two principal guests of honor, Mrs. Vanderbilt, an exceptional hostess, had invited a choice group of musicians to bear them company, among others the popular Toscanini. Josef Hofmann, another star in this group, played after dinner in his most brilliant form.

Later in the evening, when all but a few had departed, Hofmann went back to the piano and played as he probably had never played for us mortals. Humperdinck and Puccini hung over the piano, one on either side, requesting this or that favorite. Hofmann had recently returned from Russia and was deeply affected by the folk music he had found there. Like children entranced with a fairy story, the visiting composers begged for more and more, and we, the happy few, stayed on in a magic circle of enchantment far into the night.

5

AN OUTSTANDING HOSTESS in New York and Newport, on their yacht, or wherever she pitched her tent, was Mrs. Cornelius Vanderbilt, Jr. To Grace Vanderbilt entertaining, for which she had a genuine flair, was a career. She expended time, thought, and personal effort in making her parties a success; as a result they were splendid affairs.

Her annual Christmas party, with a small gift on the giant tree for each guest, was a link with the past. Old New Yorkers and newcomers drifted in, enjoying the company, music and refreshments. People one had not seen for ages assembled under her hospitable roof on this occasion. They gathered from remote corners. Frequently as they emerged from unsociable retirement you had a feeling that Angel Gabriel had blown his horn. For the last party, perhaps two years before she died, Mrs. Vanderbilt was in a wheel chair and almost blind. However, she arrived, late as usual, butler and footman in attendance. True to form, she still did things in the grand manner. Her head was held high, the customary bandeau restraining her naturally curly hair, now quite white.

Occasionally people accused her of overemphasis on royalty and titles, but to my definite knowledge, she was loyal to old friends, even when their fortunes changed for the worse.

6

A PRIVATE RAILROAD CAR is not an acquired taste. One takes to it immediately. *Mineola,* named after my husband's favorite sloop, which he raced to many a victory, was a familiar sight in the New York railway stations. The *Mineola,* staffed by our jewel of a French chef and a Negro porter, took us into Canada moose hunting; or to the Restigouche salmon fishing; to Lexington for visits to the Nursery Stud Farm to see the stallions Rocksand, Hastings, Fair Play, and the brood mares with their lovely foals wandering over the fields of luxuriant Kentucky bluegrass. It took us to Garnet, South Carolina, in quail season. I refused to shoot anything at any time, but always went along with a book in my saddlebag, in case the menfolk were away longer than usual with the dogs, hunting. My talks with the Negroes who held the hunters' horses were thoughtful interludes. One of them, Jess, a prime favorite, tall and broad of beam, always wore clothes that looked as if they had been handed down by an elder brother considerably smaller than himself. Even the cap which he wore on the side of his head resembled a souvenir from boyhood days. Jess frequently talked religion with solemnity. He was a supporter of the church, a Baptist of the first water. One day I asked him, "You know so much about religion, Jess, tell me, what is the difference between a Methodist and a Baptist?"

Jess thought carefully, as he drew on his pipe, then he drawled, "Well, Miss, I guess you 'splains it this way. The difference—it's jes a question of the amount of water they uses."

7

LONG BEFORE we were married my husband liked to consult me about naming the foals. It became a sort of "What shall we name the baby?" pastime. His practice was to use the initial letter of the dam's name and, whenever possible, some association with the breeding line. After we returned from our honeymoon, we were notified by the *Stud Book* that three suggested names for a filly out of Merry Token by Rocksand already had been taken. I had heard an Arabic greeting in Tunis, a friendly salutation that meant more than "Good Day"—It also implied "May good things be with you," "*Mahubah*—no one will have taken this name," I assured my husband. No one had. Years later I learned, according to an authority on Arabic, that the spelling provided earlier for Man o' War's dam was not correct. The pronunciation remains the same, but her name should be spelled Mahabah. When the mistake was discovered, it was too late to change. Mahubah was entered in the *Stud Book* and the mare already was famous as the dam of the classic winner, Man o' War. The name was spelled incorrectly, but undoubtedly the world will agree that, as a good omen, it fulfilled its purpose. Fair Play, Mahubah, Man o' War, all three products of the Belmont breeding stable, are great names in American turf history. I am proud and really not too modest about the fact that in addition to Mahubah and her famous son, Man o' War, I christened three other favorite winners of our stable, Stromboli, Hourless, and Ladkin. My husband was not too enthusiastic about the name Hourless for the son of Hourglass, but he said, "Never mind, a great horse makes any name seem right. Time will tell if this is a good choice."

8

THE BELMONT RACING STABLE has been famous from the days when August Belmont, Sr., and his friend, Leonard Jerome, American grandfather of Winston Spencer Churchill, founded the Jerome Park Race Course and drove their four-in-hand coaches about the city. The Belmont colors, scarlet and maroon, were established in those days. The men servants' liveries were a maroon coat with scarlet piping and silver buttons with the Belmont crest, and knee breeches of black satin. All carriages were painted maroon with a scarlet stripe on the wheels.

The Nursery Stud just outside Lexington, Kentucky, was the breeding farm. In 1910, a fine product, Tracery, a two-year-old, had been sent to England with reasonable expectation that he would win the Derby. He gave a good account of himself, but came in third in the unfamiliar surroundings. During the season of 1912, however, in truly fine style, he captured the St. Leger, one of England's turf classics. Congratulations poured in from staunch racing friends, Harry Whitney, Herman Duryea, William K. Vanderbilt in America; the Rothschilds and Lord Rosebery among others abroad.

The next year Tracery was entered for the Ascot Gold Cup, a coveted prize hitherto excluded from the Belmont trophies. The race promised a thrill, as it was the first time Prince Palatine, who had won the St. Leger in 1911, and Tracery were to meet. We had been visiting in France but, for business reasons, my husband was needed in America; reluctantly we gave up seeing the Ascot race and set sail.

On the homeward voyage a cable came from Leopold de Rothschild with the news that Tracery had been leading the field on the home stretch by several lengths when a suffragist sympathizer had dashed out of the inner field as the horses rounded the curve, brandishing in one hand a suffragist flag and in the other a fully loaded six-chambered revolver of an old-fashioned type. He caught Tracery by the bridle and shouted to the jockey to stop. On the instant he was thrown to the ground with Tracery and the jockey. The next horse and the next came down, while Prince Palatine—fortunately for him several lengths away—came from behind to win. Why the demented man was not killed, no one could understand. He achieved the desired publicity dramatically; the accident and the suffragist cause were blazoned on the front page of every paper on both sides of the Atlantic. By a miracle our jockey, though badly shaken, was not killed. Tracery's shoulder was cruelly damaged. The first expectation was that the horse would never race again.

However, he later met the challengers for another important classic, The Eclipse Stakes, over the same course. Fears were expressed on all sides that the horse would swerve when the crowd surged across the inner field, as the horses rounded the same curve, for the home stretch. The jockey told us afterward that Tracery's shoulder muscles tensed when he saw the onrushing crowd, but gallantly he maintained his stride and kept on to the finish. I cabled Mother: "TRACERY WON EASILY. WE WITNESSED VICTORY FROM THE KING'S BOX. HAD DELIGHTFUL DAY. LOVE."

We had spent the night before the race with the Rothschilds at Ascot Wing, Leighton Buzzard. King George came to dinner; Queen Mary was not present. We were informed that she seldom attended the races; not one of her favorite diversions. After dinner, our host escorted the King to the smoking room, followed by the gentlemen. The ladies remained behind, each in her place at table; turning toward the King, we slowly curtsied like drooping flowers as he left the room.

When the gentlemen assembled, King George talked to my husband about Tracery's chances the next day, and their respective stables. His Majesty inquired how many mares we had in Kentucky, to which my husband replied, "Sire, I never count them for fear my conscience would trouble me."

9

LONG SHOTS occasionally are fantastic. I remember when a sprightly young filly from our stable, Fieldmouse, pranced onto the track at Belmont Park. A family friend, Fred Beach, had been asked by one of his guests to place five dollars on the Belmont entry, which was a long shot.

En route to the betting ring, he stopped to have a drink with a friend. Suddenly they heard a roar from the crowd. Investigation revealed that as the horses paraded to the starting pole,

Fieldmouse had thrown her jockey and was racing alone around the track.

"That settles her chances for today," Fred Beach said. "Let's go back to the club. My friend will be grateful I didn't place her five dollars."

Some minutes later they again heard a roar outside, and were stunned to learn that August Belmont's Fieldmouse had come in first, winning the race at odds of 100 to 1. Mr. Beach nobly paid the $500 debt, and ruefully thereafter avoided long shots.

A race between Hourless and Omar Khayyam made a great day in Belmont Park history. To sportsmen a match race between two contending and outstanding thoroughbreds is a stirring event. To get away from the crowd, we had gone to the top of the Belmont Park grandstand, where the view was commanding. When the race started, our entry, Hourless, one of the pets of the stable, faltered; then as Omar swept along, Hourless seemed almost out of the race. Suddenly he surged forward and farther forward; coming gallantly from behind at great speed, Hourless finished a length ahead.

The cheers of 50,000 or more sports fans were almost as thrilling as the race. Silently, slowly, we descended from the grandstand after the race was over. My husband smiled but said nothing. Trembling, I clutched the railing. It seemed inevitable that in spite of the cheering multitude, people must—they couldn't help but hear how my knees rattled. If you love animals of any kind—aside from the pleasure they give you personally—it becomes agonizingly important, once entered, how they fare in a contest. The race track never gave me pleasure, but I thoroughly enjoyed the Stud Farm in Kentucky.

10

In 1917 my husband had been diligently working with the Government Remount Service, both giving and securing from others horses that were badly needed in the Army. In this connection he was offered a commission as major, with instructions to report at a given date to General Dawes in Paris for assignment.

Before leaving, he decided to sell most of his yearlings, keeping only two colts, one by Hourless and a golden chestnut by Fair Play. Ultimately, he decided to sell the whole string. He was having trouble with his trainer, and for this reason, as well as those of economy, he determined to cut drastically the entire training stable and give his whole attention to Army service.

Robert L. Gerry had always been eager to have a horse from the Belmont Stable to improve his own racing stock. My husband telephoned and advised him to buy either or both of the favored colts, saying that they represented the best youngsters the Nursery Stud had produced in years, especially the chestnut, Man o' War. Samuel Riddle of Pennsylvania was interested in buying Belmont horses, urged to do so by Louis Feustal, his trainer, who had been brought up from the age of nine in the Belmont Stable. In spite of the war, interest was keen the day of the sale in Saratoga. Robert Gerry bid $4,500 for the chestnut colt, then decided to stop. Feustal begged Mr. Riddle to bid again; he did, and Man o' War was sold to him for $5,000, the greatest bargain in turf history.

As a race horse he won purses amounting to between $750,000 and $1,000,000, and at that time was declared the greatest race horse which had ever been produced in America. When he was retired to the stud at a large service fee, he earned an income of over $100,000 annually for his owner. Acknowledged to be a great sire, he lived to a ripe old age, and when he died was honored with a funeral service and attention such as few humans have commanded.

If my husband was disappointed that this great horse did not race under his colors he never indicated it to me or to anyone. The science of breeding first-class thoroughbreds with stamina concerned him profoundly. He was always proud that as a result of his careful selection, his stable had produced the sire Fair Play, the dam Mahubah, and their great colt, Man o' War.

When he was judging at the races, my husband never bet. As chairman of the American Jockey Club and president of the Westchester Racing Association, which controls Belmont Park, he was entitled to be in the Judges' Stand for all races whenever present at the track, except, of course, when his own horses were racing. On these occasions, if he believed the horse entered had a chance, he would place $500 or double on the outcome. The winnings, if and when collected, were divided among all hands at the stable. He was a sportsman in the best sense of the word; when he won, his enthusiasm was never apparent; when he lost, he never flinched, no matter how deep the disappointment.

11

ABOUT 1912, a somewhat serious operation apparently lay ahead of me. Dr. W. Gill Wylie, a skillful surgeon, although getting along in years, was selected to see me through. He chose for the operating theatre a well-known hospital recently done over from stem to stern, where he functioned as chief surgeon. Fairly drastic medical procedures had been going on for two weeks; now, after a light supper at home, this weary patient was to be surrendered to the hospital at seven o'clock. When we arrived, we were almost blown out of the building by the overpowering odor of every kind of paint and varnish that had been invented by man. The room allotted to me was cell-like; dead white paint glittered on the walls. My anxious husband declared in stentorian tones he would have none of it, that "the whole place looked and smelled like a slaughterhouse." Taking himself to the telephone, he routed out his friend and surgeon, Dr. William Coley, from a dinner party and demanded help. Ignoring medical protocol, he insisted they must transfer me to the General Memorial Hospital to a comfortable room that had been assigned to him when his appendix was removed. Dr. Coley said it was occupied by a patient of his who fortunately was leaving the next day. My husband demanded, "Can't you get him out tonight?" The final result of this unethical spirited commotion was that two hours later, faint with weariness, I was put to bed in a small room on the ground floor at the Memorial Hospital. It was noisy, but the sounds were familiar and the room odorless. After the operation next morning, I awoke to find myself in a home-like room with chintz curtains at the window, plenty of fresh June air, and birds singing in the vine-covered walls outside.

During my convalescence, encouraged by my interest, Dr. Wylie described to me his experience as a young Bellevue Hospital surgeon. In 1872, the Bellevue board of managers decided that they must establish a training school for nurses, patterned after the Nightingale School in London; it was to be the first of its kind in America, and the person to consult about this new experiment obviously was the famous leader herself. Dr. Wylie was dispatched to London on the mission.

He found Miss Nightingale unable to keep the appointment. Not long after his return to America, he received a sixteen-page letter written in Florence Nightingale's neat handwriting, advising him what were the requirements of a training school for nurses as she conceived it—the essential principles and procedures of training and the conduct of nurses in the sick room. Dr. Wylie assured me it was better to have her letter, which in a way represented the ten commandments of nursing, instead of his planned interview. A perfect case of "Be grateful for the blessings that fly over your head."

During the war I tried to find this letter to exhibit at a special conference of nurses. Mrs. Wylie, as executor, had given her husband's medical documents to Bellevue. On investigation they thought Dr. Wylie's papers were stored somewhere in the cellar. Mrs. William Church Osborn, gracious President of the Board of Managers of the Bellevue Training School for Nurses, undertook to assist in the search. The precious Nightingale letter was finally found and permission granted to take it to the Red Cross national headquarters. We set the pages up on a metal stand constructed so that you could see both sides of each page as the great woman had written her message. And the nurses queued up for the sight as if they were going to see the Declaration of Independence or a popular movie. The significant thing about the document was and still is that, eighty-five years later, it is as sound an outline of the basic principles of nursing as if it had been written today.

12

ONE OF the early believers in aviation, my husband was a director of the Wright Company and a stockholder. He was president of the International Aviation Tournament when the first aviation meet in the East was held at Belmont Park from October 22 to October 30, 1910. An important test flight in air-mail service was scheduled from some point, Washington I think, to Long Island. Our guest of honor was the French Ambassador, J. J. Jusserand. Like most Frenchmen he was keenly interested in aviation and was pleased with my husband's support of these experiments.

A curious yet credulous crowd assembled for the arrival of the competing planes. The appointed hour came and went, and a misty fog dampened our hopes. Another hour passed, still no planes. People decided that there was nothing to this flying business after all, and minute by minute they slowly drifted away. Suddenly, phantomlike, out of the driving mist and drizzle, flying directly toward us, came first one and then another, then a third plane. The landing of men from Mars could not have been more fantastically unreal.

What amazing courage pioneer airmen had in those early days! As someone said, Jesse H. Jones, I think, "There were not adequate airports, no beacons, no airway radio communications of any kind; pilots had to depend entirely upon their skill, knowledge and intuition, with now and again a fervent prayer for just plain luck." Praise God who gives us pioneers in all professions, say I. Today youth casually takes for granted automobiles, radios, airplanes, television. Those who watched these strange adjuncts to our world emerge, one by one, enjoyed the wonder of miracles, and the thrill of participating in them.

In 1912, my husband helped to finance a French group interested in developing stabilizers. Stabilizing was then a serious problem in aviation. In 1913, we went on an inspection visit to the hangar just outside Chartres, where Paul Schmidt, a French engineer-inventor, kept his experimental machine. As our train drew into the station, we saw the plane coming to meet us. I shall never forget the optical illusion that, like a miraculous bird, the plane was flying between the spires of the Chartres Cathedral. The tiny craft, a novel escort in those days, accompanied our car, circling over our heads as we drove to the suburbs.

The wind had been strong. All airfield signals indicated "no flying." However, the inventor, Paul Schmidt, and the pilot were eager to demonstrate the new stabilizer, so the latter took off into the air. When he returned to the field he assured us it was bumpy aloft but safe, so I insisted on going up; my initial plane ride was literally a breath-taking event. The machine was not really built for a passenger. I was strapped to a seat directly back of the exposed engine, and the exhaust kept puff, puff, puffing in my face. I could only breathe with my head turned completely to one side while my hand, cupped firmly round my nose and mouth, kept the fumes partly deflected. Gasping for breath, I saw little of the world around me. When we returned to earth half an hour later my husband behaved as if his stubborn wife had been to China. Due to the wind the stabilizer had not impressed me as a brilliant success, and the fumes were decidedly unpalatable; even so, in 1913 it was a thrilling experience.

A note in my line-a-day book shows: "Sunday, May 27, 1928. Flew with Lindbergh in his new Ryan Monoplane." Mrs. Henry Davison gave a luncheon party at Peacock Point that day in honor of Lindbergh, a friend of her aviator son, Trubee. After lunch this courageous pilot of the celebrated *Spirit of St. Louis* took us one at a time in his plane for a taxi tour of Long Island.

In the years that followed, Charles Lindbergh temporarily lost his perspective when he became absorbed in the subject of isolationism. The world of politics was not his métier. Alas, as many knew at the time, isolationism for the United States was no longer a policy—it was a predicament.

Dwight W. Morrow, our Ambassador to Mexico, invited Charles Lindbergh and Will Rogers to Mexico City as good will ambassadors from the United States. Two of the Morrow daughters were there, Elizabeth and Anne. Will Rogers reported that at a party in honor of this great Knight of the Air, reserved, silent Lindbergh "walked around the two lovely girls as if they were a hole in the ice."

Years later, when Betty Morrow held open house at Next Day Hill, their hospitable home in Englewood, Anne, the eldest daughter, already concerned with writing, talked poetry with me at some length. When I left, my apology was genuine for having detained a busy young hostess earlier in the evening. She replied, "Please don't regret it. To me it was an island of safety in an ocean of conversation."

Her father and mother helped to make the history of their community bright; truly a torch has passed from their hands to hers.

13

WHEN HE LEFT Harvard University, my husband entered the banking house of August Belmont & Company and, when his father died in 1890, assumed charge of the business. He had vision beyond the average man in his group, and was an active participant in a broad variety of affairs. As a vice president of the National Civic Federation, he was an active member of the committee which in 1909 secured the passage of the Workmen's Compensation bill for New York State.

He was chairman of the board of the Louisville and Nashville Railroad Company when that railroad was brought close to perfection. When he worked, he worked extremely hard, and he played with equal concentration. His constructive interest in sporting matters was well known. He founded hunting and polo clubs. The Belmont fox terrier kennels were celebrated. He became president and guiding mind of the American Kennel Club which under his direction grew to be the national and official organization of the country.

Few people know that he introduced from Europe the use of spiked shoes for track runners. He helped to found the American Jockey Club, became its chairman, and by virtue of this office was an honorary member of the English Jockey Club.

A vice commodore of the New York Yacht Club, he was one of a small group of ardent amateur sailors that twice built defenders for *America's* Cup, the yachting trophy that Sir Thomas Lipton strove so frequently to win. When the *Shamrock IV* was defeated the second time, August Belmont privately expressed regret that Sir Thomas didn't succeed; regardless of national pride, he felt it would have been in the best interest of the sport to have the cup cross the Atlantic again. Also, he believed the odds against a foreigner in this international race were too great. A yacht, according to the original rules, must be made in the home waters of the challenger. It must be stoutly constructed to sail across the Atlantic. The chances in modern times of a foreigner beating a yacht that has only to contend with home waters are slim indeed. In any case the cup has remained locked away. I understand the rules have recently been changed and interest may be revived.

Like August Belmont, Sr., who had been chairman of the Democratic National Committee for years, my husband was a staunch Democrat. He was a director of the Metropolitan Opera and Real Estate Company, one of the founders of the New Theatre, and a member of many civic organizations. When we married, his active interests were legion. Outstanding among them were The Rapid Transit Subway Construction Company, of which he was chairman, building the Cape Cod Canal, which he had launched in 1909, and horse racing, with its many ramifications at home and abroad.

A friend of his, a distinguished lawyer, Joseph A. Auerbach, said once, "August would be a genius if he did not submerge so much of himself in detail." A priceless sense of fun with a slightly salty flavor that he called his "Perry sense of humor," coupled with a broad knowledge of affairs made him excellent company. He thoroughly mastered the details of any project assumed. A favorite expression of his is revealing—"If you want a thing done, go—if you don't, send."

One day he asked which, if any, was my political party. "I'm a Democrat," I said, "because as a girl in school I loved the pictures of Grover Cleveland's wife."

"Many a Democrat would endorse that platform," he answered. A loyal admirer of Grover Cleveland, he and Mr. J. P. Morgan, Sr., were the leading bankers who supported that President in his determination to keep the country on the gold standard.

Like taxes, the gold standard has always been one of life's mysteries to me, so I was quite sympathetic when an old friend, Julian Mason, the journalist and author, one-time editor of the New York *Herald Tribune,* sent me the following story about his wife. England in 1931 had just reluctantly gone off the gold standard, and Julian heard her telephoning to a friend in Southampton: "O, Fanny, sell every stock you own. England's just gone *on* the gold standard!"

"*Off* it, you mean," he roared.

"Never mind, dear," Florence said sweetly. "Fanny will be just as frightened one way as the other."

Naturally we attended the Democratic Convention in 1912. As a delegate, August Belmont was with the New York group on the Convention floor, and I was seated in the balcony.

William J. Bryan, although a defeated presidential candidate, still had a large following. People flocked to hear him for the challenge of his views and the excitement of his theatrical oratory, although they voted against him consistently. When he rose to address the Convention, the hall was packed; the audience, attentive. His speech was dramatic, stormy with challenge. Suddenly he launched into a vicious attack on several of the New York delegation, August Belmont among them, and upon Wall Street "interests." He wound up with a fiery resolution opposing "any candidate . . . who is the representative of or under obligation to J. Pierpont Morgan, Thomas F. Ryan, August Belmont, or any other member of the privilege-hunting and favor-seeking class." After a moment of shocked silence, the Convention burst into an uproar. Some booed, a few cheered, many hissed, while in the gallery there was a scattering of applause.

My indignation rose to boiling point, I was completely unconscious of the fact that I, too, had joined the hissing protest until a restraining hand was placed on my shoulder by someone in the row behind me. I looked over my shoulder into the kind face of Franklin D. Roosevelt.

The Democratic party was not large enough to hold me and the man whom I regarded as a prejudiced, rabble-rousing politician. The country seethed with political discussion. My husband dispassionately presented the pros and cons, but they rolled off my mind, leaving no impression. Aroused by Bryan's maneuvers at the Democratic Convention and the national turmoil in the Republican party, we went to Chicago to watch the conflict between the backers of former President Theodore Roosevelt and President Taft. We listened to resolutions debated and passed in the Republican Convention, then hurried to the hall where the Bull Moose delegates were assembled in convention to watch how these messages were received.

The atmosphere at one Republican session was tense, the hall crowded to the bursting point as Warren G. Harding began the keynote speech. Rumor had it that he was presidential timber. We listened for fifteen minutes, then we turned to each other. Simultaneously we whispered, "Won't do." My husband remained a loyal Democrat. The Bull Moose movement acquired my allegiance without effort.

Finley Peter Dunne, under the by-line of "Mr. Dooley," kept his friend, Hennessey, informed of the progress of all candidates. One report on the subject as to the relative merits of the Republican contestants clings to my memory. Hennessey finally asked, "But you said nothing about the President. What about Taft? Has he got a chance?"

"I don't know," answered Dooley. "Did he ever take one?"

Bryan's pacifist speeches were challenged by many. His fantastic theory that it wasn't necessary to make military preparations prior to World War I, his claim that "a million men if necessary would rise overnight to defend the country," brought the inevitable reply, "Yes, but with what?"

14

ONE OF the chief sports on Long Island was polo. Many of our neighbors played. The Meadow Brook Club, of which my husband was president, for years had the best polo playing fields this side of England. The turf had been tenderly nurtured, almost hand fed; the club president selected and mixed the seed himself. The practice games and matches were great fun to watch, the small teams as well as the great players preparing for international events. My husband and his three sons formed a family team. They did not demonstrate fine polo, but they certainly enjoyed themselves. August, the eldest, preferred other sports; Raymond was an excellent horseman; Morgan, tall, skinny, large-boned, rode with spirit and the utmost recklessness. They were known to the countryside as "Battery B."

Naturally the games played by such stars as Harry Payne Whitney, J. Watson Webb, Larry Waterbury, Devereux Milburn were watched with eager attention and pride by a large gathering. When it came time for the international matches, everyone with ponies selected the pick of his string for the cause. The outstanding Belmont contribution was the internationally known polo pony, Little Mary. Her skill at turning, her understanding of the game and eagerness for the sport, made her a famous lady. Harry Whitney, our team captain of the First International Match at Meadow Brook, gave my husband, when the event was over, a beautiful gold cigarette case encrusted with tiny diamonds to commemorate Little Mary's part in the game.

Our neighbors in Westbury, the Thomas Hitchcocks, had a stable remarkable for fine steeplechasers. Mrs. Hitchcock was an ardent horsewoman. She had taught many of the local boys the first principles of polo playing, including her son, Tommy Hitchcock, Jr., who became a world famous polo player. One day my husband informed me that a new expression had been added to those usually heard on the polo field. The call was, "Go *on*, Mother." Mrs. Hitchcock still played, though her game had evidently slowed down considerably.

International matches brought Edward, Prince of Wales, to Long Island. Those were great days for polo; public interest mounted steadily. The challenging British team arrived early in our midst to accustom their ponies to our climate and themselves to Meadow Brook fields and the American style of play, somewhat different from that of the British. These young fellows were good sportsmen and became very popular. The polo committee arranged to have fine new stands built at the conservative Meadow Brook to accommodate the thousands of spectators who clamored to see the matches. The splendid polo demonstrated by both teams in practice games had whetted the public appetite. It was a stirring sight when those exceptionally fine athletes—mounted on spirited horses—rode onto the field, took their positions, waited with eager attention for the ball to be thrown in to start the game.

A brilliant gathering of visitors, American and foreign, assembled for the games. Governor and Mrs. John A. Dix were our house guests as an indication that the Empire State recognized the importance of this sporting event. But the weather, oh, how badly the weather behaved! The opening match had to be postponed repeatedly. Aside from members of the family, practically no box holder saw the first game when it finally was played, with the same guests who had been originally invited. It rained so persistently, or the international field was so wet it couldn't be used, that Governor Dix and his lady, after four days, returned to Albany without having seen even a practice game.

Tension for the restricted players was almost unbearable. Their only liquid comfort, as they were in strict training, was tea, coffee, ginger ale and the like. When the games were finally played, we saw brilliant polo. Larry Waterbury, like an acrobat, could perch almost on a horse's tail and, turning with cool deliberation, make a perfectly accurate shot. The crowds responded with a vociferous appreciation that was international in sportsmanship and with an enthusiasm for the American team when it won that pointed to polo as a national sport—if we could afford it.

Aside from the imponderable weather, Long Island that late summer was gay *plus* gay. Belmont Park, looking exceptionally beautiful, was made spectacularly interesting by the presence of a great French four-year-old, Epinard, owned by Mr. Pierre Wertheimer. The noted challenger was to engage in a special competition race with several American turf favorites.

The Harold I. Pratts gave a large luncheon in Glen Cove in honor of H.R.H. the Prince of Wales before the event. The weather was perfect for an outdoor party. Mrs. Pratt was then and is now a distinguished leader in garden club affairs. The gardens of Welwyn, the Pratt home at Glen Cove, were among the show places of Long Island owing to her scholarly knowledge of horticulture. That day as we wandered among the many gardens, every flower looked its best. The heir to the British throne looked about with interest and said to his hostess, simply, "It is lovely here; it reminds me of Grandma's place on the Isle of Wight." Belmont Park was also looking its best, and some 60,000 humans jammed the club stand, and the grandstands, to watch the royal visitor and the special race.

During those weeks balls followed each other in swift succession. Clarence Mackay gave a magnificent affair; the John Sanford and Henry Sage parties were smaller, yet altogether charming; and so it went night after night. Will Rogers assured his readers, "It will take Long Island two years to get back an American accent after the warm welcome accorded to royalty and the other foreign visitors."

15

THE HITCHCOCKS also had two daughters, Helen, very young, and Tetine, married to Julian Peabody. One day Tetine invited me to meet a promising young author who was then practically unknown. In this way I came to know and like James Norman Hall. In spite of Tetine's warm appreciation and her friends' receptive interest, Hall was strangely aloof even at small parties. He went to family polo and the races with us, yet somehow he never seemed to be entirely among those present. Years later we understood this detachment and the ties that bound him to his loved far away island.

16

AMONG FAMILY FRIENDS were the Roosevelts. Probably everyone at some moment of life becomes a hero-worshiper, and Theodore Roosevelt was a hero to me. He had been an old friend of my husband's at Harvard, in the hunting field, and elsewhere. In fact, when T.R. was offered the vice-presidential nomination, he wrote to a number of associates, including my husband, although he was a Democrat, seeking advice. My husband replied that he should accept it, stating that with most men the Vice Presidency was considered a form of political burial, but that "nothing can keep you down, Theodore."

T.R. was a born storyteller, and so thoroughly relished his own stories that the magic of his enthusiasm carried you with him. I remember one occasion, when the Cornelius Vanderbilts were giving a supper party in their beautiful home at 52nd Street and Fifth Avenue. Among the two hundred or more guests invited to supper and to dance were John Purroy Mitchell and his wife, and the Roosevelts of Sagamore Hill. The Colonel told me, "Grace found herself confronted by the question of protocol, so she called me on the telephone and asked, 'Colonel, how shall I seat the table? Which is correct? Should I put you, an ex-President, on my right, or the Mayor of New York City?' "

He answered, "By all means, put the Mayor on your right." Then the Colonel gave his famous chuckle as he added, "A live dog is better than a dead lion any day."

My last vivid remembrance of him was when we went to see him in Roosevelt Hospital. He had been seriously ill, but he thought he was about to leave, "if not tomorrow, the day after or the next" on his homeward trip to Sagamore. He had acknowledged a gift of roses and urged us to come to see him, saying:

. . . I will make my time suit yours, because time is the only thing I have, and I have all there is of it. Always yours,
                                                    Theodore Roosevelt

Seated in an old-fashioned porch rocker, he seemed to be in fine form, looked well, and was cheerful. After the two men had talked for some time, my husband said, "Theodore, in spite of our political differences, I have frequently agreed with many of the positions you have taken, but I cannot follow your campaign advocating the direct election of senators. Believe me, the theory that you will by-pass the professional politician won't work. Moreover, you must remember some of the ablest statesmen are poor campaigners—Elihu Root, for instance." *

Colonel Roosevelt listened attentively to the protest, then he leaned forward, gripping the arms of his chair and barked out, "Augie, I agree. But as you know, once you have given the public a privilege which they have grown to consider a right, you cannot take it back. I repeat, I agree with you. If I could change it, I would; but"—and he leaned further forward—"if you say I said so, I'll say you lie." Then he threw back his head and rocked with glee, giving the chuckle that was so peculiarly his own.

He had less time than he thought. We never saw him again, for he died a few months later.

T.R. came into the world richly endowed—genius is born, not made. He believed it was the business of life to make full use of one's powers, and no man ever wrested so much humor and joy out of life or responded more nobly than he did to the work and responsibility involved. To know him added a sense of adventure to life. Under the white heat of his dynamic patriotism, foreigners from all parts of the world, seeking a home here, were fused into devoted citizens in these United States. This may prove to have been his outstanding contribution. Distinguished Japanese used to come frequently to see my husband.

* In 1913, the Seventeenth Amendment provided for the direct election of senators now in force. Previously they had been appointed by the state legislature by "concurrent action of Senate and Assembly."

I said to one once, "Colonel Roosevelt is a great American citizen."

"Madam," he replied, "he is a great citizen of the world."

Mrs. Theodore Roosevelt's friendship I cherished; she did not make friends lightly. One frightfully hot June day, when New York University was about to confer an honorary degree upon me, Mrs. Roosevelt came to Columbia Heights for the ceremony. When Chancellor Elmer Brown invited me to make the Commencement address, he mentioned it was the first time that the university had accorded this privilege to any woman. The Commencement Day exercises were held outdoors and my speech had just started when a terrific thunderstorm accompanied by a veritable cloudburst descended upon us, scattering the people who were on the surrounding banks and blowing over the tent under which several hundred guests had recently been assembled. The gods who control the weather obviously were masculine that day and resented a woman speaker. Through the flashes of lightning we could see Mrs. Roosevelt's little figure, dressed in black, as she always was in public after the President's death, emerging undisturbed from the swaying tent, with its background of forked lightning, as Chancellor Brown reached out his hand to assist her to the speaker's platform. At the same moment, between claps of thunder, he urged me to continue my remarks as if nothing unusual were happening.

The whole Roosevelt family were great readers of poetry; any one of them could quote with miraculous memory long passages from the works of favorite authors. Mrs. Roosevelt for a number of years had a poetry class which met a few times every summer. A literary critic whom we all admired very much, Elbert Newton, was invited to conduct the readings. Mr. Newton's letters were gems of wit and erudition, and his literary taste was impeccable. One day when Mrs. Roosevelt had been a widow for a number of years, I told her that I had kept Newton's letters to me, which periodically I read with relish. She surprised me by saying that she, too, had kept a small collection, in spite of the fact that she destroyed most letters; she had even destroyed Colonel Roosevelt's letters to her. To my startled question why had she done this, she answered, "On impulse. I had just read the letters of Elizabeth and Robert Browning, and the exposure of their intimate thoughts was horribly distasteful; I could not bear the idea that this should happen to me, so I burned everything."

Archie Roosevelt provided one of my favorite stories of the Theodore Roosevelts in the White House. The children came home one afternoon to be told their father couldn't be disturbed —an important visitor, Sir Edward Grey, was calling on state business. Disappointed, for Father was a choice playmate, they paused and heard angry sounds emerging from the study—world affairs undoubtedly were serious. Suddenly their father's voice came clear and loud. "No, no Edward, I tell you the call is chickadee-*dee*-dee."

Sir Edward's gentle voice remonstrated, "No, Theodore. It is chickadee-dee-dee-*dee*, with the accent on the last *dee*."

17

CORINNE ROOSEVELT ROBINSON (Mrs. Douglas Robinson), Theodore's younger sister, introduced me to the New York Fortnightly. These debating society meetings were at times extremely interesting, often enlightening. The topics ranged from poetry to politics, from sheer nonsense to philosophy. Two of my favorite subjects were: "What is the difference between the inferiority complex and the meekness which shall inherit the earth?" and "When does the virtue of tolerance become the vice of indifference?" My friend Mrs. Wolcott, who preferred the opinion of the stronger sex on most subjects, did not belong, but she suggested a topic for the ladies: "When does vulgar curiosity become intelligent interest?"

The Roosevelt family was well represented. Mrs. Robinson herself, Mrs. W. Emlen Roosevelt, Mrs. J. West Roosevelt all attended. My first introduction to Mrs. Franklin Delano Roosevelt took place at her home when she was presiding as hostess of the day for a Fortnightly meeting.

Corinne Robinson was many-sided in her interests; a dynamic

and vital personality, she gave herself absolutely to both the business and the joy of living. She found time to write and publish
several books of graceful poetry. Perhaps the quality each friend
felt outstanding in her was the warmth that wrapped itself
around you. She never gave half her attention; it was yours absolutely; your joys and sorrows were instantly reflected on her part
with sympathy and understanding. People of all ages and all
walks of life felt that by her own choice, she belonged particularly to them. It seems incredible that anyone could have so
many friends and yet have each one feel rich indeed in the portion received of her friendship. Your ideas, your stories, were at
their best in her presence, and her faith was sustaining to all
who aspired to do something in this world.

The distinguished, the unusually talented were happy to be
received in her home, and how she loved to gather people about
her! One day she invited me to meet Sir Esme Howard: "Only a
little party, dear—literally, no more than ten people outside ourselves," her note said. When I arrived at the appointed hour, the
babble of voices indicated many times many. Even her hospitable
table could not expand sufficiently to include the assembled gathering. The "little party" had grown to be a buffet lunch of fifty-
three.

Her last testament might be expressed in these words of the
late Sir Walter A. Raleigh, descendant of the Elizabethan:

> . . . When at heart you shall be sad,
> Pondering the joys we had,
> Listen and keep very still.
> If the lowing from the hill
> Or the tolling of a bell
> Do not serve to break the spell,
> Listen; you may be allowed
> To hear my laughter from a cloud.*

Monroe Robinson did a most unusual and moving thing several
years after his mother's death. His father had gone years earlier.

* "My Last Will" *Laughter from a Cloud* (Constable & Co., Ltd., London,
1923) p. 232.

He gave a tea to honor members of his mother's household, and invited to meet them were intimate friends who had visited the family in New York and at Herkimer, the family place in the Mohawk Valley.

Courtney, the chauffeur, and Josephine, devoted personal maid, represented the younger members of the Robinson staff and received with the host.

After refreshments of all sorts, larded with friendly toasts to each member of the household, Monroe told several of his mother's favorite stories familiar to all. Courtney also retailed a few amusing family adventures. Then Ruth Draper asked us to choose from her repertoire of monologues the ones we liked best. Never was she more delightful! Nostalgia had us by the throat, but our hearts were warm with the tender friendliness that gathering evoked.

18

ONE SPRING during a visit to Mrs. Wolcott in Buffalo, she asked if I would see a young woman in whose theatrical career she was interested. As I was leaving to catch a train to New York, we three talked in a taxi, the only available moment. The deep earnestness of the aspirant impressed me, as well as her lack of fear about the work involved in a stage career. After watching her steady progress from year to year in technical skill and public recognition, it gave me great pleasure when I was invited to second the name of Katharine Cornell when she was presented with the National Achievement Award at the White House years later. Katharine Cornell is not only an outstanding actress of rare ability and distinction, she is a most uncommonly fine woman. Alex Woollcott and I were proud sponsors that night as we sang her praises. Lord and Lady Tweedsmuir had arrived on short notice from Canada for an official visit to the President and Mrs. Roosevelt, and were unexpectedly present for the occasion. The Governor General and I had not met since the First World War, and the scholarly John Buchan had become a distinguished statesman.

When one of the medals was given to me later, I remembered a story about E. H. Sothern. Sothern was selected to receive some medal. The night of the dinner in his honor a reporter telephoned to ask if he might drive to the hotel with Mr. Sothern, who agreed. After asking many questions, the reporter said, "Mr. Sothern, why are they giving you this medal?"

Sothern looked at him seriously and replied, "Young man, if you don't know, we had better go right back, for I have not the slightest idea."

19

A HAPPY INTERLUDE between work and play was provided by Mrs. Wolcott's poetry class, which I attended intermittently for eighteen years. It was delightful, not alone for the literature that was reviewed, but for the remarkable group of women, each of whom felt privileged to be there. Mrs. Wolcott was one of the women, along with Mrs. Fiske and Alice Duer Miller, whom Alexander Woollcott (no relation) most admired. In the early thirties she gave small dinners, eight or nine—at most ten— which she called her sabbaticals—husbands and wives were never asked as a couple.

For one dinner at which I couldn't be present, Winthrop Ames was asked to come and bring Edna Ferber. At dinner Mrs. Wolcott, ordinarily a generous and skillful hostess, was angry at the Jews for some misdemeanor they were currently accused of, and she lashed out vigorously. Suddenly, sensing the freezing looks of her guests, she turned to Miss Ferber and asked, "You're not Jewish, are you?"

Miss Ferber replied, "Only on my father's and my mother's side."

20

AFTER THE START of World War I, I found myself plunged into many activities. Everywhere one went in those early war days, sympathy for the Belgians ran high. Meanwhile, President Wilson tried to restrain the mounting emotion and proclaimed the American international policy to be one of neutrality. In the hymn "Onward, Christian Soldiers," the important word to me is *onward*. My first thought was of how we could best show our feeling for the Belgians. A benefit seemed a concrete and useful way of expressing our sympathy.

My proposal was that we call upon the ever-generous stars of the theatre and have a mammoth benefit, a revue of the past twenty-five years. Each artist would be costumed in his or her outstanding popular success, and would recite an excerpt from an important scene. The program was to begin with Thomas Jefferson, son of the famous Joseph Jefferson, as Rip Van Winkle and end with Ellen Terry as Portia, reciting the "quality of mercy" speech.

Miss Terry, who fortunately happened to be in New York, agreed to settle her part in the benefit over a cup of tea. Half an hour after the appointed time there was still no Miss Terry. When fifty minutes had passed, I ordered the tea tray removed. Fifteen minutes later the star arrived, breathless, and in loving, pleading tones voiced her apologies. The oculist had kept her. Could I possibly forgive her tardiness? I hushed her with the question, "Miss Terry, wouldn't anybody forgive you anything?"

Promptly she answered, "My dear, that's been my undoing."

Enchanting, haunting Ellen Terry! Even in advancing years she made one's heart flutter.

As always when needing help in the theatre, I turned to Winthrop Ames, and it was Mr. Ames, aided by Guthrie Mc-Clintic, who actually made my idea function. It was not an easy task, presenting a benefit of what he called "my thirty-five voluntary roaring lions." Sybil Carlyle as Comedy on one side of the stage, and Walter Hampden as Tragedy on the other, presented each participant, so that the audience might be informed about the play and the character, as well as which artist was about to appear.

At my request, Corinne Robinson wrote each introduction in rhyme. As people were added or dropped out from the original list, I would telephone and say, "I must have an introduction for Jane Cowl; she is replacing Marie Tempest, whose costume hasn't arrived from England," or, "I need an introduction for Mrs. Patrick Campbell, who accepted at the last moment and wishes to appear as Mélisande."

Holbrook Blinn selected the role of the gangster in *Salomy Jane*. Ethel Barrymore telegraphed from Philadelphia:

> PLAYING IN NEW YORK NEXT WEEK AND WILL BE GLAD TO DO ANYTHING. I AM AFRAID I DON'T LOOK MUCH LIKE CAPTAIN JINKS ANYMORE BUT I WILL GET DRESS MADE HERE AND TRY—PLEASE LET ME KNOW WHAT I AM TO DO AND WHAT TIME YOU WILL WANT ME AS I AM PLAYING TWICE A DAY AND THINK I CAN ARRANGE ANY TIME FOR ONE PERFORMANCE TO SUIT YOU.

For her introduction, Corinne Robinson wrote:

> Our Ethel Barrymore
> Queen of Queens
> In Captain Jinks of the Horse Marines,
> Has made us thrill as she laughs and leans,
> To the Captain in the army.
> For she is a Siren through and through.
> And she calls to me and she calls to you,
> That is the way that Sirens do,
> To the Captains in Life's Army.*

Samuel Rothaphel, "Roxy" of blessed memory, gave us the Strand Theatre, free of charge. Everybody gave everything for the Belgians, except telephone calls and postage stamps!

One totally unexpected thing happened. Mrs. Pat Campbell had chosen as the episode she wished to present from *Pelléas and Mélisande* the moment when Golaud, the husband goaded by suspicious jealousy, tries to force from her a confession as to the relationship between herself and Pelléas. Mélisande sinks on her knees, not understanding his tempestuous emotion. Go-

---

* From *Service & Sacrifice* by Corinne Roosevelt Robinson, copyright 1919 by Charles Scribner's Sons, 1947 by Corinne Robinson Alsop and reprinted by permission of the publishers.

laud seizes her by the hair and literally drags her from one side to the other. In French, Mélisande murmurs, *"Je suis si malheureuse."* The English translation Mrs. Pat used as she raised her arms in an appeal to heaven was, "Oh, I am not happy here." The audience first gasped, then roared with laughter, then burst into prolonged applause as the curtain came down.

Joseph Choate made the intermission appeal. He said: "Mrs. Belmont has warned me that because of the high patronage under which this benefit is given, I must not forget that the United States is neutral." Then he launched into a brilliant attack on the United States' policy of neutrality, always returning to the fact that, "However, we are neutral." It was done so wittily, and at the same time with such clarity as to his own point of view, that the sympathetic audience was enraptured. The pageant on stage was beautiful, swift-moving, and crowded with nostalgic memories for actors and audiences. The benefit with contributions netted approximately $50,000.

21

MY HUSBAND had watched the encroachment on my time and sympathy of these philanthropic interests with an indulgent eye. William Locke's successful novel of the day was *Septimus,* who was called the champion of lost causes. One day he dubbed me Mrs. Septimus. When I protested that these new interests of mine were not *lost* causes, he answered, "Certainly, when you make them yours, dear, they are not lost." This flattering indulgence sustained me in and out of a considerable list of undertakings. Needless to say, people wanted me largely because my name was his; the simple addition of one letter, *s,* did not disguise the fact.

Finding a path in the, to me, new field of social service opened many vistas; some appealed, others proved outside the range of my co-operation.

I was drawn into the National Civic Federation because my husband, an officer, had persuaded Anne Morgan to organize a woman's division. Both through the Civic Federation and the

Training School for Boys at Yorktown Heights, I was introduced to corrective programs and prison procedures.

22

MY HUSBAND was a prime mover for workmen's compensation, and that subject was interesting but complicated.

So eager was he to keep me in touch with his daily thought that frequently, when I was out at a ladies' luncheon, I would find myself paged; at first I was alarmed, fearing some accident had happened, but it gradually became an accepted fact that my husband simply wanted to know if I had read a certain editorial or a leading article by a noted columnist. "And be sure to read it," was the sole purpose of the call.

His detached analysis of public affairs—even when they beat upon him personally—and his wide, accurate knowledge of many subjects drew my mind into hitherto unexplored fields. Under such guidance, education took on a stimulating aspect. Life revealed new dimensions. Where events approached his family or personal affections, he was definitely partisan. Beyond that line, he was quite extraordinarily objective.

In the presidential campaign of 1920 the country was torn with bitter controversy. Special emphasis was on the League of Nations, but the prohibitionists and other pressure groups added to the conflict. The battle of words raged with more than the usual campaign quiver full of half truths and exaggerated promises. Fears of foreign influence and entangling alliances were waved constantly before us like agitating banners. When votes were counted, the Democrats had repudiated their erstwhile acclaimed leader, aided by the Republicans, to be sure.

With characteristic understanding, my husband said, "They have pulled Wilson down today, but mark my words, those who have defamed him will shrink in stature while his position will increase in history." We discussed at some length, not how to make the world safe for democracy, but was democracy safe for the world?—"But evermore came out the same door" as in we went.

My husband had come into my room one morning some time before that election and, handing me the paper, said briefly, "Read the President's speech!" I read with ever-increasing interest Woodrow Wilson's statement containing the now famous phrase, "the right of small nations to self-determination."

When he returned for the paper, he asked my opinion. Deeply moved by the high plane of the President's thought and his expression, I said that it was one of the noblest statements I had ever read. Solemnly he replied, "Many people, like you, will be moved by the language, for the ideal is beautiful; but that theory, if literally carried out, would start an endless chain of revolution round the world."

Looking back, his words—which sank deep into my mind then—today seem prophetic.

23

THE NURSERY FARM at Babylon, Long Island, had been a source of interest and relaxation for all of us through the years since my marriage. August Belmont, Sr., bought it about 1851 and used to take his intimate cronies there to fish and play whist. Some of the yearling race horses received early training on the mile race track laid out in the fields. The practice was continued in some measure until 1914. It was fun to watch them work out around six in the morning.

Two slow-moving brooks fed Belmont Lake, which about once a year was stocked with trout. The old house stood on one side of the lake; on the other, all the farm buildings. The preserve held deer and quail. Of the 1,300 acres, about 400 were in cultivation. Somewhere I had read in an English magazine that Jerusalem artichokes fed to pigs increased the price of pork sixpence a pound. So we planted Jerusalem artichokes. They grew like weeds and threatened to destroy some of the other crops. Hopefully we agreed that the flavor of our home-smoked bacon was improved; the price of pigs in America, unfortunately, did not increase.

Farming, especially if you care for animals, is an absorbing occupation, probably because battling with the elements is one of man's traditional occupations. While we were motoring one day from the races at Saratoga to South Williamstown, a friend led us to an abandoned farm near his place which was for sale. The site was at the foot of Graylock Mountain and so very lovely on that August day that without due process of thought we acquired it.

The tumbledown hundred-year-old farmhouse was to be reconditioned as a summer home for my mother and as a sort of retreat for me. My husband selected an array of animals from the Babylon farm to stock the place. When they arrived in Williamstown the town turned out to see the circus-like parade as they descended two by two from the modern ark—a railroad boxcar—horses, cows, sheep, pigs, crates of chickens, geese, ducks, guinea hens. It was quite a show as the procession started for South Williamstown followed by many curious neighbors part of the way, their enthusiastic comments drowned out by the cacophony created by the confused and excited animals.

A gurgling brook, made interesting by an occasional trout, flowed past, but no water flowed into the house. Finally an excellent spring some 500 yards away was discovered. A dam perforce was erected and the water piped from this source came from a hill near by, called oddly enough, Jones's Nose. From Gladbrook, where I went to see my mother and discuss farm matters with a new superintendent, I wrote home, "It looks as if you have a first class horse among the yearlings, but it is so hard to tell, isn't it? They are almost like children, they suggest such tantalizing hopes for the future."

The Nursery Farm cows were grades, providing butter and milk for all requirements of the house and farm. His father had always kept Jerseys, so the farm in our day included a few Jerseys—for sentiment, my husband said. For cream, I insisted and recklessly bought Guernsey thoroughbreds for Gladbrook.

Farming can be a painfully expensive form of adventure for the eager amateur. I learned the hard way why this had been an abandoned farm. Later I wrote, "At last I know the meaning of a sinking fund." My husband said the definition was still out of line, financially speaking.

To be welcomed and followed, as if you were a parent, by a gosling that had been fed, with an eye dropper, on milk and pellets of bread after being abandoned by mother goose; to be greeted with hilarious sounds of joyous welcome by chickens you have guarded from incubator days; to be trusted by baby lambs you have fostered: these are among the pleasures of a farmer. My husband and I shared our experience as collaborators; in fact, so real was our mutual interest in farming, that for our fifth wedding anniversary he gave me eight beguiling white angora goats for Gladbrook. As a retort courteous, I presented him with a separator to measure butter fat in the milk at the Nursery Farm.

Possessions had come and later, one by one, they had gone without making any significant impression on me. My husband had made me a partner in the Nursery Stud several years before he died. This wise move was intended to insure the continuity of the Belmont stable entries in important future races, as well as an interest for me. When in 1925 I had to authorize the dispersal sale of the Belmont Stud and the racing stable, parting with the cherished thoroughbreds hurt unbelievably. Thoroughbred race horses are beautiful animals. My reason spent hours arguing with my sentiment. I was very eager to keep a chestnut colt that I had named Ladkin, and two or three other favorites of my husband's, in order that the Belmont scarlet and maroon colors might remain on the turf. It became apparent that this was not possible, and Morgan Belmont agreed with my decision to sell all of them.

Economic factors also made the sale of the farm at Babylon imperative. Furthermore, owing to the heavy burden of the Cape Cod Canal, even the future of our family fortunes seemed highly precarious. When I put the Nursery Farm up for sale, the announcement read:

> 1,300 acres of land northeast of the railroad station; fronting one mile on each side of Belmont Avenue. One

hour by express train from Pennsylvania Station; 600 acres
cleared land; 700 acres woodland, lake and stream. Farm
buildings, barns, hoghouse, concrete stalls; gardener's cottage; chauffeur's house; herdman's house; hired men's apart-
ments; incubator and sheep house. Hospital building for
sick animals. Main garage concrete steam heated to hold 40
cars. Two icehouses. Race horse barn 30 x 150 feet used
during horse shows on property. A milk house with cooling
room and heating plant; gasoline engine, separator, etc.

The separator was still functioning.

Temporarily I held back a few acres and the caretaker's cottage, clutching at a thread of ownership. Once you ally yourself with the land, it takes a firm hold on your affection. One
wakeful night during the dreary sale negotiations, I sought the
Bible. Would it provide even a straw of guidance, shed any
light on the sad and difficult road ahead? I opened the Book;
immediately on the page before me I read the first of Psalm
137: "By the rivers of Babylon, there we sat down; yea, we wept,
when we remembered Zion." True, the message offered no guidance, yet it was strangely apt and the feeling of understanding
brought a warm awareness of comfort. It seemed like a trouble
shared, and surprisingly important.

24

DURING THE YEARS of my married life, I have already said that
I often had occasion to note my husband's vision and his strong
feeling of civic responsibility. In spite of an overconcern with
details, he had a keen perception regarding essential projects
that would benefit the community.

By the construction of the subway system under his leadership, he had given New York City the opportunity to become
a great metropolis. Shortly after our return from Europe in 1910
he took me to see the northernmost extension of the subway,
which had recently been opened. Already apartment houses
were springing up along the route pressing close to the new

The author as Audrey in a dramatization by Harriet Ford
of the novel by Mary Johnston

As Grace in *London Assurance*

As Bonita in *Arizona* by
Augustus Thomas

As Kate Hardcastle in *She Stoops
to Conquer*

As Glad in *The Dawn of A Tomorrow* by Frances Hodgson Burnett

In the title role of the play *Merely Mary Ann* by Israel Zangwill

Left: As Mary Ann, painted by Louis Loeb

In the potion scene from *Romeo and Juliet*

As Constance in Robert Browning's *In A Balcony*

In the title role of Israel Zangwill's *Nurse Marjorie*

stations. He pointed to this rapid development with regret because no space was reserved for small parks to serve the incoming tenants. He realized the congestion that would result and said that the city would later have to buy back the land for breathing areas for the people at vast expense because the subway was steadily increasing land values.

The building of the Cape Cod Canal by a private corporation with August Belmont as president was a courageous undertaking of serious importance. Like the subway, the canal had been pronounced impractical by other men of vision and ability.

The possibility of cutting a canal through the Cape Cod Peninsula had been urged from the time of George Washington. Several attempts had been made to carry out the idea, each failed for lack of consistent leadership and proper financing.

The plan for the canal ran through the eight-mile shoulder of "the bare bended arm of Massachusetts" through a natural valley from Buzzards Bay to Barnstable Bay. Due to severe storms, exceptionally strong currents, shoals and the dense fogs that frequently prevail, there is no place on the entire Atlantic coastline more dreaded by mariners than that portion embracing Cape Cod. A huge black-and-white company map of the proposed channel created a dramatic picture. It pinpointed in red ink the locations where vessels were known to have been wrecked rounding the Cape, and the dots were so numerous one had the impression that red pepper had been sprinkled over the area.

My husband's grandfather, Commodore Matthew Calbraith Perry, was born in Rhode Island, and an early ancestor, Edward Freeman, came to Sandwich in 1634. When asked by friends why he wanted to build the canal, my husband mentioned his ancestry, the important fact that this channel would cut off seventy miles through notoriously unsafe waters around the coast and thereby prevent loss of life; and that such a canal would be of service to the country in case of *war*. People listened respectfully when the first items were listed, but at mention of service in time of war, invariably they laughed. In those days war that could touch the United States seemed a laughing matter.

Work on the canal was hopefully begun June 22, 1909, as August Belmont, with appropriate ceremony, turned the first shovel of earth with a silver spade. An empty pork-and-bean can received the warm earth as it was lifted. The function was held on the lawn of the one-time Perry Estate at Bournedale, where his great-uncle Oliver Hazard Perry, hero of the Battle of Lake Erie, had lived. A group of Massachusetts officials and members of the Canal Company attended; also, close friends, among whom were Francis R. Appleton of Ipswich, Robert Bacon, and other Harvard associates.

The work proved unexpectedly difficult. Engineers had assured the company that only sand and rocks of *moderate* size would have to be removed. It developed that underneath the surface sandbed they encountered huge boulders of granite, costly to blast and difficult as well as costly to transport. At last, after more than five years of intensive, unbelievably difficult work, accompanied by discouraging tidal and financial problems, the opening day was set, July 29, 1914.

Scores of congratulatory messages from home and abroad were received, including one from President Wilson:

> WHITE HOUSE,
> WASHINGTON, D.C.
> July 28th, 1914

> ALLOW ME TO CONVEY THROUGH YOU MY HEARTY CONGRATULATIONS ON THE COMPLETION OF A GREAT WORK WHICH SHOULD BE OF DIRECT BENEFIT TO THE COMMERCE OF THE COUNTRY.

> WOODROW WILSON

The elder J. P. Morgan asked if his *Corsair* might be the first vessel to go through the canal. It was the first steam yacht, but the Company officers with my husband on his seventy-five-foot yacht, the *Scout,* went first, followed by the schooner *Rose*

Standish, which carried the Governor of Massachusetts, David I. Walsh and other official guests, myself, and a large party of friends, Robert Bacon, former Secretary of State, Mrs. Bayard Thayer of Boston, the Hermann Oelrichs, the Stuyvesant Fishes, Suffern Tailers of Newport, Francis R. Appleton of Ipswich, Massachusetts, and a host of others. Frank Appleton, an old Harvard friend, had named the New York subway the Interborough.

The ceremony over, we returned with Robert Bacon to By the Sea. As we sat talking over the events of the day, my husband asked Mr. Bacon if he thought the assassination of Archduke Franz Ferdinand of Austria and his morganatic duchess at Sarajevo would lead to European war. Mr. Bacon replied cautiously, as a trained diplomat would, that things had looked threatening for some time; that the Germans had cried wolf often before, and this incident might pass over.

The opening of the Cape Cod Canal after two hundred years of discussion was an historical event and a beautiful sight to see. The harbor at each end was crowded with boats and yachts of every size and variety, including a few old whalers and schooners in full sail. All of them were gaily flag-bedecked. Thousands of holiday-minded citizens watched from the banks that sunny day in July.

We expected that newspapers the following day would give it wide publicity, and stress the importance of the waterway to trade and to pleasure craft along the eastern seaboard. Instead we awoke next morning to find on the front page of *The New York Times:*

RUSSIA EXPECTS WAR, MOBILIZES 1,200,000 MEN

CZAR ALSO SUMMONS RESERVISTS TO THE COLORS

BELGRADE BOMBARDED AND OCCUPIED BY AUSTRIA

KAISER IN COUNCIL ON NAVAL PREPARATIONS

Page six reported:

"Open New Canal for Use of Trade—Marine Procession in 30 Minutes Makes Cape Cod Journey, Once of 11 Hours; Rob Cape of Terrors—New Safety for Shipping, President Belmont Asserts —Repays Him for All His Efforts.

A few days later Germany declared war on Russia; her lava-like infiltration of Belgium on August 4 brought the British into the strife and a world war came into being.

The United States took over the operation of the Cape Cod Canal after we entered this conflict three years later and it became a refuge for shipping on the Atlantic Coast from marauding submarines. On July 21, 1918, a German U-Boat attacked the Lehigh Valley Railroad tow off Cape Cod; badly damaged by shellfire, the barges sank. Actual war and the rapidly increased size of battleships completely changed the operating picture for the Canal Company. It became apparent that to be useful the Canal must be wider and deeper.

From 1919, when the Navy turned back the Canal to the company, bill after bill was presented in Congress urging that the property should be purchased by the Government and made a free waterway instead of a toll canal. Three Presidents and their secretaries of Army, Navy, and Commerce urged the passage of a bill to acquire the property, yet when August Belmont died, December 10, 1924, nothing definite had been done by Congress. Morgan Belmont and I, as executors, were left with this as a major problem, in addition to all the other sad duties that confronted us. We never could have secured a satisfactory settlement had it not been for the guidance and generous assistance given us by old friends of my husband, and friends of mine with whom I had worked in the Red Cross and other projects. They helped us to hold off Canal creditors and reorganize Congressional support. In 1926, the Government finally purchased the Canal for half what it had cost to build, with an obligation to widen and deepen the waterway for free transportation.

The financing had been prolonged and difficult. My husband had had to solicit creditors frequently, urging them to renew their loans and make new commitments. Among others, he went with the utmost reluctance to Mrs. E. H. Harriman. To ask a woman to add to her existing obligations was particularly distasteful. Mrs. Harriman's answer was immediate. "My faith in the project as a patriotic service remains intact. Besides," she added, "I always keep a little money in the bank ready to help a friend in case of need." With this statement, she pledged $500,000. Was it Will Rogers who said, "People are funny"? Probably, but then too, people are wonderful!

Toward the end of 1934, Lt. Colonel John J. Klingman of the Corps of Engineers wrote from the Boston U.S. Engineer Office of the War Department regarding the Government's plans for widening and deepening the canal and at the need to secure title to several parcels of land, one of which belonged to me. He suggested:

> . . . in view of the fact that the Cape Cod Canal is a lasting memorial to Mr. Belmont's enterprise and organizing genius, you might wish to assist in the further development of this great project by donating to the United States the parcel of land referred to above . . .

I had bought the site in question from the estate in order to erect a memorial. Finally, an exchange was made for a smaller piece of land on the opposite bank. The Army moved onto a cement base a boulder of white granite which had recently been dug from the canal and was the largest the engineers had ever seen. It is an extremely simple marker, surrounded by native shrubs. However, it can be seen from the highway by those who pause to look.

A bronze tablet fastened to the boulder bears the inscription:

IN MEMORY OF

AUGUST BELMONT

FEBRUARY 18, 1853—DECEMBER 10, 1924

WHOSE VISION, INITIATIVE, AND INDOMITABLE
COURAGE MADE POSSIBLE THE FIRST COMPLETE
CONSTRUCTON OF

THE CAPE COD CANAL

CONNECTING BUZZARDS BAY AND CAPE COD BAY
WHICH WAS OFFICIALLY OPENED FOR TRAFFIC
JULY 29, 1914.

FROM HIS MATERNAL GRANDFATHER
COMMODORE MATTHEW CALBRAITH PERRY
HE INHERITED A WARM ALLEGIANCE TO THE
INTERESTS OF NEW ENGLAND AND HIS DEEP
CONCERN FOR THOSE WHO GO DOWN TO THE SEA
IN SHIPS.

PART THREE

Make no little plans; they have no magic to stir men's blood, and probably themselves will not be realized. Make big plans: aim high in hope and work, remembering that a noble, logical diagram, once recorded, will be a living thing, asserting itself with evergrowing intensity. Remember that our sons and grandsons are going to do things that would stagger us. Let your watchword be order, and your beacon, beauty.

> —DANIEL HUDSON BURNHAM (1846–1912), *architect*
> *of World's Fair buildings, Chicago, and*
> *the Flatiron Building, New York*

Asked if he could summarize the lessons of history in a short book, Dr. Charles A. Beard, American historian, replied that he could do it in four sentences:
1. Whom the gods would destroy they first make mad with power.
2. The mills of God grind slowly, yet they grind exceeding small.
3. The bee fertilizes the flower it robs.
4. When it is dark enough, you can see the stars.

> —DR. ARTHUR H. SECORD,
> *University of Michigan*

To hear the inventor Michael Pupin, tell the story of his landing in the United States, a youngster with only a few pennies in his pocket, was to find yourself drawn into the web of a druidic spellbinder. Here was an immigrant whose scientific mind made generous returns upon the investment of shelter and education afforded him by the New World. As he talked, miracles of science cast off their shroud of mystery and took on simple outlines. Even the quantum theory temporarily became clear to his listeners with ears unfamiliar to such tales, while the rich tones of his Slavic voice added a poetic effect to the story. When he came to dinner, it was a pleasure to watch him quietly draw the guests under his spell.

One night we had all been discussing industrial progress, the latest spectacular developments in aviation and radio. I asked Professor Pupin how he thought the world a hundred years hence would evaluate our period. What would they call it? My thought was that he would reply, The Machine Age, or some such title. To our surprise, he answered, "This will be known as the Age of Idealism. Consider the picture galleries, the conservatories of music, orchestras, the institutions of learning—nurseries of the aesthetic activities of the American soul—made possible during my lifetime in America by the individual donations of private citizens. Yes, this will be known as the Age of Idealism, at least so far as the United States is concerned. The beautiful miracle of the American Red Cross service and the rapid awakening of social conscience on a national scale offer a demonstration on the part of a people that is unique in history."

Out of the horrible tragedy and suffering of war, mankind produced one great good: the magnificent development of the Red Cross movement throughout the world. When the United States went to war in 1917, President Wilson, on the recommendation of Cleveland H. Dodge, a Red Cross pioneer, established a War Council to take charge of Red Cross operations: Henry P. Davison as chairman, Cornelius N. Bliss, Jr., Charles D. Norton, Edward N. Hurley, Grayson M.-P. Murphy, with William Howard Taft and Eliot Wadsworth, the Chairman and Vice-Chairman, respectively, of the Central Committee as ex-officio members. John W. Davis was Counselor. For six months prior to this action Eliot Wadsworth, summoned from Boston, had been at work striving to bring organization out of chaos at headquarters, where they were short of funds and short of personnel.

Almost immediately the War Council announced a drive for $100,000,000. Many people thought the goal was unobtainable, but the Red Cross Chairman was sure this figure would be needed, and without hesitation, set about to secure it. His confidence and leadership prevailed.

To start the big drive, men and women organized fund-raising committees on a national scale. Mrs. E. H. Harriman invited me to join New York's Team No. 1, of which she was captain. I told her I didn't know how to raise money. However, she insisted; as it turned out, my principal task was not soliciting funds, but making speeches for the cause. Once more "on the road," a lengthy schedule of one-night stands was before me. From February 25 until May 27, 45 speeches were listed in 38 cities in 10 states. Private life again was just around the corner. My husband murmured anxiously that he wished he knew of some eight-hour law that might include me.

Mr. Davison's capacity for organization undoubtedly was unique, yet it was his vision, coupled with an ability to impart his own warm confidence to his followers, that made him a superb leader and transformed the impossible into the attainable. No one who did not live through those years will ever realize all he and his associates on the War Council did for the Red Cross. Clara Barton was the founder of Red Cross in the United States. After persistent effort and dramatic demonstrations of the need, she forced the initial idea through Congress and gave the American Red Cross its charter, the nation-wide rock on which it rests today. But the person who took the ideas contained in that charter and made our Red Cross a living thing, who gave it a far-flung imaginative program, well adjusted for war requirements, and who later adapted the program to serve a League of Red Cross Societies in time of peace, was Henry P. Davison.

Numbering less than a million members when the War Council came into being, within two years under his leadership 20,000,000 people were registered, while several million men and women were actively working through this philanthropic agency to carry out the Red Cross charter mandate "to . . . aid the sick and wounded of armies in time of war . . ." and "to mitigate . . . the suffering caused by pestilence, famine, fire, floods, and other great national calamities."

The public dinner to announce final campaign results was a great occasion. President Wilson had issued a beautifully worded Red Cross Proclamation authorizing the drive. After the triumphantly successful reports were presented, this document was auctioned off, a crowning contribution to the fund. The auction was as thrilling as a match race at Belmont Park. It finally narrowed down to a contest between two men, Cleveland H. Dodge and William Fox, Chairman of the Motion Picture Committee; this group, under Mr. Fox's leadership, had done an outstanding campaign job. Bids for the Proclamation mounted higher and higher; seven, eight, nine hundred thousand dollars! I sat next to Mr. Dodge at table. For years he told the story that he had had no intention of going on with the bidding, but that I nudged him until his ribs were black and blue, insisting, "Go on, go on! You must get it for the Red Cross." That is undoubtedly an elastic description of the facts, but be that as it may, Mr. Dodge called the last bid—$1,000,000. The Proclamation was his, and the Fund totaled over $114,000,000.

Henry P. Davison's electrifying declaration that we needed $100,000,000 to serve the American Red Cross and the securing of it, Colonel House called "perhaps the finest piece of executive management accomplished during World War I." In three annual drives, over $400,000,000 was raised, including the value of donated supplies.

2

MID-SEPTEMBER, 1917, I sailed for Europe, a Red Cross worker assigned to the European area for the purpose of reporting how existing activities were functioning, and to bring back recommendations regarding future development, supplies, and services needed. Also, with my passport lodged—and this was a prize—a letter of introduction to General Pershing from Theodore Roosevelt. That letter is still in my possession, thanks to Colonel Frank McCoy, who was on Pershing's staff at Chaumont. At the time I confided that this introduction meant infinitely more to me than it would to General Pershing and might I have the letter back? Magic or sleight of hand may have been used, for finally Colonel McCoy forwarded it to me.

9 EAST 63RD STREET
Sept 12th 1917—

My dear General Pershing,
        This is to introduce a most valued and most charming friend, Mrs. August Belmont. Her husband, as you know, is one of the leading men of New York, and a tower of strength to the Government in this war. Mrs. Belmont is one of the few really able people who are also gifted with the power of expression. She wishes to help in every way, and then, on her return home, to put before our people, as vividly as only she can do, what the real needs of our troops are. She has a man's understanding, a woman's sympathy, and a sense of

honor and gift of expression such as are possessed by very, very few either among men or women.

I hope my boys are giving you satisfaction.

With heartiest thanks for all your kindness, I am,

faithfully yours,
Theodore Roosevelt

On the S.S. *New York* were Major General Clarence Edwards, his staff, and soldiers of the 26th division. There were only three women on board, Gertrude Robinson Smith, en route to France in the interest of a French war project, someone whose name I do not remember, and myself. The officers of the 26th were good companions, and what we saw of this contingent made us proud of our army.

Information of submarines along the route necessitated a zig-zag course. Enemy raiders disguised as "tramp freighters" were reported to be roaming about dangerously. Although there was a general feeling of tension, no untoward event happened until we were approximately twelve hours off the Irish coast, when we were instructed to don lifebelts. Through field glasses a tramp ship was dimly visible on the horizon. The passengers hung over the sides of the ship, watching and waiting. Suddenly, like an electric current which touched each individual, we learned the tramp was a camouflaged American destroyer assigned to escort us to port. Patriotism roamed the decks. The Stars and Stripes seemed not only to "still wave" but actually to enfold us.

Landing in England produced the impression of discovery. The United States was predominantly Francophile, with little talk of British activity, and as we toured from project to project, the extraordinary organization the British had set up became apparent. Everything and everyone gave you confidence in the strength and quiet efficiency of this important ally.

At Mr. Davison's request, Ivy Lee, a giant among men who provide expert advice on public relations, had been guiding the publicity for the American Red Cross War Council.

He kindly gave me a letter of introduction to Colonel John

Buchan, who later, as Lord Tweedsmuir, became Governor General of Canada. It so happened that I knew and admired several of his popular books. John Buchan had a literary grace that made his works easy and delightful reading. Frequently his prose touches the fringe of poetry and leaves the reader expectant that a couplet may weave its way into the next line. He was spontaneously friendly, with exceptional charm of manner. Obviously, he liked to write; and he seemed to enjoy, without a trace of self-conscious embarrassment, admiring comments on his literary output. He discussed his books with a detachment that was disarming.

The letter to Colonel Buchan was an open sesame of importance. Doors sprang open as he asked for appointments; those of hospitals, including St. Dunstan's where they were caring for the British blinded in battle; training camps; even the very secret Woolwich arsenal.

The Colonel arranged an interview for me with Edward Carson, a witty Irish-born lawyer who was a cabinet member. I had heard of him first some years before from George Smalley, a noted newspaper correspondent, who wrote me gossipy letters from 1900 to 1915, telling of people and theatres and his attendance in Portsmouth, New Hampshire, at the Russo-Japanese Peace Conference. In September, 1913, he wrote of the Ulster Conference in which Edward Carson played a dominant role. Carson was noted for his eloquence, wit, fire, and settled purpose. Mr. Smalley said, "He was an organizer as well as an orator. His Provisional Government was a masterpiece of political mechanism and ready to set going tomorrow, though not meant to be launched till next summer after the Home Rule Bill had become law, if it does."

He told me two stories that I remember. Carson asked a rough witness: "Do you drink?"

"That's my business."

"Have you no other?"

When Mr. Birrell, chief secretary for Ireland, taunted him with being a lawyer yet breaking the law, Carson replied: "Yes,

Bill and I both are lawyers. The only difference is that I have been a successful one."

I can see Sir Edward now as he sat at his desk, a fine-looking man, clasping and unclasping his hands; his long, slender artistic fingers looked something like those of Winthrop Ames. Ireland's attitude in the war so far was a subject of controversy; how she would behave in future was an important question in America. To my anxious query as to whether we could count on Ireland's support in the war struggle, he said, "Individually, yes; collectively, who can say? Some argue this way, some that. The Irish don't know what they want and they won't be happy till they get it."

He was right to this extent: Northern Ireland was a gallant part of the British war effort, but even from southern Ireland, individually, they gave a grand account of themselves. Young men came in large numbers to enlist. Actions speak louder than words and, on occasion, they are more desirable.

3

ENGLAND OPENED EVERY DOOR to provide the information I desired. Mrs. Whitelaw Reid was being generously helpful in the war effort both there and in France. Among other gifts, she and her daughter, Lady Ward, had equipped an officers' hospital so perfect in its appointments, my recommendation was that American officers should have their identity discs marked, "Please send me to Mrs. Reid's hospital."

After walking through miles of hospitals I wrote home, "This war has discovered no Florence Nightingale, but a modest woman who does anything and everything the hospitals require. She has no name, only initials. Her service unit is called Voluntary Aid Detachment and she is known as the V.A.D." How to get a similar service into the American Army Nurse Corps was a problem.

The next introduction from Colonel Buchan was to Viscount Esher in Paris, a great aristocrat, who was good enough to arrange a passport for me to the British Zone in France, almost impossible to secure. His son, Sir Maurice Brett, was in charge of British forces in Paris. British regulations were very strict. I felt it was important to visit British base hospitals, etc., and find out what supplies their volunteers made that were useful. In Paris I found Mrs. J. Borden Harriman. She was in France, managing a contingent of Red Cross Women's Motor Corps, and she was permitted to go with me. This lovely woman later served her country with distinction and effectiveness as Minister to Norway during the Franklin Roosevelt administration. We were housed with the chief nurse of the British Expeditionary Force, Miss Maud McCarthy, a remarkably wise woman trained in the Queen Alexandra's Nurse Corps.

4

MY HUSBAND, commissioned as major, arrived in Europe in time to join me in a visit to Chaumont. His specific orders had not come through, so on October 31 we made our first war trip in France. General Pershing was away from his headquarters on an inspection tour. After waiting a few days, when many interesting things were shown to us by Colonel McCoy, Winthrop Chanler, and others, we proceeded with a special permit to Rheims. The route was camouflaged with screens of potato sacks tied together and strung from tree to tree at exposed spots along the route. Everywhere signs read, "*Attention! L'enemi vous voir!*" Every so often the earth trembled as a result of the bombardment. We reached Rheims in a cold rain. The Hotel de la Haute Mère Dieu had been partly bombed. The kitchen wing was intact, and beautiful French copper utensils gleamed incongruously as they hung on the walls in the midst of devastation. In the courtyard, ominous in appearance, a huge unexploded *obus* had landed erect, nose down. Inside, about to have dejeuner, sat three men, dressed in worn velveteen jackets and flowing ties and looking as if they were ready to sing the first act of *La Bohème*. A sculptor, an architect, and an archaeologist, they were preparing plans for the rebuilding of Rheims, even

The author at four

In the library at 11 King Street, London

With Mrs. Francis C. Bishop
at the races

Author beside chauffeur, her mother in rear seat with
Mrs. Burnett on her right

Coaching with August Belmont in Newport (Mr. and Mrs. August
Belmont, Jr. in the rear seat)

On tour for the
American Red Cross

Governor David Walsh of Massachusetts (center) with Mr. and Mrs.
Belmont at the opening of the Cape Cod Canal

In front of the gold curtain at the Metropolitan Opera House

With Lauritz Melchior and Edward Johnson at the Metropolitan

At the tenth anniversary of The Metropolitan Opera Guild on
the stage of the Metropolitan

With Morgan Belmont, presenting the Belmont Cup to
William Woodward at Belmont Park

With three members of The National Council on Home Nursing

With Edward Johnson and George A. Sloan

as guns shook the ground and rattled the kitchen utensils. Shattered pieces of glass from the cathedral windows were placed in trays of sand; broken bits of angel wings, or a saint's nose and a gargoyle's horn were assembled, identified if possible, and keyed as to where they should go when it was safe to replace them.

We had brought some *pâté*, butter, and a sacrificial offering from friend Winthrop Chanler at American headquarters—half a loaf of *white* bread. The artists had wine, and a few fresh eggs which the concierge scrambled and stretched in a miraculous fashion. We shared supplies, murmuring frequently a toast which seemed a prayer, *"Vive la France."* The meal over, the trio escorted us to the cathedral. Deeply moved, we looked at the brutally damaged edifice, with seven gaping holes to the sky, and before it the statue of Jeanne d'Arc astride her horse. It had rained persistently all morning, but as we marveled at the beauty of the historic ruin, the sun suddenly broke through the clouds and a shaft of light fell across the shoulder of the saint. It conveyed a sign of blessing, even a promise: "God's in his heaven: All's right with the world."

We visited with the charming old archbishop Luçon who steadfastly refused to leave his suffering people for a place of safety, and proudly wore the *fourragère* of the defending regiment over his cassock. Then we drove to Chalons to talk with General Gouraud. This dedicated man was remarkably simple. His devotion to the poilus serving under him went to the heart. He arranged for us to see a secret observation hut not far from his headquarters. On the wall of this narrow building was an enlarged map showing the entire front line. Through exceptional binoculars we spotted the encampment where enemy Big Berthas were placed. We saw the smoke curl upward as the gun, aimed toward Chalons, was fired, and shortly afterward felt the earth shake when the shell struck near by. The Germans had been trying for days to locate this observation post. Next we toured under Red Cross guidance over a considerable area, which, according to strict military regulations, one identified vaguely as The Front.

5

WE RETURNED TO PARIS, visiting en route hospital units such as
Roosevelt and Yale, which had been assigned to the French. In
Paris, a hot bath and sheets were once again obtainable. Never
had they been more welcome, for I had caught the prevailing
influenza and was unable to move for days.

That November General Pershing called a war conference in
Paris of Allied government officials and heads of military and
naval missions. Mrs. Whitelaw Reid decided this assembling
of leaders offered an excellent opportunity for the Red Cross
representatives Grayson M.-P. Murphy, Commissioner for Europe, James H. Perkins, France, and William Endicott, England,
to meet, in an informal way, officials of the groups, which our
Red Cross hoped to serve.

The brilliant dress uniforms of the military chiefs assembled
at Mrs. Reid's dinner with their multicolored orders and decora-
tions, made me think of birds of paradise, the males in glowing
colors that far outshine the female. Mrs. Reid placed General
Pershing opposite her as host of the occasion. I was seated between Arthur Balfour, who was on the hostess's right, and Admiral Sims. There was an elegance about tall Mr. Balfour that
was unusual, but slightly overwhelming. In fact, he was so impressive that, at first, shyness banished any feeling of ease I
might have felt in talking to this distinguished man of the world.
Finally I asked Mr. Balfour if he knew what G. B. Shaw was
doing. I had tried to see him while I was in England, but for
the first time in many years Shaw had gone to Ireland, to attend, of all things, an Irish Convention. Mr. Balfour answered,
"No, I don't know what he is doing. Whatever it is, it is bound to
be witty." And he added with a disarming chuckle, "I rather
think it might be mischievous."

Admiral Sims talked easily and well. As he chatted away, he
revealed nothing secret, yet somehow conveyed in a subtle way
that he had taken you completely into his confidence. I'm happy

to say the Admiral always declared his belief in Red Cross as an agency of service. For obvious reasons the Navy was more self-sufficient than other units of the armed forces. But he welcomed every civilian effort that attempted to serve the Navy. "The Red Cross is easy to recognize," he said. "Its symbol, two pieces of red tape, imposed one on the other, form the cross, and this is the only red tape I know about the organization."

In my diary there is noted December 2, 1917: "We lunched with Colonel and Mrs. House—Hotel Crillon, one o'clock. Guests present: Rt. Hon. Arthur Balfour, Lord Milner, Mrs. Barclay Parsons, General Pershing, Lady Paget, The Hon. Winston Churchill." There is no other comment. Probably I thought enough said.

My husband left Paris two days later. His orders were to negotiate with Spain the purchase of mules for the Army. Spain, being neutral, was reluctant to sell these useful animals to a belligerent. An important part of his mission was to negotiate a contract providing for the shipment of various supplies for American forces in France, either from or through Spain in exchange for our raw materials needed there, such as cotton, oil, and coal.

6

IN MID-DECEMBER, my trip to the war zone was with Gertrude Ely, a forceful member of the YMCA, who was inspecting the YMCA huts assigned to the Americacn Army. A young singer, Jack Barker, went along to entertain the troops at each recreation hut. I talked to assembled soldier groups of what the folks at home were doing to back them up. During one visit at a Dijon hospital, enemy planes flew over. When the alert sounded, lights went out; it was a bright moonlit night. The hospital, with its huge Red Cross on the roof, must have been clearly visible. The recreation hut held over a thousand men. Impulsively, we sang "Where Do We Go from Here?" Other popular songs followed, one after another until the all-clear sounded, and the lights came on again.

When Gertrude Ely and I left Paris our motorcar was packed to the roof with Red Cross supplies—cigarettes, candy, sweaters, mittens, everything that could be squeezed in. Before the last hospital stop our supplies were exhausted, yet when we started to leave, the men crowded round the car as if they couldn't let us go. "Sorry boys, there isn't a thing left," I said. "What can we do for you?"

After a pause one doughboy spoke up. "Just go on talking. It sounds good. We haven't heard a woman's voice tell about home since we left in June."

In my diary I noted:

An interesting effect of a trip to the front is the change of values. Under ordinary circumstances you sing the National Anthem with zest, or people mumble it if they cannot remember the words; but after a trip to the war zone, "Oh, say, can you see, by the dawn's early light," comes out with a ring of tenderness it never had before. And when suddenly you see our flag, the Stars and Stripes, waving, almost unconsciously you say, "How beautiful it is!"

Before leaving on these trips I had asked Major James H. Perkins, then Red Cross Commissioner to Europe, in what way I might help him, in addition to securing information for home use. He was profoundly discouraged. The Red Cross warehouses were bulging to the bursting point with supplies of every kind, but the Army refused to make requisitions. First, "The Army will provide whatever is necessary. Things are not here yet, but they will be. The Army will provide." Second, regarding hospital comforts, pneumonia jackets, bathrobes, comforters, "This is war. Men at war cannot be pampered."

The American Army was hardly engaged as yet, but touring through British and French hospitals left scars on the heart. The Germans had recently taken to using mustard gas, and gas burns seemed the cruelest wounds of all. At one French hospital, Mission Ambrine in Compiègne, largely financed by Dr. Henri de Rothschild, I found Elsie de Wolfe serving as a nurse, specializing in mustard gas dressings. The French advocated a medicated wax called Ambrine. American and British doctors doubtfully debated its use. Ambrine had to be heated to flow over the burns. The torture in the eyes of men whose wounds were being dressed in the hot wax was hard to bear. Inwardly one raged against the abominable cruelty of it all.

7

THE NAME of Dr. Alexis Carrel first impressed me as I walked mile after mile past hospital beds in the three war zones. The Carrel-Dakin antiseptic treatment for wounds was new and remarkably successful; a bottle with tubes leading into the patient's wound hung like a strange climbing plant on almost every bed.

After the war, we met Dr. Carrel when he came to the Rockefeller Institute for Medical Research to continue his experiments. One episode during our acquaintance occurred at a friend's house, where he recounted the story of his visit to Lourdes. He had gone, tape measure in hand, with the avowed purpose of proving that the statements regarding cures of skin cancer at the shrine were greatly exaggerated. The growth of tissue is gradual; time, and then more time, is required to heal open wounds. He waited at the station to meet a trainload of pitiful sufferers and, accompanied by his assistant, measured the grievous sores of those who arrived. After prayers at religious sessions and the healing water of the Lourdes spring had been applied to the supplicant, Dr. Carrel again measured the same sore. Quite beyond scientific understanding and human belief, in a number of instances the circumference of the wounds had shrunk appreciably.

He was deeply stirred by what he had witnessed. I do not feel that he was a converted believer in the miracles of Lourdes, but he was a scientist who never closed his mind, one who felt that in an unbelievable world, all things are possible. Faith may not be knowledge, but it certainly is power.

8

THE RECRUITING of nurses into the military service in those days was largely Red Cross responsibility, and in the States I had made innumerable speeches in hospitals and on public platforms, persuading women to enroll. During my five months abroad for the Red Cross, I found that the greatest affliction our nurses in Europe had to bear was mud, evident everywhere in quantity. They had come abroad with the standard graduate nurses' white-starched uniforms, which were a torture to keep clean, and which seemed out of place in the barracks of wartorn France. Ultimately, these uniforms were changed to a gray seersucker, not pretty, but so much more serviceable! The nurses were also troubled because they were not permitted to take care of the men in the casualty huts immediately behind the front lines. The influenza epidemic was taking its heavy toll, and newly made cemeteries attached to each hospital base added to the heartbreak of war. Never shall I forget the raw cold that struck to the marrow, and the eternal mud over my boot tops—mud—everywhere.

Fortified by all I had seen and heard on this tour, I thought it imperative to talk informally with Surgeon General Bradley of the Expeditionary Forces. Mrs. William K. Vanderbilt, who had been appointed Red Cross Director of Canteen Service in Europe, was living in her house in Paris and asked him to dine with us alone. I urged that the American registered nurses should be allowed nearer the front (corpsmen were used in the advance stations). The General, with a smile, asked me if I had seen a cartoon in a recent issue of *Punch*, which showed a hospital ward of soldiers and a flapperish girl in high-heeled shoes prancing down the center. Several beds held a placard: "Too ill to be nursed." Like Queen Victoria, I was not amused, and suggested that the placard should read, "Too ill to be nursed by men."

I also cited the service rendered by the Voluntary Aids in the British hospitals. The General said that the question of aids was a matter for the nursing service to consider. As to the requisition and use of Red Cross hospital supplies, he definitely agreed to modify Army restrictions. Mrs. Vanderbilt had gently but firmly supported every recommendation. "General Bradley," I wrote home, "looked so tired that I was embarrassed to have badgered him."

In January before leaving Paris, I wrote:

My dear General Bradley:

Thank you for your kind letter of Jan. 28th. In regard to the V.A.D.'s many of us feel they will surely be needed before we reach any great distance on our war journey; and we want to help you in the big task by standing "ready" if there are little things we can do!

My recommendations are these—as the situation stands at present it seems inadvisable to bring V.A.D.'s over here as a military adjunct. But the Red Cross can devise various means of placing some of these who have had their training—where they will not waste their time or take up unnecessary space. They may in some instances place them with other hospital organizations which are in need of assistance and which will fit them the better for service when they are called to our Army. The Red Cross should control them until such time when you are ready—when the suitable ones should be gathered together and transferred as a whole to your Department.

The laundry at Etaples interested me immensely, as did the fact that Colonel Barefoot the D.D.M.S. told me had they had their own from the beginning the Armies would have saved millions of pounds sterling. I will report to you later when I can find out more on this subject, for there is another side. Sir Wm. Morrison at the Quai de-Javel British Ordnance Dept. told me it was better to have the French existing laundries if they were not too far off and were run by capable women, not ordinary labor. It is surely an if which holds the heavens up.

Edward Carter, who directed the YMCA in Europe, invited me to remain in France and join their splendid group of women serving with the armed forces, outstanding among them, Eleanor, wife of Theodore Roosevelt, Jr. My husband wrote from Spain urging me to wait for him. He was reluctant to have me cross the ocean alone. But his return was still indefinite, and after five months (from September to mid-February) of inspecting work being done by the British, French, and Americans, I felt that my duty was to return and make my report at Red Cross headquarters. Black clouds hung over France as the Germans advanced steadily toward Paris. I had a deep conviction, based on the armies I had seen, that the Germans would be stopped before long. This was the core of the message that I brought home.

The only memorable incident on the return voyage, as we zigzagged our way across the ever-threatening gray ocean, was meeting a dedicated young Maryknoll missionary named James Keller, who later founded The Christophers. Having served in China, he had been sent from his American base to comfort a group of unhappy coolies who had been recruited to dig trenches on an implied promise that France was a land of sunshine. That particularly cold and wet winter, life in the trenches was unspeakable misery for any human, especially for those disillusioned Chinese in their cotton clothes, unable to make themselves understood or to find companionship outside their dreary camps.

9

FROM THE DAYS when the Treasury Department and the leading bankers of America called on every available citizen to help them put over the first Liberty Loan drive, speechmaking seemed to fall to my lot. Benjamin Strong, Governor of the Federal Reserve Bank of New York, wrote in April, 1918, inviting me to speak at Carnegie Hall, where a rally would be held to launch the Liberty Loan campaign. The Archbishop of York was the announced guest of honor. Several dignitaries, representing various important agencies, would each deliver two-minute messages of welcome. The Archbishop, returned from the battlefields something of a war hero, was the principal speaker. George Wharton Pepper of Philadelphia and I were to represent America. With plans rearranged, I hurried from a speaking date in Buffalo. A capacity audience filled Carnegie Hall.

Under any and all circumstances it was a trial to face an audience without the help of fine words, written by brilliant authors, such as those at my disposal in the theatre. That night it was twice as difficult—with the presence on stage behind the speakers of right honorable gentlemen, city notables, trustees of the Cathedral of St. John the Divine who had marched in to form an honor guard for the Archbishop.

First came the chairman's welcome, tributes to the Archbishop, and his address; then came my turn. When I was seated again, a program was passed to me on which the Archbishop had written:

> I feel like a wounded soldier I saw in an Advance Dressing Station who said after the Nurse had left him "Thank God for the sound of a woman's voice."
>
> Cosmo Lang

I always cherished a feeling of gratitude for this gracious churchman and followed with interest his career. He finally became Archbishop of Canterbury and played a prominent part in the abdication of King Edward VIII.

Another invitation came from Rabbi Stephen S. Wise, who held his Free Synagogue services at Carnegie Hall. In May, 1918, he asked me to take over the period usually allotted to his sermon.

Never had I heard such quality of voice, such beauty of interpretation, as when Dr. Wise read, "Comfort ye, comfort ye my people, saith your God." Later he wrote, "I am very grateful to you and congratulate you upon the privilege of going throughout the land and awakening the American people to a sense of the loyalty and nobleness of our youth and their own opportunity to serve them." This kind message encouraged me.

I found myself in a new role for women, such as speaking from church pulpits, from the floor of the New York Stock Exchange (the first woman so privileged), from forums of every sort and kind. Like a buffeted tennis ball, I never knew which court I would land in next; my subject, of course, was America's war effort and the Red Cross at home and abroad.

Speechmaking before large crowds invariably gave me stage fright; my husband could not understand why anyone with years of experience in the theatre should suffer so. "Don't let them frighten you," he said. "Remember the old saying, 'A lusty bluff well chucked is better than a wavering truth.'" Was it an old saying? I don't know. Outwardly the bluff was effective; inwardly, fear held sway and butterflies worked overtime.

In 1918, out of a clear sky, a letter came from my one-time business manager, George Tyler, making a fund-raising suggestion. He forwarded to me the manuscripts of three old successes: *Merely Mary Ann, Salomy Jane,* and *The Dawn of a Tomorrow.* The plan outlined called for a six weeks' tour with the play of my choice, an all-star cast, in a cross-country tour of one-night stands. Expenses would be at a minimum—members of the cast and others would donate their service to this patriotic cause—and ticket prices would be high. Should the proposal be accepted, he guaranteed $100,000 for the Red Cross or any other war cause nominated by me.

My husband offered not the slightest objection. He said he had always been proud of my career in the theatre. Generously and wisely, he left the decision to me. Time to think it over was granted. The issues, however, were soon clarified.

The next Red Cross engagement took me to Wilmington, Delaware, as a result of the following letter.

THE AMERICAN RED CROSS

PENNSYLVANIA DIVISION HEADQUARTERS
N.W. COR. 16TH & WALNUT STS.
PHILADELPHIA, PA.

April 26th, 1918

My Dear Mrs. Belmont:

Supplementing my appeal to you to speak at Wilmington during the Red Cross Campaign week, I want to tell you that these people talked to me again only yesterday and told me that if you will consent to talk to them down there, you will arouse such interest as will enable them to raise at least one million dollars; whereas if they have to conduct the campaign without the inspiration of your presence, they do not see how it is possible to raise more than five hundred thousand. Can you possibly resist such an appeal as that?

You should I think feel highly flattered to think that one address of yours is worth five hundred thousand dollars to the Red Cross. And still after listening to you the other afternoon, I feel that I would cheerfully and gladly give five hundred thousand dollars for the privilege, providing, of course, I had the five hundred thousand to start with. Between you and me, . . . it would be a glorious thing to literally talk people out of five hundred thousand dollars for the Red Cross.

I understand that Mr. Tamblyn of the Atlantic Division is represented as your booking agent, but I am taking this up with you personally with the hope that you may be able to grant us this favor.

Very sincerely yours,
Charles Scott, Jr.
Division Manager

The meeting was packed with patriotic citizens. Enthusiasm for the American Red Cross was mounting. The ceremonies over, Pierre du Pont, chairman, reminded the audience that theirs was a small community with a quota of $500,000. Then he proposed that in honor of Mrs. Belmont, Wilmington should double this quota. The whole audience shouted approval. To the glory of Wilmington, be it said, they turned in $2,155,000 when the time came, as evidence of their patriotism.

Obviously, there were other and more effective ways of raising essential money than by returning to the theatre for a guarantee of $100,000. The following day I wrote Mr. Tyler, thanking him for his generous offer and telling him of my decision not to return to the stage.

For the original plan was substituted an all-star tour built around Laurette Taylor in Hartley Manners's play, *Out There.*

Laurette wrote a gay account in the autumn of 1918, "*The Greatest of These——*," describing this barnstorming event, and sent me a copy. Of this successful venture she said:

> It has been a wonderful journey for the soul. The dirt, the heat, and the noise, nothing has penetrated *there* except the glorious consciousness of helping. I am sorry it is ending, and I say again, the people of the stage know the art of giving.
>
> Now, on to Columbus! Christopher! What a large country our own United States is! As an English comedian who travelled it for the first time said, "Why give him credit for *discovering* America? How could he miss it?" *

10

SINCE ACCOMMODATIONS in Washington were scarce, Mrs. E. H. Harriman had taken a large apartment at Stoneleigh Court for herself and other Red Cross friends who had to be in Washington from time to time. On August 22, 1918, a telegram arrived at Stoneleigh Court, where I was staying: "NEWS BUREAU TICKER ANNOUNCES YOUR APPOINTMENT AS ASSISTANT TO THE NATIONAL WAR COUNCIL. A QUEEN BEE SURE ENOUGH. AUGIE."

Frankly, this appointment was less important than it sounded. It had been a concession on the part of the Red Cross to an insistent call for a woman on the War Council to represent the woman's point of view. A free-lance in every sense of the word, and not a feminist, I belonged to no woman's organization. However, after the appointment, nothing further was heard from any women's groups, partly because we were all occupied with the war, and partly because I eagerly sponsored and represented, to the best of my ability, every woman, professional or volunteer, who wanted to serve the Red Cross.

On the invitation of Henry P. Davison, Chairman of the Red Cross War Council, to join the headquarters staff, I moved to Washington for the duration, and rented Mrs. J. Borden Harri-

---

* "*The Greatest of These——*" (New York, George H. Doran Company, 1918), p. 50.

man's house while she went overseas. My husband, as major in the Remount Service, was assigned to General Dawes and had gone back to Paris. Also two of his sons were overseas, so Army regulations prevented my return to Europe. The heat that summer of 1918 in Washington was intense, and the humidity broke all records; the air was so lifeless, one felt it must have been used since the days of Adam and Eve. But no one counted the hours we spent at national headquarters in the memorial building, which the staff somewhat disrespectfully called the Marble Palace. Personnel of the War Council had changed somewhat. Mr. Hurley had gone to another post. He was replaced by George C. Case of New York and his able partner Joseph M. Hartfield was Counselor, replacing John W. Davis who had been appointed Ambassador to Great Britain.

Mr. Davison had taken a large, hospitable house, Twin Oaks, later the headquarters of Secretary Stimson. Here, when the offices had finally closed for the day, members of the War Council and department heads would meet to consider present and new projects and to discuss lengthy cables from overseas. Our chief believed clarity and speed were essential to evaluate the service of commissions already in operation abroad. These cables were incredibly long, and the sessions frequently extended well beyond midnight.

I was supposed to concern myself with any program that involved nurses, and women in general, but practically my first definite assignment was to serve on a small committee to select designs for Red Cross service badges and medals, and establish recommendations regarding their distribution. The immediate need was for a general war service badge and insignia for uniforms. Designs were chosen also for three medals: gold, to be awarded for valor; silver, for exceptional service; bronze, for special service. Suddenly the committee ran into a hurricane of difficulties; all headquarters, in a babel of opinions, was divided into small pieces as we tried to establish simple rules and procedures for awarding these three medals.

The problem was, to whom should medals for valor and exceptional service be presented? By whom and upon what evidence could such recognition be evaluated? We studied Army regulations as to medals, service stripes, and so on. Our own Army and Navy gave every assistance. The policies of foreign organizations and various service groups were considered. After burning much midnight oil, we finally agreed to recommend to the Central Committee that *no medals* be given to Americans for valor or for distinguished or exceptional service. What constituted distinguished or exceptional service presented too many problems in the face of so much self-sacrifice in all walks of life, from production rooms to foreign fields. One exception was made. We recommended that the bronze medal should be awarded in America to the families of those who died in Red Cross service overseas.

Service badges were approved. Responsibility for distribution was left with the chapters, their workers to receive badges according to the length of individual service involved. Headquarters handled its own staff, and foreign workers' badges were distributed by the Red Cross commissioners in other countries. These commissioners might also recommend to the awards committee at Red Cross headquarters names of foreigners who had rendered outstanding service to the American Red Cross in the various overseas areas of operation. They received silver and bronze medals. Important citations were composed by President Wilson's brother-in-law, Dr. Stockton Axson, a modest gentleman with a scholarly gift for using the English language.

Of the gold medals, two were struck off. One was immediately awarded to Dr. Richard P. Strong, who headed the Red Cross Sanitary Commission to Serbia in 1914–15, when typhus was raging. He and his staff performed heroic service in that country. Years later, the other gold medal was presented to Mabel T. Boardman on her fiftieth anniversary of active service.

Miss Boardman's historical connection with Red Cross undoubtedly was responsible for the general impression in Congress that she knew better than anyone else what was best for Red Cross. The chief menfolk at headquarters in 1917 were somewhat shy of crossing swords with her. Indefatigable when she was right, she could be equally indefatigable when wrong.

Edward Hicks, a cousin of Elias the Quaker, once wrote of the "great importance of superior women always being right, for when they get wrong they are so difficult to manage."

The War Council did not seem able to manage Miss Boardman, so to simplify swift-moving developments of the gigantic war program, they by-passed her.

Hers is a long and extraordinary record of unswerving loyalty to the cause she espoused in her youth. In years to come people will write legends about her, but there are two distinct and extremely important parts of her contribution to the growth of the American Red Cross. First, the pioneering care with which she tended the young and recently chartered organization; then, after 1922 the building of a body of trained volunteers, ready to take up their appointed tasks, ready faithfully to carry them out. A born leader, a dominant personality, she inspired a vast group of women to achieve a regularity of service and a standard of loyalty in performing accepted tasks that is rare even in professional fields. She was well known as a generous hostess to the succeeding diplomatic and Congressional groups in Washington. Her family tradition was hospitality.

11

EARLY IN THE WAR Home Service was created and grew under the direction of expert social service workers, as the armed forces grew, to prodigious proportions. Rapidly spreading throughout our chapters, it combined with the Department of Military Relief to serve the troops in training camps, on active duty overseas, and with their families at home. It was truly a manifestation of the charter pronouncement that the American Red Cross "act . . . as a medium of communication between the people of the United States of America and their Army and Navy." Administered by professional social workers, supplemented by volunteers and their various functions, generously financed in every chapter and national budget, the Home Service Department, more than any other, justified the title bestowed upon our Red Cross, "Greatest Mother in the World."

Information along innumerable lines was provided; guidance for mothers, young and old; funds when Government checks were delayed; other loans; help in unraveling worrying snarls due to governmental and military red tape; exchange bulletins between man and family where matters of illness, birth and death were concerned. There was practically no human problem Home Service and the Department of Military Relief in the field didn't face. To finance these services to our armed forces cost more than half the money raised in the different fund drives, but the manifold benefits provided meant relief of mind and body to millions of men, women, and children. Above all, Red Cross contributions cast no shadow of charity. One star on a service flag gave everyone a right to use this expert guidance and the far-flung channels of communication maintained between home and the fighting men everywhere; a people's gift to its armed forces. Newton D. Baker, then Secretary of War, spoke of the Red Cross as, "the nation's shock absorber," a prophetic statement indeed!

Jesse H. Jones was chairman of the Department of Military Relief. Everyone at headquarters was intrigued by this tall, handsome, quiet-voiced Texan. They were pleased, too, with his unmistakable ability in administering this hitherto unknown form of Red Cross assistance. Jesse Jones never talked unless he had something to say; then he was brief and always to the point. He was somewhat of a mystery man, but we all liked him.

12

DR. JOHN H. FINLEY—author, educator, and editor of *The New York Times*—(the only man I ever knew who walked around the Island of Manhattan) when he returned from a visit to Canada in 1918 reported on a piece of work being done in a few schools there, and urged that the American Red Cross should draw the youth of our country into service. Mr. Davison seized upon the idea outlined in this modest Canadian experiment, and the Junior Red Cross started on its triumphant way. In 1956, it recorded more than 45,000,000 children enrolled in the 60 nations of The League of Red Cross Societies. Of this number, 20,000,000 are in the United States.

13

THE PRESSURE put on national headquarters in wartime was stupendous. Literally millions of people, with no particular training, were eager to do something—anything to serve their country. Mistakes were made, many times and oft. Realizing how rapidly the organization developed, it is surprising that there were not more mistakes.

The question of uniforms caused hours of discussion. The women's hats, adopted after lengthy consideration, were appalling. In the midst of seriously important decisions would come questions such as, "What should be the size of the Red Cross on a worker's uniform worn in the production room?"

That gave our male leaders a setback. Finally, instructions were issued. "The red cross on workers' uniforms should be in proportion to the bust measurement."

Another time, there was almost a riot in Red Cross production rooms throughout the country because workers decided they didn't like the supplies Red Cross was sending to the French civilians. "Soldiers are being killed in France," they said, "but there is no reason why we should put all these children in black." They had to be persuaded that black aprons were the standard uniform of French children; they wouldn't wear colored ones.

14

A SUGGESTION made to Mr. Davison immediately after the war he had turned over to me, to wit, that a Red Cross museum be started before important souvenirs were discarded or lost to sight. Irene Givenwilson, who had a splendid record as Director of one of the large American canteens in Issoudun, France, accepted the appointment as curator. Wisely she called upon museum experts to assist. Herman Bumpus of Tufts College was invaluable as chairman; and Dr. Frank Chapman of the Museum of Natural History in New York became guide, philosopher, and friend of the project. A few of those who paid any attention scoffed; nevertheless, the museum, under the guidance of Miss Givenwilson, grew apace at amazingly little cost to the Red Cross. Most of the money we raised outside the budget, with the help of Mrs. Davison.

An early souvenir presented was a large lithograph of Clara Barton. Immediately we ran into difficulty. Mabel Boardman protested hanging the picture in the Red Cross building. She had been a leader in the group which brought about a reorganization in 1905. Ultimately Judge Payne and I persuaded Miss Boardman that regardless of her personal feeling, nothing could change the fact that Clara Barton had established the Red Cross in America. Finally Miss Boardman, by silence, gave consent to our hanging the picture. In December, 1923, on my recommendation, the Central Committee recognized the museum as a permanent activity of the organization. Before World War II, when the museum went into storage to make room again in the Marble Palace for war workers, 50,000 visitors were recorded annually.

15

IN 1919, Mr. Davison returned from Red Cross conferences in Europe and, using several of us as guinea pigs, tried out a new idea. The vision of a world league of Red Cross organizations possessed his mind; he urged a Red Cross in every country with a permanent peacetime program. The Geneva Convention under which Red Cross organizations operate was based upon emergency service in time of war. It so happens that the charter granted by the Congress of the United States to the American Red Cross was broader than the Geneva Convention, making provision for it to "carry on a system of national and international relief in time of peace and apply the same in mitigating the sufferings caused by pestilence, famine, fire, floods and other great national calamities, and to devise and carry on measures for preventing the same."

Mr. Davison advocated a revision of the Geneva Convention to include Red Cross activities in time of peace. He believed that, in co-operation with the International Red Cross and with an enlarged scope, Red Cross organizations of the various countries would each stimulate and develop peacetime activities for the betterment of mankind. It was a challenging idea. From this seed, the League of Red Cross Societies was born. Mrs. William K. Draper of New York, a noted Red Cross worker since Spanish War days, joined those of us who staunchly believed in the idea.

Meanwhile, a fairly serious struggle was taking place in America. The so-called old guard insisted our Red Cross was a war and disaster organization; that when war was over, the proper procedure was for the organization to retire to its tent, only to emerge like a fire engine on call of "fire, flood or pestilence." A large group, on the other hand, felt that activities developed during the war experience, a responsibility to war veterans, coupled with the education in public service that had been achieved, must continue. Certainly the need for such service was conclusively apparent. Hastily the War Council appointed a committee of some eighteen or twenty persons, drawn from various departments at headquarters, the general manager serving as chairman. Jane Delano, director of the Department of Nursing, and I were the only members of the distaff side that I remember. The purpose was to ascertain the opinion of these workers regarding an active future program and to incorporate their recommendations, if any, in a preliminary report.

The group expressed unanimous conviction in favor of the policy to carry on. Hopes and ideas were exchanged, but to everyone's surprise, Miss Delano presented a plan for the creation of a Red Cross Public Health Nursing Service on a national scale. It was complete in every detail: the wise nurses had given much thought to a postwar program. They had consulted educators in the field, and they were ready. Once again *pre*-vision was *pro*vision.

Being well known to the chapters, between which I had been shuttling, speechmaking to their members, trouble-shooting or explaining policies, and also an enthusiastic advocate of the peacetime program, I was appointed chairman of a small committee to ascertain the opinions of Red Cross workers throughout the country.

Our first move was to issue a questionnaire to the 3,700 chapters. Dr. Neva Deardorff, a distinguished social service specialist, was brought to headquarters to assist in co-ordinating and evaluating the replies. A few of the chapters had already folded at the cease fire, but some 73 per cent answered. Of these, perhaps 62 per cent favored the peacetime program. From the replies, special emphasis on problems of health in the smaller communities was apparent. One woman, a rural chapter chairman, wrote to me: "We are deeply interested in the suggestion of a public health program. The only health work in our community is being carried on by the Ladies' Shakespeare Society."

Using this survey as a guide, our committee recommended a peacetime plan with postwar services to veterans, a public-health nursing program, educational activities, first aid, home care of the sick, and a well-rounded program for volunteer service to fit chapters of various sizes. We offered a composite pattern of the best existing procedures in operation in the chapters, to which we added a Braille service in line with a fine service operating in Chicago, Philadelphia, New York, and several other chapters.

Delegates assembled in Washington to consider the future course; a strong many-sided peacetime program versus a stand-by for emergencies policy. The discussions were spirited. A number of delegates held to the generally accepted theory of service restricted to war and disaster.

Finally one Southern chapter chairman walked to the platform and after a fiery speech energetically stated, "Our country has grown to expect a major service of this Red Cross, an' I say we cain't deliver that service by just havin' Miss Delayno arrivin' on a fire engine." This lurid picture seemed to shed a final light on the argument. The full peacetime program was approved by the War Council, adopted by a good-sized majority of chapters.

Dr. Livingston Farrand, an expert in the field of public health, was appointed by President Wilson as Chairman of the American Red Cross on recommendation of the War Council at the time of its retirement. The Central Committee once more took control of the organization. Eliot Wadsworth of Washington, George E. Scott of Chicago, Cornelius Bliss and I of New York were appointed members of the reorganized governing body.

Our Survey Committee had recommended that a Volunteer Service Department should be formed with a place in the organization comparable to that held by Military Relief, Home Service, and Nursing; further, that Volunteer Service should have a national director at headquarters, with a representative in the division offices and chapters. The post of national director was offered to me. However, my husband had been demobilized by now, and knowing it would be impossible to administer the work from New York, I declined. A highly recommended college graduate and war worker was appointed Director. She did some excellent spade work in organization that first year, helping the chapters of varying sizes to find their programs in peacetime. But there were strong tides of opposition at headquarters. Also, she could not afford to be a volunteer, and that fact contributed to her defeat and led to her resignation. Miss Boardman succeeded to the post in 1922, and with ability and devotion, produced a national band of effectively trained workers.

The major demonstration, led by Dr. Farrand, to show the value of public-health nursing grew until Red Cross had placed nearly 2,000 nurses in probably 1,200 rural communities. Another notable demonstration was made in New York City at the East Harlem Health Center. Co-ordination among the multiplicity of public, private, and religious health and welfare groups was a necessity, but it took Red Cross leadership and prestige, which the local chapter provided, to bring it about successfully.

Thirty years later, thanks in large measure to these two major experiments, there is a Federal health program co-operating with public-health nurses in every state. New York, thanks to Mayor LaGuardia, took over the East Harlem Health Center. Today there are 30 such centers in the 5 boroughs, 22 of them with their own buildings, 8 operating on an area basis. Truly, good seed fell on good ground.

With customary vision, Harry Davison had recognized that the time might come when it would not be possible to find a desirable chairman who could devote full time to Red Cross national affairs without compensation beyond the amount the Central Committee might feel justified in awarding. To meet this probability, he raised a chairman's fund of $100,000. The income was to be added to a salary appropriated by the Red Cross. He also bought a charming house to be used by the chairman. Dr. Farrand lived there for two and a half years until he resigned. Judge Payne, with a background of exceptional service to his country, was appointed by President Harding to succeed him. He was a volunteer who had his own home in Washington; therefore, the Red Cross house was rented.

Due to the rapid expansion of Washington in wartime, the neighborhood changed drastically; ultimately, the house became a doubtful asset. We decided to sell, and the proceeds became part of the chairman's fund. Income from this, added to a modest salary voted from Red Cross sources, made available nearly $18,-000 a year.

Judge Payne's legal experience was valuable in clarifying problems that developed in advancing the League. Some Red Cross leaders had grave doubts of its value. Under the Judge's leadership a formula was found, not an easy task, for co-ordinating the work of the many national societies, the International Committee, and the League. The International Red Cross Conference, which meets every four years or every two years in case of need, is now the deliberative body of the entire Red Cross world. Its decisions govern the traditions and common purposes of the Red Cross movement. This co-ordination has been arrived at without encroaching upon the independence of any group.

The International Committee, controlled entirely by the Swiss, remains the guardian of the purpose of the Red Cross. It informs the national societies whenever a new group is established in conformity with the Geneva Convention. It remains a neutral intermediary, respected and recognized as necessary in time of war. Matters that concern prisoners of war are centered in this unique organization.

The International Committee and the League work closely together, yet each preserves its individuality and its own field of action, corresponding somewhat to war activities on one hand and peacetime activities on the other. But they collaborate, especially in matters which relate to the international distribution of relief through Red Cross in time of war or other disaster and information about health education and Junior Red Cross.

Judge Payne, a newcomer, was an excellent Chairman. He took us firmly through the postwar deflationary period without suffering a qualm himself. The American Red Cross had become gigantic business, and getting it back to a fairly normal basis was a painful operation for all departments of service. Fourteen divisions were reduced to three. Growing pains in reverse—people cherished their jobs. Hearts as well as hours were bound up in production of surgical dressings, for which, gratefully, there was no longer dramatic need. But in so many cases one's kinship with glory had been to produce the prodigious quotas called for by national headquarters, and the essential pruning in many departments caused considerable distress. The Judge—wisely, yet at times sternly—brought the organization through demobilization to a foundation which could be safely held. With increasing devotion he led the Red Cross into a peacetime program that was strong in purpose, useful in service, and defensible in budget. Twice my resignation was offered. Twice it was gently but firmly refused.

Rear Admiral Cary T. Grayson was appointed Chairman of the Central Committee after Judge Payne died. Speaking at the next Red Cross convention banquet, he told this story:

Back in the days of the First World War, I was asked to join a scheme to help the Red Cross. A lady from a western state wrote me a letter saying:

"We are working for the Red Cross, and we are conserving and saving, and we have decided that in time of war men could get along out here with at least half of their shirt-tails, and we could use the other half to make aprons for the working girls in the Red Cross. We have had pretty good success, but two weeks from now we are planning to have a bazaar, and we are going to make, at that time, aprons for the working girls in the Red Cross from promi-nent men's shirt-tails. I want you to use any influence you might have with President Wilson to get one of his shirt-tails to make an apron for that bazaar. P.S. If you could note any particular functions that the shirt-tail attended, it would help us out."

So to get that shirt-tail was my first Red Cross mission.

The news of Rear Admiral Grayson's appointment as Chair-man by President Franklin D. Roosevelt came as a complete surprise to the members of the Red Cross Central Committee. No member had been consulted in the matter. To many of us, Dr. Grayson was a well-known and valued individual. Several questioned, Had politics played a part in the appointment? Did it mean that the position might become a political plum?

Admiral Grayson's knowledge of medicine combined with his willingness to listen, his personal tact, made him popular with Red Cross leaders over the country. Also, his sympathetic un-derstanding of nurses' problems left the staff and those who espoused the public-health program particularly sad when he died suddenly, two years and a few months after his appoint-ment.

Not even a rumor of his successor reached us until President Roosevelt appointed Norman H. Davis to the Chairmanship. This statesman was well known in America. Also, his service in the field of diplomatic international affairs made his selec-tion more than acceptable to nations participating in the League of Red Cross Societies.

The chairmanship carried only a modest compensation at that time, but the subject of salary was frequently discussed by chap-ter representatives. It was of paramount importance to Mabel Boardman. Several years later, June 8, 1942, she wrote to me:

. . . It troubles me to hear said that politics have come into the Red Cross. When the President can appoint a man to a paid office the accusation no matter how untrue and unjust will arise that each appointee is beholden to the man who appointed him and must do his bidding. That is one of the reasons I have always opposed salaries. Our chairman has devoted himself to his work and I am sure acted in the most conscientious manner but people will talk—and idle gossip is hard to down. When several Presidents appointed chairmen from the other political party and no salaries were paid—such remarks did not occur. Well good night dear. Let's hope for the best. . . .

16

DURING THE WAR, Washington became the hub of American affairs, a highway for transients of many nationalities. People arrived suddenly from somewhere, usually en route to a known or unknown somewhere else. For war workers who were anchored there, the long days were crowded. Occasionally, however, small, interesting late dinners brought one in touch with the fixed planets of Washington life, in addition to the shooting stars.

Whether or not you agreed with his policies, Senator Henry Cabot Lodge was one of the planets, a distinguished man, and a cultivated and delightful talker. He acknowledged a copy of one of H. G. Wells's books about the war with the following:

Mr. Lodge, Chairman
UNITED STATES SENATE
CONFERENCE OF THE MINORITY
December 24, 1918

Personal

My dear Mrs. Belmont,

You are very kind to recall our conversation and send me Mr. Wells's book. I have read it. Mr. Wells is a brilliant novelist and has written some remarkable novels, but when he undertakes to deal with politics or international questions it seems to me he is as unfit for the work as I am for writing a novel. He condemns *all* soldiers in one paragraph although he never was a soldier. He condemns *all* public men and represents everybody in public life as either a cheap sort of politician or absolutely imbecile. He has never held public office and never had to deal with public questions practically. He has made a study of human nature for his novels and he ought to have some general idea of it, but of human nature in the mass he seems curiously ignorant. Therefore he leaves it out of his calculations. The book seems to me rather incoherent. It starts out to be an argument in favor of a League of Nations, but not much of the book is devoted to that. He has a good deal to say, writing before the war was over, about what the peace should be, and with his terms of peace for Germany I largely agree. He devoted a whole chapter to proportional representation in which he finds a panacea for all political ills. That chapter seems to be addressed to Great Britain. I wish some machinery could be devised that would elect nothing but the best men to Congresses and Parliaments. I have seen a great deal of invented machinery put to work for those ends and it has left everything about as it was. People who get elected to Parliament or Congress are those whom the voters want as a rule. If they were not satisfied they would get somebody better. The machinery is not what prevents them. If there is a failure to get the best in representation it is because the people who desire only the best do not go into politics and work the machinery themselves, but they allow it to be done by professionals and then they wonder that selections are not satisfactory; and so, to avoid it, they undertake to make the machinery more elaborate, which of course simply strengthens the professional.

He then has another chapter about how certain nations including our own are to take possession of Africa and pool all its raw materials. I do not know whether that would promote the peace of the world or not, but it seems a strange line for a man to take who is an enemy of imperialism. In the same way, when he comes to the question of voting in the League, he takes up two of the points that I made—the one about the voting by States, each State one vote, and the other a vote based on population—and he sees very clearly that neither would do, so he gets around the question of voting by getting rid of the voters; that is, he proposes the League shall substantially consist of England, the United States, France, Italy and Germany—that is, there shall be an imperialist control of the world divided among five nations instead of being centered in the hands of one which is what Germany proposed. I see but little advantage in the change and I think if it did lead to quarrels they would be of a very desperate character. I am still waiting for somebody to explain to me the condition of the League of Nations which shall make it a working body. I agree with its purposes as fully as anybody can, but in seeking to promote universal peace I do not want to establish an organization which is likely to lead to further discords. In any event I think it is most harmful to try and force the establishment of a League of Nations before we settle with Germany. If that is done we are likely to get a very poor treaty with Germany and a great deal of dissension among the Allies.

With renewed thanks and kindest regards, believe me

Very truly yours,

H. C. Lodge

17

THERE WERE different opinions about Colonel Edward M. House, among Democrats as well as among Republicans, but my husband and I thought he was a patriot with a middle-of-the-road approach to the agitating problems which confronted our country. His tact was phenomenal. When talking of world affairs, he eased into a controversial situation as gently as if he were approaching an elderly partner for dinner. Of course, he was slightly prejudiced in favor of Democrats.

He had a profound conviction about the importance of the League of Nations to the world, but was objective in his discussion of the subject. I really was fond of the Colonel and always enjoyed tiny bits of information that he would murmur into my ear, saying, "Eleanor, this is just between you and me and the angels."

When the bill designed to bring the United States into the League of Nations was defeated in Congress, knowing how zealously he had worked for its passage, and realizing how its defeat would affect him, I went to see him promptly. It was a call of sympathy, as one might seek to comfort a friend when a member of the family had died. After voicing genuine personal regret, I blamed the Senate, as did many others, but he walked up and down his library, unusually agitated and said, "Definitely no. They are not entirely responsible. The bill might ultimately have gone through if the President had not insisted so stubbornly that not an *i* should be dotted nor a *t* crossed in amending the bill." It was the only reproach I ever heard him utter about his leader.

One day at lunch, when Colonel and Mrs. House were entertaining visitors from overseas, the subject came up of the famous statement made when the American Army landed in France, "Lafayette, *nous voici.*"

This perfect salutation that had warmed the hearts of Frenchmen everywhere was attributed, as usual, to General Pershing. It so happened that I had been in France when the wreath was laid on the tomb of the Unknown Soldier. Therefore, I maintained that this phrase was not pronounced by General Pershing —who could not be present, owing to an important war conference—but by a member of his staff whose name unfortunately escaped me. Everyone near by insisted to the contrary. We turned to the Colonel, who answered, "Pershing did not say it, but I too have forgotten the name of the man who did."

A few days later a card came from Colonel House saying, "You are right. It was not General Pershing, but Colonel Charles E. Stanton who said, 'Lafayette, we are here.'"

As a matter of fact, on previous occasions at war meetings I had heard General Pershing himself deny authorship. The third time he made no denial; as he returned to his seat beside me on the platform, I said, "General, you did not make your customary answer to the introduction."

The General replied, "I have found that it doesn't do any

good. Who can talk down a legend? Besides, it embarrasses the presiding chairman to be corrected."

18

AFTER THE PEACE CONFERENCE, Henry White, former ambassador to France and one of the delegates, occasionally came to visit and discuss the various problems involved; as he talked of the peace treaty and reparations, I expressed the opinion that the world had learned nothing from previous wars or from Christianity if the conquerors tried to enforce such crushing penalties on the defeated. Mr. White argued that owing to the strong current of postwar feeling, the terms in the treaty were the best that could be obtained, besides, definite provisions had been made for modifications. He offered to make these points clear, and kindly sent me a copy before his next visit. At first I put my name on the cover; then the idea occurred to me to secure a few original signatures. Gradually I collected autographs and finally had an extremely interesting copy of the Versailles Treaty with the signature of every member of our delegation, as well as those of the Big Four: Woodrow Wilson, Lloyd George, Clemenceau, and Orlando. Altogether, some twenty-six autographs of the original signers are on the document, as well as others concerned with the war and with the Peace Conference: Arthur Balfour, Alanson Houghton, General Pershing, and Viscount Allenby, who headed the campaign in Palestine.

A number of people helped me secure the signatures. Colonel House obtained that of Orlando and several others. Mrs. Charles Dana Gibson, sister of Lady Astor, agreed to ask Clemenceau when he was dining with them. With the returned treaty came a note saying:

Dear Eleanor,
    I led the Tiger to the desk and handed him a quill pen. "Madame," he said, "how did you know that I use a quill pen?"
    I said, "*Monsieur, je sais tout*," and he signed.

Some of the signatures cut from letters were given me by Austen Chamberlain and Godfrey Thomas, from their own files; Godfrey Thomas was personal secretary to the Prince of Wales.

To collect these autographs gave me enjoyment. It was a genuine pleasure to pass the material on to the Yale Library to be placed with the Colonel House Collection and other papers of that fateful period in world history owned by the university. While not an exact duplicate of the original treaty, this copy may be important because the Germans destroyed one of the few in existence when they captured the *wagon-lit* in the Forest of Compiègne in World War II, where it was housed.

19

REMEMBERING the expressed convictions and hopes of our people during World War I, I find myself surprised that any considerable number believe that the leadership which took us into that war was a group of international bankers. Memory must be short, indeed, if we can forget the many motivating factors which stirred us so deeply from 1914 to 1917. Given firm convictions and an occasional platform, anyone is bound to record a number of beliefs. I quote from a speech of mine in May, 1936:

> We did not go to war because Germany violated the neutrality of Belgium, but it had a profound effect upon the American mind; we did not go to war because, in her effort to subdue her enemy, Germany initiated the use of poison gas to the horror of the civilized world; our participation was not due to the sinking of the *Lusitania*, though these ruthless acts aroused a passionate feeling of righteous indignation—the contemptuous disregard for treaties, for the rights of combatants, the cruel submarine warfare, paved the way to our conviction as to what was right and what was wrong, and when Germany finally assumed to dictate to this country where our ships could go and what they could carry, that last act, interfering so drastically with United States policies at that time, finally brought us into the war.

Could any group of international bankers have drawn this country into war on the opposite side?

The ghastly horror of the recent war [1917] provided three things at least that we need at the present time: unity of purpose, a willingness to make sacrifices for the common good, and self-control. Perhaps the greatest of these is self-control. We have every right to cross the street, but we surrender a section of that right to cross just as and when we please, partly with the fundamental idea of self-preservation, and partly in the general interest of others. In the interest of peace abroad, could we not surrender a little of our freedom to ridicule and insult publicly other nations in regard to their leaders, their policies, their motives? Good will is recognized as an important element in peace. Why discard it for a temporary and quite unimportant relief to some individual's feelings, humorous or otherwise? A voluntary surrender of the outer boundaries of liberty is not an unreasonable price to pay for real freedom, whether that freedom lies in the use of power, trade, liquor, or words. In fact, one might go so far as to predict that, if democracy fails, it probably will be for lack of self-control more than any other thing. If democracy is worth the price our ancestors paid for it, is it not worth some sacrifice on our part of the outer fringes of our liberties?

20

A RED CROSS on a field of white is the recognized emblem of mercy throughout the world. This emblem should be reserved by decree of Congress for the exclusive use of the Red Cross in America, as it is in other nations. It is my definite opinion that its use for shoes, medical supplies, or any commercial product should not be permitted, no matter how good the product may be. Once I hurried into a stationery shop, "strong as any army with banners." There was a poster in the window; under the Red Cross emblem was the caption, "*Red Cross Hospital* for Fountain Pens." My righteous indignation must have impressed the storekeeper. In any case, he destroyed the sign and handed me the fragments as a souvenir of conquest.

Norman Davis, when he was chairman, made a gallant effort
to secure exclusive use of the Red Cross emblem. He and I were
authorized by the Red Cross Central Committee to appear before a special Senate committee called together to urge action
on this appeal.

A committee of the Senate heard our case on several occasions. Finally the chairman introduced me and asked for comments. I said:

I have been twenty-five years associated with the Amer-
ican Red Cross, a member of the Central Committee of the
National Organization, and a member of the Board of Di-
rectors of the New York Chapter of the American Red
Cross. I have served continuously since April, 1917. I was
abroad five months in World War I, as an observer to
British and French Red Cross and different parts of the
Front, where our American Red Cross was serving with the
Forces. My work has taken me from New York to San Fran-
cisco, from Maine to Texas. There are few states in which
I have not been on behalf of the Red Cross. Experience over
these twenty-five years enables me to know the value and
significance of this emblem. I have been to Canada several
times, also to international conferences of the League of Red
Cross Societies and the International Committee of the Red
Cross.

The most recent conference was held in London in 1938.
At that time, some 425 delegates from fifty-eight nations
represented more than forty million people who belong to
the Red Cross throughout the world. The conference had to
be transferred from Spain, where it was originally planned,
because of civil war in that country. When we met in St.
James' Palace, China and Japan were also at war, but in
that room where the delegates assembled were representatives of the Japanese and Chinese Red Cross. Also, there
were two Red Cross Committees representing Spain. One
of them urged that the other newly organized group belonged to the rebels and had no legal right at that convention; they insisted that those delegates be instructed to

withdraw. The International Committee representative informed the chair that both committees were rendering effective and impartial service to the Spanish wounded. Sir Arthur Stanley, of the British Red Cross, the presiding chairman, therefore ruled that both were entitled to be seated, and under the Red Cross Flag, these committees remained with the other delegates throughout the conference.

I then introduced Virginia M. Dunbar, assistant to Mary Beard, Director of the Red Cross Nursing Service, who read into the record a resolution passed at a convention of three national nursing organizations on the subject of the bill under discussion. Major Julia C. Stimson, president of the American Nurses' Association, the first woman to be created a major in the American Army, signed the resolution. Their organizations went on record as unanimously supporting and urging the bill to restrict the use of this emblem. Then my testimony continued:

We believe that the emblem of the Red Cross on a white ground was created as a symbol of service to suffering humanity. We believe that this emblem does not belong exclusively to the United States; that it was committed to the care of the United States when a group of American citizens in 1881 undertook to carry out the humanitarian work started in Geneva in 1864, which undertaking was confirmed and ratified by treaty, and since that time has been promoted throughout the world in this and other Red Cross Societies. . . .

Implicit in our agreement to become party to the Treaty of Geneva is the understanding that we would use this emblem for the purpose for which it was created. In my humble opinion, the right to use or to assign the use of this emblem does not rest with any individual. It does not even belong to the United States. Our country shares the right to use it with other nations engaged in Red Cross work.

There is no doubt that to reserve the use of this symbol to the Red Cross and the Medical Corps of the Army and

Navy would inconvenience commercial concerns, which today are using this emblem as a trade mark, but for many years now, they have enjoyed a good will which in no way can be considered as belonging to their products. The respect and the affection in which the Red Cross emblem is held does not accrue from any commercial product, no matter how excellent that product may be. It has been developed over the past thirty years through cruel suffering and hardships shared in war, famine, fire and flood. The deep-rooted confidence in the Red Cross has spread through every town and village of the country, into the homes and classrooms even of our children, because of the prompt and effective help given to those who suffer. This help has been made possible by the hard work and the sacrifice of men, women and children, our millions of members.

If the historic work of the Red Cross is to be carried on in time of war, it is essential that all nations, belligerent and nonbelligerent, should respect the emblem of its service. How is it possible to insure that respect if in a great country such as ours this emblem is permitted as a Trade Mark on a large variety of purchasable goods ranging from matches to dynamite?

If other great nations, including Germany and Japan, can afford to reserve this emblem for the purpose for which it was created, surely this country, which has contributed so much to the development of the Red Cross program throughout the world, in peace as well as war, can do no less.

However, our mission did not succeed. The extended length of time over which the Red Cross had been used as a commercial symbol made restriction difficult unless compensation was granted to the commercial users. The misuse of this noble emblem remains one of those unpleasant problems that most politicians manage to by-pass. Important unfinished business, this subject should be faced some day by our Government. Both past and future service of the American Red Cross warrant the exclusive use of its symbol to the cause of mercy.

21

ANOTHER DOOR of memory opens and reveals the Red Cross International Conference held in London, June, 1938. One important item which caused long and heated discussion was the question of bombing nonmilitary objectives from the air. This session was incredibly difficult, tense with expressed and suppressed feeling. Eliot Wadsworth, a member of our delegation, presided with sound judgment and parliamentary skill. Our national Chairman, Norman Davis, introduced a resolution which appealed in the name of humanity to competent authorities in all countries to prevent or restrict bombing from the air, and urged governments, in cases where military operations endangered the lives of innocent civilians to arrange effective measures for their evacuation to safety zones under Red Cross protection. The delegates from Japan refrained from participating in the discussion. Those from Italy and Germany argued against the resolution, their point being that all phases of war are horrible, therefore war should be outlawed and not any one aspect of it. Great Britain, Czechoslovakia, France, and all the other nations assembled endorsed the American resolution, which finally passed unanimously after two days of argument.

The delegate from China was memorable. His plea was for the children. His experience showed that while many are maimed and killed in air raids, a worse aspect of this horror is the malnutrition and disease which follow in the wake of war. He pointed out that the shattered nerves of the children who survive continual bombing would eventually make for frightful mental conditions in the world of tomorrow. He referred to the churches and monuments of great beauty which are destroyed in such raids, as the heritage of the whole human race, the only tangible evidence of man's struggle for thousands of years to raise himself from the mud.

The conference closed with a thanksgiving service of solemn beauty in St. Paul's Cathedral. Nearly 500 delegates from 54 nations were seated in the center of the cathedral. Then, to beautiful music, the procession of uniformed Red Cross workers began. Every county in the British Isles was represented. Nurses in great numbers from the various hospitals filed in. Ironically, the Cathedral was later damaged and many of the hospitals represented in this beautiful service were laid to ashes as a result of brutal and relentless air raids. The Lord Mayor and his staff arrived in official regalia. On a balcony high up, immediately under the dome of St. Paul's, we saw a blaze of color from Red Cross flags in the hands of children, the Junior Red Cross of England.

Every seat in the great cathedral was occupied. At that moment a color guard composed of nurses marched slowly up the aisle in a hollow square, in the center of which a stately young woman carried aloft the Red Cross banner. The flag was received and blessed by the Archbishop of Canterbury, who then placed it upon the altar, where it remained until a benediction closed the ceremony. Then it was borne out while the organ pealed forth a glad *Te Deum*.

22

OUR DELEGATION and others left this Conference with grave anxiety. Undoubtedly war clouds were gathering over Europe. One day I asked a British M.P., "Tell me, aside from your recognized government leaders, who is the ablest man in England today?"

He answered promptly, "Lady Reading."

Some years before, following the Shakespeare Theatre ceremonies at Stratford, the Lamonts and I spent a night in Deal Castle with the Readings. On his retirement from the Foreign Office, he was made the Earl of Reading and appointed Lord Warden of the Cinque Ports. After his death, Stella Reading turned her exceptional ability to public service. Norman Davis, Red Cross Chairman, gave every assistance in her effort to develop for England activities, patterned on our Red Cross program, that were not available to British Red Cross due to its charter.

In anticipation of the war crisis. Lady Reading organized the Women's Voluntary Services. When war came a year later, 1939, this army of women, under her leadership, rendered to Great Britain one of the unique contributions made by any group in their country's history. Following are extracts from her letters, telling of the voluntary services, their advantages and disadvantages. These comments apply equally to voluntary services in our own country.

WOMEN'S VOLUNTARY SERVICES
FOR CIVIL DEFENCE
41 TOTHILL STREET
LONDON
s.w.1

LONDON, 22nd November, 1939

My dear Eleanor,

It seems such a long time since we were together and discussed the many things, foreboding in our minds, but hopeful in our hearts would not occur—now we are really in the throes of work and you can imagine the immensity of it.

This machine has absorbed its first big shock extremely well and you can have no conception what it felt like to send out 12 telegrams putting the machine into operation and calling out for work 120,000 women on evacuation services—all that has been done during the last year has been more than amply justified in the way that the initial burden was absorbed; and now the other services are each in their turn making demands and being carried out in the way that one had foreseen might occur. After evacuation came the big demand on the Hospital Supply services, followed with great rapidity by the demand for communal feeding and canteen work.

. . . I feel very proud of our administrative staff of 5,000 and our army of over half a million volunteers who are carrying on their very unglamorous tasks extremely well. . . .

Travelling round the country, I am amazed at the leadership which has sprung forward—you will remember in discussing it with me, how I told you that the one thing which frightened me in 1938 was that women were constantly saying "tell us what to do and we will do it." I can assure you now that the boot is on a completely different foot and the tempo is they tell *me* what to do and *how* to do it. I feel from a democratic point of view this is frightfully valuable for it means that 5,000 potential leaders have come into being and there is no chance of control being tied up in one pair of hands ! ! ! . . .

Yours always devotedly
Stella

12th December, 1940

My dear Eleanor—

. . . The work of W.V.S. brings the members into contact with the very worse sides of the war. It is indescribably sad and heart-rending. So often they have to smile and pretend they are gay because their hearts are too full of pity to be able to talk of the things that are happening. The girls on mobile canteens feeding rescue squads have a particularly hard time with the terrible sights they cannot avoid, but by their courage they bring normality back to the man. I am proud of them all. However grim or difficult or merely dull the job in hand may be they carry on, adjusting and readjusting themselves and their arrangements from day to day, according to where the need for help is greatest.

We are down to essentials with no frills. Sensible clothes, sensible food, sleep, and every few weeks one or two days' rest in the comparative quiet of the Home Counties, which are now more or less huge dormitories. It is becoming a public duty to keep well so as to be able to carry on with one's job, and not overload the medical services. (Already, practically every hospital in London has been bombed, also many clinics and treatment centres.) Even woollen combinations are being revived to wear under siren suits in the shelters. I saw a very soignee woman buying some warm woollen combinations the other day. Her expression was wonderful—a mixture of mortification and revulsion. At length however, she sighed, smiled sweetly at the assistant and said: "Well, I suppose it is all in a good cause. It is no use getting a chill and being a nuisance now!" . . .

Later she wrote in an article for the Junior League of New York:

Too many people think of volunteer service as cheap labour. Real voluntary service is nothing of the kind. It is the gift of one's skill, one's time, and one's energy, given by an understanding human being for a special reason. It is essential to be realistic, practical, and honest about the contribution to a nation of voluntary service. What are its strengths and what its drawbacks? Its strengths lie in an enthusiastic approach to the subject, a spontaneous steeping of self in the job, a sinking of self in the undertaking with complete indifference to obstacles and absolute lack of acceptance of difficulties. Its weaknesses are possible lack of continuity, absence of any form of binding contract to complete the job, and the variety of personalities amongst the people carrying out the work.

Most people employing voluntary labour omit to realize that the people giving voluntary service are just as responsible people as they are themselves—in fact that they do not work for gain is their own decision and their own responsibility. . . . They have learned that voluntary service is given in the largest measure, not by the woman of leisure but by the woman who, recognizing the need for the work, if necessary, makes the time in which to do it.

. . . We do not consider our work is for today, neither do we feel it is for ourselves or for each other. We believe that in all its manifold smallnesses, our work is to establish the things which, in their fulfilment, will be of value and help to the sons and daughters of the future—for whose survival and existence, in decency of living and happiness of undertaking, wars have been fought and peace has been won.

23

In America World War II brought many Red Cross volunteers back on a full-time basis. The military forces made drastic demands on the nursing organizations. Hospitals, public welfare and private nursing groups were heavily drawn upon. Recruitment was now officially a Government responsibility, but our Red Cross Nursing Department helped screen applicants and rendered valuable assistance of various kinds.

At headquarters the nurses were troubled by a persistent nightmare. With the thousands of trained women drawn from civilian fields, what would happen if, as in 1918, the country should be swept by an epidemic? One important possibility for self-help lay in spreading the knowledge of home nursing in communities.

Mary Beard, Director of the Nursing Service, and I studied national reports. These revealed that only 57,000 individuals had taken the home nursing course the previous year. We planned to take immediate action to renew public interest and to launch a big program of development. Miss Beard invited Olivia Peterson, a state public-health teacher in Minnesota, to join her department. Then she asked me how much co-operation laymen in the chapters would give in recruiting the classes, and how many we should aim to train in one year. Always an enthusiast, with complete confidence in Red Cross volunteers, I plucked from the ether half a million as our goal!

Red Cross had kept always to itself in teaching home nursing. I proposed that we should seek the co-operation of government departments. Several of them were in some measure teaching home nursing and home economics in the schools, and through the Farm Bureau in rural communities. Joint participation in this field was something new.

Norman Davis approved Miss Beard's program and pledged $250,000 to carry it out. He appointed a National Council on Home Nursing, myself chairman and Olivia Peterson, director. This nurse proved the perfect choice for the task, with a positive genius for getting along with professional and lay workers, Government experts and Red Cross. She kept her eyes on the goal of training 500,000 in home nursing during the year; also, she kept her feet on the ground in establishing her organization. Volunteer experts were needed to teach volunteers to carry out the training program. It was an emergency; speed was essential. However, she kept steadily before the committee the fact that standards were important, that we must get the best possible nurse teachers to assist with the classes. On the national scale required, they had to be volunteers, but a small professional paid staff was secured at headquarters to guide the teaching. One month later, a call was issued from National Red Cross to division areas and chapters to recruit volunteer nurses who would teach after hospital and other business hours. Some 26,000 nurses volunteered as instructors. By October, twelve months later, the Red Cross had issued about 397,000 certificates to those who had completed the course. I am sure our chief nurse was troubled in her professional soul by the fact that many of these nurse volunteers had never been teachers before; indeed, a number needed refresher courses in simple principles of home nursing, which chapters provided. However, co-operation with Government services was genuinely effective. The nurse volunteers did a useful, patriotic job, and the public had benefited in health education.

The following year the Nursing Department revised and simplified textbooks on this subject, and proceeded in a deliberate scholarly way to improve the courses in Red Cross chapters.

24

MANY PROBLEMS presented themselves at the outset of World War II, but now there was a great established organization with an army of trained volunteers accustomed to work with a corps of experienced professionals; they were prepared to meet the known and the unknown emergencies that are the weird sisters of war and disaster.

At first mobilization of the armed forces and the groups that served them seemed slow to gather momentum. The slogan "This is a phony war" cast a spell over the public mind. Yet the Government was moving and great camps were mushrooming, in places well beyond city limits. For the most part Army and Navy Regulars had been sent to foreign fields. New forces were in the making, unfamiliar with Red Cross and its position with the military. Camps held as many as 20,000 or 30,000 men. The major problems were how to reach them in the scrub-oak forests, on sand dunes, and in the desert acres where they were located, and how to provide them with services that would make life more bearable. The situation was further complicated by the fact that these camps were remote from large cities with their many trained volunteers; the nearest Red Cross unit, if any, usually was a small, understaffed branch, with little money and few facilities. Furthermore, chapters were under instructions not to cross into one another's territory.

A sense of frustration was the dominant feeling at headquarters and in the field. After discussing the matter with the Military Relief Department and Pauline Davis, National Director of the Volunteer Service, our chairman requested me to visit several camps, consult local chapter leaders, and report my findings to him.

To ensure prompt co-operation of busy military leaders, I asked Frances McCoy, a devoted Red Cross worker, to assist in making the initial contacts. Her husband, Major General Frank McCoy, was loved as well as respected in the Army and everywhere he was known. The Corps Commander at Fort Jay arranged a friendly reception on the part of commanding officers at several posts. Fort Dix, New Jersey, and Pine Camp, New York, were visited. The same pattern of confusion existed. The need was the same; above all, the officers were eager for the services we proposed.

Public pressure was urgent in every direction; thousands of citizens were eager to help, but a plan for channeling their potential usefulness was lacking. No one knew who should do what, when or how. Hurrying to Washington, I presented to Mr. Davis our suggestion that to service each large military or naval installation, Red Cross should form a council of chapters, made up of representatives from the chapters within a thirty- or forty-mile radius encircling the cantonment. The council would have a chairman and treasurer, and the Red Cross field director assigned to each military post would act as secretary.

The purpose of such a council would be to supply these camp

hospitals and recreation centers with material comforts beyond basic government provisions. The council would allot to each chapter its share in an over-all program of services and supplies which would be approved by the camp commanding officer. For the forces the councils were intended to fill in the gap between existing and living; at the time, the Army and Navy were of necessity primarily occupied with the job of feeding, clothing, and housing their personnel. Each chapter would use its volunteer services of Motor Corps, Gray Ladies, and Production at designated times. Each chapter should be urged to call on other local groups of every kind for co-operation in meeting the needs as outlined in the Camp and Hospital Service program.

Mr. Davis immediately invited me to form a council in three or four key places to test its effectiveness. A professional social worker, Robert E. Bondy, Administrator of Services to the Armed Forces, a colossal task, set up an organization within the Red Cross structure to operate the councils. He established the procedures necessary and skillfully controlled the zealous volunteers who were clamoring to serve. One tropical July day, Fort Dix became our first guinea pig. Pine Camp was next; then came Yaphank on Long Island, followed by the Naval Base at Newport, Rhode Island, where Mrs. Archibald MacLeish joined Frances McCoy, my able partner, and myself. By that time the Red Cross headquarters had become convinced that an effective way had been found to serve the armed forces.

The councils secured comfortable furniture, equipment for recreation rooms for the well and the ill, radio systems with individual headphones for those hospitalized; pianos and other musical instruments, many of which The Metropolitan Opera Guild provided in the New York area, gardens and plants through garden clubs, almost anything you can think of from ash trays to games, to love birds, were processed through camp and hospital councils in a steady and ever-increasing stream.

Camp Edwards, Massachusetts, and the Brooklyn Naval Hospital had been added, when Mr. Davis, in October, authorized the council plan on a national scale. I hesitated to accept the directorship offered, feeling wearily the strain of intensive work.

Shortly thereafter, a severe nasal hemorrhage sent me to a Washington hospital for three weeks and into retirement for months. From hospital I wrote urging Chairman Davis to push the program and appoint a new chairman. Fortunately, he secured Mrs. MacLeish as national director.

At Camp Dix four years after the first council was formed, Robert E. Bondy reported that under the able leadership of Mrs. MacLeish and her committee, 223 councils, made up of 2,200 chapters, were participating in the service to camps, hospitals, and naval units throughout the United States.

In all, 52,000 nation-wide organizations were co-operating through these chapters. The work was carried on by 4,000,000 volunteers. Twelve thousand sunrooms and dayrooms for recreation were completely furnished. Thirty-seven thousand birthday gifts were provided for hospital ships plying back and forth to the War Zone. From July, 1941, to June, 1946, a total of 75,000,000 individual items were contributed. Recreation chests were shipped to points overseas, when groups were isolated and recreation for the well in addition to those hospitalized was of vital importance.

Estimated gifts, cash and in kind, of close to $90,000,000 flowed through those channels. On receiving a copy of the report, Cornelius Bliss, a leader in Red Cross affairs wrote: "Congratulations! You must be proud of the accomplishments of your brain child." Pride did not enter the picture, only overwhelming gratitude to those who had carried out the broad development of the councils, and admiration for their persistent devotion through innumerable difficulties.*

It is my conviction that no Red Cross Service was more appreciated by the general public. The contribution to morale was imponderable; the human and spiritual comfort provided was vast. The public desire to serve was fulfilled. It was a greatly diversified record of accomplishment made by people of various faiths, various functions in life—different in every way except in their universal desire to serve men and women in our armed forces.

* These notes are taken from the *Red Cross Service Record, Accomplishments of Seven Years, 1939–1946.*

At the present time, 1956, there are still 123 councils serving the armed forces, and when Camp Kilmer was opened to receive Hungarian refugees, the Red Cross council was reactivated and 30 chapters co-operated with the government and several other important agencies to serve these homeless people.

Norman Davis said to me, "In the past two world wars, England and France held the line until our country made up its mind that the issues at stake were vital to the United States, and we finally prepared to fight for them. My concern is what will happen if the decision of war must be made again, and there is no one to hold the line while we prepare."

PART FOUR

J'ai chanté dans du noir.
—Ma chanson s'éleva dans l'ombre, et la première.
C'est la nuit qu'il est beau de croire à la lumière!

—EDMOND ROSTAND, *Chantecler,*
Act II, Scene 3

ADA DWYER RUSSELL, sterling artist that she was, remained on the stage some three years after my retirement, during which time she made an outstanding success in a play called *The Deep Purple*. Then, a few months after a major operation, she yielded to Amy Lowell's insistent request that she should leave the theatre and take up permanent residence with her in Brookline and assist her on a business basis with the books to come. Ada had been established for some years at Sevenels when my husband died suddenly on December 10, 1924. The cause was a violent infection, seemingly the result of a hypodermic injection containing a simple drug which was frequently administered to increase red corpuscles.

SEVENELS
BROOKLINE

Dearest Nell,

I cannot let Ada go on to you without sending you my love and very deep sympathy. You know how I wish there were anything I could do, and you know also that our house is always a welcome resting place for you whenever you will come to it and for as long as you will stay. I know that to be with Ada will be the greatest comfort you can have and I want you to feel that it is not only Ada who longs to take care of you and comfort you, but I also, as far as is in my power. Come to us then, Dear, as soon as you can, and always consider this as another home.

Lovingly always,
Amy

Wednesday night.

It was characteristic of Ada Dwyer that when she agreed to become a permanent part of Amy Lowell's home, she tried to share with her those she loved best; and Amy endeavored with as good grace as possible to make these friends her own. One result of this was that I went frequently to Sevenels and, whenever possible, Ada came to my home; or I saw them both on their many trips to New York. After my husband's death Sevenels offered a respite from sadness and the multitude of serious problems that confronted our family.

These two interesting women became friends after meeting at an informal lunch club of Boston ladies when Ada was playing in *The Deep Purple,* and it was renamed "The Purple Lunch Club" in her honor. When Ada took up residence in Sevenels, and the theatre no longer called for her nightly presence, the Purple Lunch Club became an annual dinner party that met February 9 to celebrate Amy's birthday, and Ada's of February 8. The change to dinner was inevitable because Amy never could be on time for lunch, and frequently was an hour or more late for a seven-thirty dinner.

Ada spent hours in the public library and the bookstores hunting endlessly for the reference material Amy needed, coming home, especially during work on the Keats biography, laden with the fruits of her search. All items were traced and carefully listed for the author's scholarly inspection.

Handicapped as Amy had been from youth with a serious glandular malady, which made her form huge and disproportionate, she still moved with grace. Her hands and feet were quite beautiful. Amy's head was small and well proportioned. When dressed, she wore a false braid of hair like a tiara, in an effort to keep her head in balance with her body.

She was a brilliant conversationalist, with decided and occasionally controversial opinions. Heywood Broun wrote in the New York *World,* May 16, 1925:

> . . . Since Dr. Johnson there have been few so much addicted to conversation and so able in the art. . . . I have always hoped for a Heaven. Mostly I want it for myself, but I also like to think of it in relation to Amy Lowell. I like to think of her arrival. St. Peter and others of importance would be brushed aside, I believe, when she came to the great gate. Nor would she, in those first moments, ask, like the others, for the King of the celestial city. Rather I see her striding by the saints and crying out, "Where is John Keats?"

Poets and interesting people of various patterns came to see Amy. They remained to love Ada. The hostess, nearly always late, relied on her friend to welcome guests and keep them entertained. Ada's sympathetic understanding made her an unusually good listener, so the time passed pleasantly for these creative folk. Because of her pleasant mixture of humor and kindness, she was easily the perfect buffer between Amy and small annoyances. Even the time-consuming attentions of devoted admirers were tactfully screened by this friend.

John Drinkwater, who was a frequent visitor at Sevenels, said Amy was "representative of a vivid experimental America," and her "inquiry and discovery had their roots deep down in New England soil. . . . She was a distinguished poet and a great American."

She was also a great lady, in spite of her cigar smoking and frequent exhibitions of ungovernable temper. She loved poetry and was its advocate at a time when poetry was not generally popular. It has always seemed to me that for poets of her day she performed the service of a barker at a circus, as from the lecture platform, in the press, and almost the street corner, she cried aloud, "Poetry, Poetry, this way to Poetry."

Every item that concerned the East riveted Amy's attention, such as pictures of Egyptian tombs made by her friend, Joseph

Lindon Smith, the poetry of China translated by Florence Ays-
cough. Amy eagerly questioned my husband regarding the opening of Japan by his grandfather. "Guns as Keys: and the Great
Gate Swings," which deals with Commodore Perry, was the result. The following brief excerpt holds a prophetic line, ". . .
and pry off the lid of Pandora's box once more":

> . . . Let the key-guns be mounted, make a brave show
> of waging war, and pry off the lid of Pandora's box once
> more. Get in at any cost, and let out at little, so it seems,
> but wait—wait—there is much to follow through the Great
> Gate!
>
> They do not see things in quite that way, on this bright
> November day, with sun flashing, and waves splashing, up
> and down Chesapeake Bay. On shore, all the papers are
> running to press with huge headlines: "Commodore Perry
> Sails." Dining-tables buzz with travellers' tales of old Japan
> culled from Dutch writers. But we are not like the Dutch.
> No shutting the stars and stripes up on an island. Pooh! We
> must trade wherever we have a mind. Naturally! *

We were discussing Shaw's prodigious output one day in the
early twenties, and the value of his work in general; she agreed
it was exceptionally witty and interesting, but his flippancy irritated her. She prophesied that he would not live as a great play-
wright. "Fifty years from now he will be a back number and
will not be read." The plays apart from the prefaces probably
were in her mind.

In reply to my question as to which of the young men who
eagerly came to talk books and poetry with her would, in her
opinion, make a mark in the future, she selected: John Farrar,
now a publisher, then editing *The Bookman;* Archibald Mac-
Leish, who was soon to produce a challenging book of poetry,
The Pot of Earth; and Hervey Allen, who had not yet written
Anthony Adverse.

Prophets, like weathermen, cannot strike it right every time;

* *The Complete Works of Amy Lowell* (Boston, Houghton Mifflin Co.,
1955).

her average is good, but thirty-five years later Shaw has top billing. His plays, frequently revived, are remarkably successful on stage and the new medium, television; while *My Fair Lady—Pygmalion* set to music—has been called "one of the best musical comedies of the century." How G.B.S. would have reveled in that comment! I wish he might have seen *Fair Lady*—who knows, he might have lived another ninety years.

2

ON A VISIT TO SEVENELS, where Amy was born, and the long-time home of the seven Lowells, I followed my usual custom of paying the hostess as discreetly as possible for my outgoing telephone calls. I left something more than enough with the parlor maid, and received a note with a check for one dollar (still uncashed) enclosed:

> Received from Nell
> This money. 'Tis well
> She pays her debts with promptitude,
> With an exactitude almost rude
> I wish to state that she had paid
> A dollar in paper crumpled & frayed,
> With sixty cents in tarnished money
> But any money's welcome as honey—
> I admit these verses do not go well
> But my name is valid! Amy Lowell—

I had also sent her a book, and a letter followed on the heels of the above.

BROOMLEY LACEY,
DUBLIN,
NEW HAMPSHIRE

August 7, 1915

Dear Nell,
      What must you think of me for the casual way in which I received the book? Do you know, it never occurred to me

when you said you were sending out a book, that it was not intended for Ada. Indeed, I should have deluged you with thanks, had I known, instead of letting you go out of the house with a joke poem. It was very sweet of you to think of it, & I shall enjoy the book very much, I know. I have already enjoyed the pictures, which is all I had time for before the world upheaved with Ada's departure & my removal up here.

Life has been anything but beer & skittles since I saw you. First, Ada went, an occurrence which one would suppose happened sufficiently often for me to get used to it; but, having got used to her presence, I find it quite impossible to accustom myself to her absence.

* Then I moved up here, & my waitress, overcome by the isolation of the place, inconsiderately left the next morning. An accommodator arrived upon the scene, & chopped her hand open on a finger-bowl. So, although I still have her as an ornament, she is of no other use.

Then the elements took a hand, &—it rained ! ! ! The local carpenter assures me that he saw to it that the roof was in excellent order & that there were no leaks anywhere, before I got here. The house evidently opened itself to me, for it acted like a sieve. The rain came through plaster ceilings at such a rate that we had to put bath-tubs under them, & I expected, at any moment, to see the ceilings themselves descend with a crash to the floors. But this was not all, my old friend, the neuralgia came on with fine vigour (possibly living over a pond, for there is one in my cellar, is not good for neuralgia) and I have been in a good deal of pain, & eating phenacetin all the time. Surely Ada's vacation is not proving exactly a joy-ride for me. Not that she could have stopped the leaks, or staunched the brook in the cellar, had she been here, but all these things are worse when our only human propinquity is a group of startled & unhappy servants. I knew the Summer would be a trial, but I never bargained to pass it between the upper and the under waters, suspended in a damp middle space, as it were.

. . . Ada will be better, I am sure, now she is on the spot,

---

* Also quoted in *Amy Lowell: A Chronicle* by Samuel Foster Damon (Boston, Houghton Mifflin Co.).

& Lorna's tea-party cannot possibly go on without her. She writes in good spirits, says the journey tired her a little, but that she is getting rested, that most of her particular friends are away so that there are *no* invitations. She tells me that Mrs Chatfield-Taylor's sister, Mrs McCann has a "bug", & has been in bed six weeks. I verily believe Ada would have been in bed now, if we had not had that inoculation. I do hope she will pick up, it worries me to have her off there, but I do believe it was the best thing for her to go. She would have worried so about Lorna if she had stayed, that that would have made her sick. And you—what naughty thing have you been doing to have a pulse like that? It is none of my business, I know, but please forgive me if I say—"Go slow!" Remember, operations are tricky things, & you cannot trust the feeling well which follows them, for quite a little time. Be a good, self-sacrificing girl, & "go gently", even if you don't want to.

You should not have troubled to have that doggerel copied, although it was very kind of you to do it. It is not worthy of your scrap-book. I will send "The Paper Windmill" just as soon as my secretary comes up to copy it.

Forgive this long screed but you see we had a nice time for those twenty four hours, didn't we?

Again, many thanks for the book.

Very sincerely yours,
Amy Lowell

"The Paper Windmill" referred to a story my husband had told her. Talking one day about the images that are made upon a child's memory, Amy drew attention to how clear these outlines remain. My husband agreed and told us something he remembered that had happened to him in Holland, where his father was United States minister to the Netherlands. The nurse had taken the small boy out into the square near the American Legation. They came upon a vendor selling bright colored paper windmills. The child was fascinated by their dancing and twirling in the breeze. His nurse bought him one; grasping the treasure they hurried home, but his disappointment was devastating when he found that the paper toy, which had seemed like a dancing butterfly in the breeze, became lifeless when brought into the house. Amy liked the story, and as a result wrote "The Paper Windmill."

3

DURING A VISIT at Sevenels, following my five months' trip to Europe on the mission for the American Red Cross, I described my experiences, including an air raid which Daisy Harriman and I had witnessed from the balcony of my bedroom at the Hotel Vendôme. Contrary to instructions, we watched, fascinated, the sky fight, before descending to the ground floor. Also, that night was probably the first raid on Paris made by a German Big Bertha. Amy, impressed by the description of the airplanes and the sound of the shells from Germany, wrote a poem. Later, she sent me a copy of her book *Can Grande's Castle*, inscribed "Nell, with much love from Amy . . . with gratitude for pages 224 to 228 . . ."

These pages reflected her idea of an air raid, for which she expressed a poet's gratitude in the following letter:

May 22, 1918

Miss A. Lowell
Heath Street
Brookline, Mass.

Dear Nell:

I never knew such honesty in my life. I am going to take your stamps and bind them into a fillet across my brows. As a sample of perfect integrity of character, they are priceless. Seriously, I never knew anything like it. You might at least have accepted the paper pad in return for your description of the air raid, for instance.

And, by the way, the poem is done, and Ada thinks the air raid is good. It will amuse you to know that I read aeroplane books for a week, but in none of them did I find anything like the vividness of description or the poetical perception which characterized your account. You ought to write a book, or better still from my point of view, you ought to talk, and talk, and talk to me, and then let me write books. I shall not send it to you, however, but let you come upon it in my new book, which of course I shall send you as soon as it is out. It is just going to press.

We have Lorna and the baby here now for some weeks, and they are coming back again later to pass the Summer with us. You see how foxy I am. By this process, I keep Ada instead of losing her to Salt Lake City. We have a sand pile in front of the house, and Mr. Man, with his hair cropped short like a real boy, disports himself in it from morning till night; but it is a sad comment on the inferiority of woman that he prefers the men in the garage to any of us.

I wish you would come here, and inhabit my other barn-like spare room while they are here, and join the group. Then, indeed, Ada's family would be all together. Do think it over, and in the meanwhile, with many thanks for the stamps, and a great many more thanks for the air raid,

Affectionately,
Amy

4

ON ONE VISIT, these friends followed me to my room for a final good night. Amy asked, "What would you like to read?" The answer, "A detective story," brought forth the fact that her principal guest room held quantities of detective stories. But she added, "I put three or four especially good ones on your bed-table." One with a cheerful red cover caught my eye; the title, *Mystery of the Boule Cabinet,* looked inviting. Good detective stories always rest me; when I am overtired, they unhook my mind from disturbing problems. The next day the book went home with me, for I assured Amy confidently that this story held a play.

Realizing technical knowledge of play construction was needed, I invited Harriet Ford, an old friend from *Audrey* days, to become my partner in the venture. Incredible as it may seem, Burton Stevenson, author of this mystery story and others, was the man who assembled the great anthology of poetry, *Home*

Book of Verse. When our play was finished, Winthrop Ames, contrary to his custom, permitted me to read it to him. Promptly he accepted it for an Ames production and appointed his young assistant, Guthrie McClintic, as coproducer; it was his first such assignment.

Harriet Ford and I had changed the title *Mystery of the Boule Cabinet* to "The Next Room." We felt it was simpler to pronounce when ordering tickets; besides all the action took place there. Mr. Ames telephoned after the first rehearsal to suggest a slight modification: "Do the authors think that *In the Next Room* might be more intriguing?" he asked. We happy authors thought the suggestion was excellent; furthermore, the play now held a good omen, for that simple addition made thirteen letters in the title.

The nervous tension on the opening night of *In the Next Room* was great; my mind is a blank where it is concerned. Guthrie McClintic insists that when responding to calls for "speech," "author, author," from an enthusiastic first-night audience, I said after a few words of thanks on behalf of my associates, "I had no idea that my re-entrance into the theatre would be made on a crime wave." The thirteen letters may have brought us luck; in any case, the play ran for several years in this country and in England; also it forged another link in friendship's chain with the Ames family.

The New York opening at the Vanderbilt Theatre on November 27, 1923, brought forth a generous bundle of good wishes.

To the superstitious it may be interesting to know that thirteen has followed my life in many ways. I was born on the thirteenth, there are thirteen letters in my name, and in my mother's name. My first appearance on the stage was on the thirteenth, with actor-manager Daniel Frawley, whose lucky number was thirteen. He signed every contract, wherever possible, on the thirteenth. My first opportunity came in Honolulu, where the Frawley company had gone to play thirteen performances. My stage career lasted thirteen years. On the twenty-sixth of the month, without any premeditation as to date, I married a man with thirteen letters in his name. His major project at that time was to connect Buzzards Bay with Barnstable Bay by a canal thirteen miles long. As I've already mentioned, the title of my mystery play had thirteen letters in it. Totally unimportant all this, probably without significance, but in such matters, who can tell where meaning begins?

My mother claimed that she was not superstitious. However, any pin on the floor that pointed in her direction offered an irresistible attraction. A ladder was something to walk around; one should never go under it. When questioned, she said, "Certainly I am not superstitious, but I don't want to take a chance."

5

DURING THE YEARS when Ada Dwyer lived at Sevenels, Amy wanted to dedicate first one volume of poems or another to her good friend, who steadfastly refused the honor. Finally, when *John Keats* was published, the author was insistent. The dedication read: "To A.D.R. This, and all my books. A.L."

When this, her finest work, was published in England, the critics were somewhat cool, occasionally even unfavorable. This hurt Amy keenly because she had expended her entire vital force on its production. Therefore, it was with warm satisfaction that she read me a letter from Thomas Hardy, which began: "My Dear Cousin." He was very understanding about the British critics. He considered all writers of one family, and he was proud to claim relationship on the basis of her Keats.

6

THE SEASON of 1923–24, Duse was brought to the United States under the management of Morris Gest. Her final performance in *Lady from the Sea*, at the Metropolitan Opera House, was one of the great moments in the American theatre, an imperishable memory. Alas, she was already a dying woman. She could eat next to nothing and was pitifully frail. The only thing that seemed to sustain her was champagne, which unfortunately was very difficult to procure, for at that period America was in the throes of Prohibition. Amy instantly appointed herself *sommelier* to the great Italian actress. She would come from Brookline to the Hotel Belmont, just opposite Grand Central Station, where she always stayed "because it was the nearest to Back Bay." Here an understanding headwaiter secured champagne for her, surely at an exaggerated cost. These bottles, carefully packed in a suitcase, were consigned to a traveling friend and shipped by hand to Duse wherever she happened to be. The thought of Amy Lowell of Sevenels, descendant of the Lowells of Massachusetts, acting as bootlegger for Duse appealed to my fancy and touched my heart. The last consignment was on its way to Pittsburgh when the great actress died there.

After Duse's death, her casket was placed in a small chapel in the beautiful church of St. Vincent Ferrer in New York. Such was the sympathetic public interest that tickets had to be issued for the funeral service. I secured three from the Italian consul and took Amy and Ada to the service. Seated in the fourth row, we must have seemed—as in spirit we felt ourselves to be—part of the small band of chief mourners at that beautiful service. When it was over, we three devoted admirers tearfully followed Duse on her last American journey. The progress was delayed by the crowds that pressed forward at each crossing, so we could not watch as the casket was placed on the Italian steamer which was to carry her home. While deeply moved by the event, Amy never wrote the sonnet she longed for.

7

AS THE YEARS PASSED, Amy protested the periods when Ada would go, as per agreement, to see her family in Salt Lake City or to visit Lorna and her children, three of them, who followed each other in rapid succession. Amy then decided to bring Lorna and her boys to Brookline away from the summer heat in Washington. The following letter tells of one visit.

BROOKLINE. Monday
night August ? 1923

Dear Nell,

Your bounty is beyond words, and the worst of it is that I have, with the most meagre assistance, eaten it all up. I have been afraid to weigh myself since the deed was— Ah, but I do like Sherry's chocolates! And I never had so large a box before. The joy is only so much enhanced because it partakes of the nature of forbidden fruit. With every delectable drop, I feel a pound going on, and only when I recollect how short is life, how fleeting, do I reflect that it makes very little difference whether a skeleton was once fat or thin. This consoles me greatly, and I eat on, unmoved and unmoving. . . .

Both Ada and I feel a distinct desire for recreation, so I think we may drop into your town somewhat sooner than we expected—October perhaps, or early November. There are such things as P.E.N. dinners. You have heard of that literary dining-club got up last Winter? I think they have monthly dinners, and I think we shall time our trip to coincide with one of them. I ought not to break away, even for a day, but I have been attending to Keats for so long that I do crave a brief vacation. However, we may not come.

Ada read me your mournful letter. Poor Nell, you have had a time! I am sorry the play is sticking. But don't get discouraged, things often do that. I do think that you will have to write the dialogue yourself if you want it to snap. . . . You will get confidence as you go along. I do believe dialogue is the easiest part of a play. It seems so to me, at least, who know nothing about it. A funny thing happened to me, the other day. I received a telegram from Robert Edmond Jones, asking me if I had ever thought of writing for the stage, and if I had he would like to have a talk with me. I wired back that I never had written for the stage, but that I would like to see him sometime, and there the matter rests, shelved, I imagine, for he never wrote a line. Of course I never intended to allow him to inveigle me into writing a play, knowing quite well where I get off, as they say, but I wanted to know what his idea was. Has the supply of O'Neill plays fallen off, or what is the matter with him, do you suppose?

I do hope you will become so exhausted with the labour of authorship that you will have to take a rest, and that you will take it chez nous. I do so like to have you here, and of course Ada remains on the grill from the moment you come till the moment you go. Your coming here would be the best kind of vacation for us. Now I must go and eat my supper, being 4 A.M. The others would send messages, but they are fast asleep.

Affectionately,
Amy

P.S. Ada has appeared on the scene, and says this is spelt all wrong from beginning to end. She is so savage at dawn, and she has no business to be awake anyhow. It is the bad habit the children have taught her.

8

PROUD OF BEING INVITED to give a poetry lecture in May 1925, in Cambridge, England, Amy frankly admitted with anticipation that it might lead to a degree from that ancient institution of learning. In spite of her very real pride, she was actually humble about her own work. She read every available item of new poetry as it came along. While highly critical at times, she was also generous with praise when something pleased her. She read aloud "The Eagle and the Mole" when Elinor Wylie first published her book of poems, *Nets to Catch the Wind*. To my comment that I liked it, she answered, "I like some of her poetry so much that I wish I had written it."

More and more as her writing increased, Amy's night was turned into day. During visits she often would pause at my bedroom door about eight o'clock, when the breakfast tray made its appearance. She was then on her way to bed in her third-floor room under the eaves of the mansard roof, hers since childhood. She had spent the eight or nine hours since we last met in solitude—except for her black cat, Winky—reading and working in her library, a room of rare beauty and comfort.

Impressed with her rapidly growing list of achievements, coupled with her scholarly *Keats,* a number of old Boston neighbors, and many literary friends, decided that early in April, before she left for Europe, they would give her a send-off party as evidence that a prophet is sometimes recognized in his own country. The invitation read: "A complimentary dinner in honor of Amy Lowell." Being in deep mourning, I hesitated to accept; however, they insisted and assured me it would not be a social gathering in the usual sense of the word. It promised to be an outstanding demonstration of the growing appreciation which people held for this remarkable woman. I have always been grateful that I attended.

Recently Ada had confided a serious anxiety about her friend's health. Even so, I was startled to see the change that had taken place in two months. Amy was tired to the point of collapse and reluctant to face the ordeal of what she knew would be a long-drawn-out dinner party. She was never on time for anything except a train or a lecture she was giving, so that we three arrived nearly an hour late. Her extreme weariness added to the usual difficulty of dressing; the long, complicated bandage she wore always had to be carefully adjusted and wound to an exact position, or the whole procedure had to be done over again. She lived with a sword of Damocles over her head, in constant fear that the hernia from which she had suffered for so long, would open wide. She never took cocktails. The party was to be a large one, and altogether, it seemed advisable that night to be more unpunctual than usual.

The ballroom and dining room of the Hotel Somerset were overcrowded. Old friends, Mrs. Bayard Thayer and Mrs. Montgomery Sears, had gathered flowers from their own greenhouses; and Albert C. Burrage had provided exceptionally beautiful orchids (a favorite of Amy's) for the main table. The beauty of the flower arrangements was breath-taking.

At least a dozen speakers rose to do her honor, including

Professor John Livingston Lowes, Elinor Wylie, Hervey Allen, Foster Damon. They presented verbal tributes in speeches witty, grave, gay, and altogether brilliant. It was a great occasion. As the Providence *Journal* reported next day, "there were literally as well as literarily four hundred present."

The ever-mounting volume of praise seemed inexhaustible. The hour was late, past midnight, when John Farrar's turn came, so discarding his prepared address, he said simply, "I wish Miss Amy Lowell long life and happiness, but the best wish I have for her is that one day a biographer would write of her with as much love and understanding as she has written of John Keats." Her publishers were represented by Roger Scaife, who introduced the guest of honor. Amy responded very simply and read her fine poem, "Lilacs."

An exhausted but thoroughly happy and grateful woman returned to Sevenels that night, where, for at least an hour, we talked over every detail of the triumphant occasion. That night she did not sit up writing, but laboriously climbed the two flights to her bedroom when Ada and I said good night.

In spite of increasing ill health, she and Ada steadily went ahead with preparations for the European trip; both dreaded the ocean voyage. Late in April, because of a threatened recurring hernia operation, the trip had to be abandoned and all engagements canceled. Amy grew weaker and weaker, and lost weight in an alarming way; however, she insisted on getting up for part of each day. May 12, she was sitting in front of her mirror, trying to get dressed. Her faithful maid and the nurse were struggling to adjust her bandage while Ada waited, holding out the braided crown to put upon her head. Suddenly in the mirror she saw Amy's face change as the long-dreaded stroke came. Amy herself, watching her reflection in the glass, gasped, "It's a stroke," and fell back into their arms. She died without regaining consciousness. Ada telephoned me and I went immediately to Sevenels to render such assistance as was possible. Amy had stipulated that she wanted no religious service and no formal gathering. We filled the house with lilacs from the garden she loved so well, and when the time came, only her family, her maid (Elizabeth Henry), Ada, and I went with her ashes to the family plot.

Ada was appointed as literary executor and carried out her mission with skill and understanding. Two things she regretted—that Harvard, after much discussion, finally revoked a previous acceptance of Amy's library at Sevenels in which to house the books she left to the University. Fire hazard was, of course, the reason, but Amy had so much wanted the exceptional library preserved that it was disappointing.

Also, they both wanted to have a special edition of her poem, *Hedge Island*, illustrated in color with old English coaching prints that hung on the bedroom walls at Sevenels. These prints were beautiful examples; they showed spring, summer, autumn and winter coaching subjects. Amy had spent years collecting them. It was finally decided that the illustrations were too expensive. It would have made a precious book.

9

MY SECOND TRIP to the top of temptation's high mountain came some years later when George Tyler sent the manuscript of a new play by an author unknown to me. The central character was appealing—the play potentially a winner. After considerable hesitation, my decision finally was in the negative. When regretting this offer and the play, which I believed might be a money-maker, I urged that he secure Katharine Cornell for the leading role. Unfortunately for him, she was already under contract to someone else; he refused to produce it without one or the other of us in the title role. When he declined the play, Mr. Tyler advised the author, Rudolf Besier, to present it for Miss Cornell's consideration. Thus, Elizabeth in *The Barretts of Wimpole Street* became one of her many artistic and financial successes. Through this chain of events Mr. Tyler lost a fortune he never possessed, and for his sake I regretted it deeply.

There was one actual return to the theatre, but it was temporary. This public event, unconnected with charitable appearances, afforded me satisfaction on several scores. For one thing, it was poetry. In the spring of 1927, Edwin Arlington Robinson had just finished *Tristram*. Unfortunately for poets who must eat to live, long poems—*book*-long poems—do not sell well, as a rule. If asked, as E.A.R. undoubtedly was, why he had attempted a long poem about such an oft-repeated legend, he might have given the same answer as George Mallory, who said he climbed Mount Everest "because it is there."

Edwin Robinson's friends decided something beyond the ordinary must be done to capture public attention for this major work of a fine American artist who, in spite of praise a-plenty, had received an uncomfortably modest financial return for his accomplishment. An idea was born in the minds of the editors of The Literary Guild—Carl Van Doren, Glenn Frank, Zona Gale, Joseph Wood Krutch, Hendrik Willem Van Loon, and Elinor Wylie. They planned to take a theatre and invite the best known Toms, Dicks, and Harrys of the literary world, critics included, to hear a dramatic reading of *Tristram*.

A devout believer in the magnificent contribution poets provide for the minds of men almost free of charge, I felt under obligation to accept the insistent invitation extended to serve as the *Tristram* Reader.

The poem had to be cut considerably for the occasion. E.A.R. would not touch it, but left the matter to my "discretion." The theatre was packed. The author refused to be present, saying the strain would be too great; besides, essential as the cuts were, they would hurt him "unbearably." He came to the reception in his honor afterward and shyly beamed and basked in the outpouring of enthusiastic praise heard on every side for his fine work.

To the natural question why had he discarded the love potion, usually a pivotal point in all versions of the story, he assured me, "People in love do not need a potion to get themselves into mischief."

Mark Van Doren called this verson of an old, old legend the "best in English since the Middle Ages."

A friendly reaction following the *Tristram* reading comes to mind. The Lawrence Whites were old friends. He was a clever architect, head of McKim, Mead & White, who also, for pleasure, translated Dante's *Divine Comedy*. After the reading, a bunch of American beauty roses came from them with a note from Larrie that began graciously, "To our Lady of the Enunciation."

It is surprising that the public launching of a new poem is not tried more often. Artists of the stage, both dramatic and lyric, are ever generous with their ability to interpret. Poetry, like music, is not complete without sound. To reach fruition, both need to be heard.

In a way this event had been anticipated by Amy Lowell, who wrote me in 1922:

> What you say about "Lilacs" delights my soul. How I wish you would read some of my things! I should like to hear you do it, and, with my natural eye to the main chance, I cannot think of anything which would do me more good. I could teach you the rhythms of "Lilacs" in two shakes of a lamb's tail, if you care to learn them any time.

The following gracious letter may be some evidence for this idea.

THE
LITERARY GUILD
OF AMERICA, INC.

May 31, 1927

Dear Mrs. Belmont,

It is not to intrude upon your privacy or to reopen the matter of the evening in honor of Mr. Robinson which was brought to such a successful conclusion, that I send you this letter. But I wonder if anyone has told you of the extraordinary things that have happened to TRISTRAM.

Mr. Robinson told us that he expected to make about $500 out of the poem when it appeared, which is apparently about the amount of his royalties on previous books. Already I think his royalties on TRISTRAM have amounted to more than $5,000.

204 THE FABRIC OF MEMORY

The Macmillan Company had no idea that the poem was going to become popular and printed the usual number, so that by ten o'clock the day of publication every copy was exhausted and the bookstores were clamoring for more.

During the first ten days two other large printings were made and I think the bookstores took 10,000 copies, bringing them to the extraordinary figure of a thousand copies a day for the first ten days. The demand for the poem since then has increased, and during the last week both Brentano's and Macy's had it heading their list of best sellers of non-fiction.

In as much as Mr. Robinson had already twice won the Pulitzer prize and had for years received the highest critical praise, the popularity of this poem seems to be the most literally due to your good offices in its behalf. I am thoroughly convinced that if you had not read the poem and focused attention upon it as you did, that once more it would have been brushed aside with a few superlative reviews from the critics.

There has been an enormous amount of publicity about the poem and the reading that has come in from all over the country. I do not know whether you would care to look over it or not, but I have it in the Guild files and should you be interested in seeing it I should be delighted to have my secretary bring the material up for you to see. If you are out of town, or do not care to see the clippings, do not trouble to acknowledge this letter.

I merely wanted you to know how completely the purpose which led you to consent to read the poem had borne fruit.

Sincerely,
John William Rogers

One fact has always given me pause. It is said that if he is lucky, a poet of pronounced ability can earn perhaps $3,000 to $5,000 a year. An outstanding scientist, who unpacks his well-stored mind for a university, who charts new planets in the sky, or reveals hitherto unknown secrets of the universe, is fortunate if he obtains $12,000 a year and a modest house for his family to live in, while a ranking sportsman may command $75,000 a year, and even consider the figure a concession. Surely this shows an unbalanced conception as to essential values—or perhaps my opinion only reveals a lack of conviction as to the relative merits of baseball, but of course baseball is important.

10

POETS AND ARCHEOLOGISTS have this gift in common—an unflagging imagination. On the recommendation of my good friend Olga Stokowski, I had taken a furnished cottage near hers in Seal Harbor, Maine, one summer. The owner had died some months before and Mr. John D. Rockefeller, Jr., had bought Nantibe, as he bought many pieces of property on the Island of Mount Desert, with the idea of ultimately adding the land to the Acadia Park, which he gave to the nation. This great patriot became my neighbor and my landlord.

In addition to Nantibe, a small house with a superfine view of the ocean, the place had a guest house or studio on the ledge below, hidden from sight, with a living room, bedroom, bath and tiny kitchen. C. Leonard Woolley and his wife, Katharine, both Oxford graduates, bore a letter of introduction to me from the Thomas Lamonts, with whom they had been staying in North Haven. They were relaxing after a lecture tour following his dramatic discoveries in Ur of The Chaldees. The studio was ideal in that they made their own breakfast when ready for it, came to meals at home, walked or picnicked with us as they wished. Both seemed exhausted by hard work and the emotion of these truly important discoveries; these included a quantity of exquisite golden objects, many of which were already housed in museums in Pennsylvania and Egypt.

Leonard Woolley was writing a book, and occasionally in the evening read a chapter to me as he finished it. They came for a few days; however, at my urgent request, they stayed three weeks. Serena Blandish blithely said, "A girl who is asked to tea and stays to dinner never gets asked again." I would have invited the Woolleys repeatedly. They were fascinating guests. Expert botanists, as so many Britishers are, they discussed the unusual flora of Mount Desert, which they were seeing for the first time, with more knowledge than most of the garden club inhabitants.

It seems that T. E. Lawrence of Arabia had been a member of the Woolley expedition a few years before; they talked about him casually. To them he was just a minor member of the expedition; to us who listened, every shred of information about the much-publicized man of mystery was of asborbing interest.

Leonard Woolley described Ur as being "half-way between Baghdad and the head of the Persian Gulf, some ten miles west of the present course of the Euphrates."

He talked with genuine modesty, coupled with scholarly interpretation, of recent results achieved following several years' hard labor on the project.

As he described the graves of the queens of Ur and reported how the expedition had found definite evidence of the ancient deluge, and reconstructed that civilization of 3500 B.C., centuries melted away. The kings, queens, and their attendants, their temples, the mud huts of the community, were as real as our hilltop in Maine; Noah was present in the shadow. Time, no longer ruthless, seemed a friendly doorkeeper who wafted us in and out of past centuries at the bidding of this gentle, erudite narrator.

A few watercolor sketches and black and white photographs revealed objects of exceptional artistic value, but he colored them all for us with vivid descriptions of paintings on pottery and mosaics inlaid with lapis lazuli and precious stones.

As bit by bit he reconstructed this era from golden objects, twisted or crushed flat, at times mangled almost beyond recognition; slabs of stone with a few hieroglyphics, dust of various shades, impressions in the sand—something I had heard William Butler Yeats say came to mind, "I once read in a fabulous book, that Adam had but to imagine a bird and it straight came to life. He created all things out of himself by an unflagging fancy."

Poets come from a long line of prophets. They are not just vague dreamers who struggle to reveal, or often conceal, meaning in various forms of rhyme. Some of them have been rebels against tyranny; some, exponents of faith in liberty, stirring those who hesitate to courageous action. They are magnificent historians, but their greatest gift may be that the best of them find expression for the hidden feelings of the human heart.

Again I urge that poetry like drama should be spoken. Noble words well pronounced can be so wonderful! Who that saw it will ever forget Stephen Benét's historic poem *John Brown's Body*, how it came to life when it was presented by distinguished actors? How effectively the cadenced words, unencumbered by scenery and costumes, provided story, mood, scene, and emotion. Think of the extraordinary value of Bernard Shaw's *Don Juan in Hell*, the tremendous impact of his words when spoken without scenery, costumes and with scarcely a gesture for emphasis!

I shall be forever grateful to Ada Dwyer that she planted in my mind a seed of appreciation for poetry. She shed a special radiance difficult to describe upon each relationship. She had a genius for friendship. Everyone felt it who came within range of her sparkling eyes and gracious smile.

Perhaps this radiance was compounded of unfailing interest in the friend's interests, a sense of loyalty and understanding. Her heart was ever approachable. She laughed and wept easily, being, as she said, "of the Dwyer persuasion." Among my treasures is a letter from this old friend. Words flowed swiftly when she spoke, and the same effect of prompt response came from her letters—for she rarely paused to dot an *i* or cross a *t*.

August 9
1938

MRS. HAROLD RUSSELL—685 CHESTNUT HILL AVENUE—
BROOKLINE, MASS.

My Dearest Child—

It was such a pleasure to hear your voice last evening— & you sounded—not tired or weary—notwithstanding the terrific heat we have had for nine days & nights. It has not

been very pleasant summer so far— I have been rather lonely
—& the rains was such a dreary time—I have read, sometimes, two or three books a day— It evidently was a success
for the camp near Lorna for the younger children— They
are happy & well is the report. . . . No words anyway, can
convey what you mean to me—to love a person as I love
you—is its own and adequate reward—because it sanctified
and made significant & beautiful and exciting and alive,
everything we did together—into the fabric of my being has
been woven a thing that couldn't perish—a fabric of shared
memories that is imperishable—& that's that—
Darling:—
When you go to Jenny Tiffany at Newport wouldn't it be
easy to come here from there— If not—do the easiest thing
for you—you have been chasing the continent—& crossed the
Ocean almost time to rest a bit isn't it? Arms round very
tight

Your Dada

Rejecting all religious creeds, Ada lived the life of a noble
Christian. Over the years of our friendship she gave me books,
cut poems out of magazines, and frequently copied for me in
longhand some special item. The last poem she sent has with
the years taken on new meaning.

IMMORTALITY *

If you were gone from me to some far land,
Distant, remote and I could never hear
Within the dreary stretch of year on year,
A word of you; if I could never stand
Beside you, see your face, or touch your hand
Again, forever, would I have to fear
That all of you I cherish and hold dear
Was lost beyond my power to understand?
Surely without the help of sound or speech,
Or the swift blessed happiness of sight,

* Katherine Garrison Chapin, *Outside of the World* (New York, Duffield
and Company, 1930).

I know that you would find me still, and reach
To me, and share my sorrow, my delight,
From far I still could hear the words you said.
And will this not be true when you are dead?

Winthrop Ames once wrote me, "Almost everybody over forty
knows that the dead . . . never rest in their graves—if indeed,
they ever go into them at all."

PART FIVE

"I wouldnt have your conscience not for all your income," says an unemployed workman to the millionaire in *Major Barbara*.

"I wouldnt have your income, not for all your conscience," replies the millionaire. . . .

"Well, you have made for yourself something that you call a morality or a religion or what not. It doesnt fit the facts. Well, scrap it. Scrap it and get one that does fit. That is what is wrong with the world at present. It scraps its obsolete steam engines and dynamos; but it wont scrap its old prejudices and its old moralities and its old religions and its old political constitutions. What's the result? In machinery it does very well; but in morals and religion and politics it is working at a loss that brings it nearer bankruptcy every year. Dont persist in that folly. If your old religion broke down yesterday, get a newer and a better one for tomorrow."

—*Major Barbara*, G. B. SHAW

"Beggar that I am, I am even poor in thanks . . ."
—*Hamlet*, Act II, Scene 2

PART FIVE

When this country had joined the great war in 1917, the American Red Cross became my major activity. However, other issues presented themselves from time to time which aroused my interest and to which I gave a moderate amount of service.

The Prohibition Amendment stirred the country out of proportion to its importance. Unfortunately, it became apparent to all thinking people that prohibition did not banish the evils of intemperance, but in many sinister ways exaggerated them. As one speaker said, "Prohibition is nothing more or less than an intemperate temperance remedy."

Will Rogers, a public benefactor with his amusing and shrewd comments of the day, said, "People are divided into two classes now; those who have still a little, and those who have a little still."

A bit of doggerel was quoted on all sides with glee.

"Four and twenty Yankees feeling rather dry,
Marched into Canada to get a little rye.
When the rye was opened, the Yanks began to sing,
Who in hell is Coolidge? God save the King."

213

I discussed the subject of prohibition with David F. Houston, one-time Secretary of Agriculture, then Secretary of Treasury under Woodrow Wilson. He wrote me in the summer of 1930:

D. F. HOUSTON
34 NASSAU STREET
NEW YORK

Monday, June 2.

Dear Mrs. Belmont,

The prohibition problem is not new. I know that it was discussed in the British Parliament in the 17th Century. Jefferson wrote letters about it. I would not be surprised to learn that Adam and Eve talked it over. They had apples. Why not cider—hard cider? Who knows what Adam's condition was when he fell for the snake and laid the blame on Eve. I prefer to think that he was not himself.

Lincoln discussed prohibition; and, of course, he was frank. He is reported to have said:

"Prohibition strikes a blow at temperance. It is a species of Intemperance itself, but it goes beyond the bounds of reason. It undertakes to make crimes of things which are not wrong in themselves and therefore strikes a blow at the foundation of government."

If Lincoln did not say this, he ought to have done so. It sounds like him. He was a man of great common sense. He understood the limitations of human beings and of law making.

It was a great pleasure and privilege to be in your home a few days ago and to see you at the Davises yesterday.

Faithfully yours,
D. F. Houston

Mr. Houston was also critical of the rapidly rising income tax. He felt the trend was dangerous, as it largely "penalized the thrifty."

Mrs. Charles H. Sabin, Chairman of the Women's Organization for National Prohibition Reform, wrote me in February, 1931, that on April 14, their annual conference for prohibition reform would be held in Washington. She invited me to make the keynote speech. This organization had been established in 30 states; it had a total membership of 250,000 women, representing every field of endeavor and coming from every walk of life. The invitation appealed to me. My husband had objected to national prohibition. From his viewpoint, the Eighteenth Amendment was absolutely the wrong way to go about securing temperance.

In my speech at that conference, I said:

> Prohibition has been labeled a moral issue, and it takes exceptional courage to lead a campaign against a movement which is labeled that way. If you want to know just how much courage it takes, ask your Congressman.
>
> There must be no misunderstanding in the public mind about this question of labeling. Temperance is the issue, and that *is* of moral importance; prohibition is not, as I see the matter. In this we are in absolute agreement with the advocates of prohibition. In fact, we share with them a common cause. We believe in temperance; we want temperance; we are here because we know we are not getting it. Instead of opposing a moral issue, we have allied ourselves with that issue. We do not agree as to the method of achieving the result. We agree with the President of the United States [Mr. Hoover] that prohibition was "a noble experiment," only how can we call the experiment a success when we see rum, racketeering, and rebellion against the law on all sides?
>
> You cannot change the habits of a people by legislation. Only education can do that. We must take human nature as we find it.
>
> I firmly believe the experiment of prohibition does not and cannot produce national temperance. When scientists find an experiment does not produce a given result, they don't abandon the goal. They scrap the experiment and try to find another way. Personally, I consider it a disgrace that today, when the world is facing great problems of economic adjustment that may, even in a few years, shatter this thing we call peace, when we ourselves are in the midst

of a national crisis of unemployment, the most important political question is prohibition. It is degrading our private and our public life. Somehow we must remove this cancerous sore from our politics; we have got to clean house.

On July 15, 1932, I with several others, resigned from the Advisory Committee of the Women's Organization for National Prohibition Reform. In wholehearted agreement with the organization in the plan for reform, we were opposed to the policy their National Executive had adopted of swinging the organization into the Democratic campaign behind President Roosevelt. I wrote:

We believe in the organization policy, to support Congressional candidates who favor repeal. The real point in our disagreement with the action of the Executive Committee is, we do not believe that at this time of crisis in business with unemployment causing universal suffering and the threat of world chaos, that the repeal of the 18th Amendment should be made the issue, or even the issue of paramount importance in the coming presidential election. After all, the essential point remains, allegiance to the Nation should be above allegiance to any party or any organization, no matter how patriotic it may be.

We commit ourselves to neither candidate; we simply declare our independent right, after considering the many serious problems which confront the United States, to work and to vote when the time comes, each as her judgment shall dictate, for the man whose policies seem best qualified to bring about the return of a normal condition of employment, and to promote the general welfare of the country as a whole.

2

MY FIRST ENTRANCE into the field of public welfare had been made during the run of *The Girl Who Has Everything*. The title inspired begging letters; one proved irresistible.

Dear Miss Robson,

I have read in the paper that you were the lady who had everything. I am a little girl 12 years old and I am very sick with spine trouble and I have got a little sister that is blind. I would like a new dress and a pair of shoes for Christmas and my little sister want's a doll and carrage. My father is sick and we cannot get anything for Christmas.

I hope you will not forget me.

I am yours truly . . .

Please do not put this in the paper for my father and mother don't no I wrote this letter.

Greatly distressed, I set out to relieve this misery. A huge basket of food was prepared, books and toys. Several members of the company added their generous cash gifts to mine, and an old-fashioned Lady Bountiful responded to the call for help. The experience was disillusioning. The story proved to be absolutely false. Food was abundantly in evidence; the three children looked quite healthy. But drunkenness and dirt were everywhere apparent. However, the lesson learned was important, that investigation and distribution by specialists are essential to the wise use of public relief funds.

3

THE GREAT DEPRESSION which started in 1929 called for dedication on the part of Americans, and throughout the country, thousands upon thousands answered the call. *Dedication* is a big word, but occasionally it takes a big word to describe human beings in action. In 1930, at the request of welfare agencies, a committee of New York's leading businessmen organized a Central Emergency Unemployment Relief Agency to deal with the increasingly important problem of men and women thrown out of work through no fault of their own. Seward Prosser, the chairman, asked if I could undertake a benefit at the Metropolitan Opera House; the committee hoped in this way to raise $50,000, he said. I suggested that a committee of women should be appointed to assist the Men's Committee, seeking direct fund contributions instead of through a benefit. Mr. Prosser authorized me to investigate, although the campaign was half over. Luckily we secured Mrs. Reeve Schley of New Jersey to head the women's group. With the co-operation of people we knew and people we did not know, $385,000 was added to the fund raised by the Men's Committee when the campaign ended six weeks later. That spring Mrs. Schley left us for work in New Jersey and I was appointed to succeed her.

In December, the Welfare Council placed before us the plight of unemployed single women. While both men and women heads of families were being cared for by funds raised in October and November by Mr. Prosser's committee, no provision had been made for thousands of practically destitute single women and dependent young girls. After consultation with the leaders of my committee, we agreed to raise the necessary funds. Mr. Prosser tried to dissuade me. He said that the big campaign in November for $6,000,000, which yielded $8,000,000, was over; the Red Cross and the Salvation Army had concluded their drives; New York had given generously. He felt our women's committee had made a fine showing, and that if we failed now in a new undertaking it would discourage workers in the future. My reply was it didn't matter if we failed to reach a goal, but it would matter if we failed to try, as agencies working for girls reported the need was serious. *Any* money contributed would help. Mr. Prosser gave the undertaking his blessing and agreed to stand back of us. A goal of $500,000 was suggested; my counsel that we should make it $350,000 prevailed. This sum would enable the Work Bureau to create for single women 1,000 jobs at $18.00 a week, for a period of four months. My personal belief in drives always has been to take a possibly attainable goal—then work with all your might and main to exceed it.

The committee was enlarged, with myself as chairman. Mrs. Courtlandt D. Barnes was chairman in charge of special gifts. Her knowledge of the known, generous giving community, her tact and devotion, made her like someone descended from heaven to

handle this difficult task. In two months, the campaign closed
with $597,000—of which the ever-generous John D. Rockefeller,
Jr., contributed $100,000. The downtown financial groups were
led in each drive by the House of Morgan.

Among the thousands of letters I received during the campaign, the following was not in the usual pattern:

> Dear Mrs. B. I think the time is ripe for the District
> Attorney to investigate what you and Mr. G. [Harvey
> Gibson] are doing with the money. Girls to be turned out
> of department stores on Saturday night. Where can a woman
> find a place to live in New York? The Y.W.C.A.? All their
> buildings filled with swimming pools, not a bed to sleep in.
> A few of us are going to get busy.
>
> Judges of the Court

4

FROM OCTOBER to December, 1931, registration lines were dis-
tressingly long, and the Emergency Work Bureau extremely
active: 39 registration bureaus for men and 12 for women were
in operation in the 5 boroughs. Of the total placed that year, 77
per cent were laborers; 11 per cent white-collar men workers,
and 12 per cent women. The Bureau estimated that one out of
every thirteen families in the city was seeking employment. Their
report stated that during that year, from October to the following September, 1932, 43,924 were placed: 23,954 laborers; 9,991
white-collar men workers; 9,979 women. A total of 2,260 different groups were on our list to accept workers: nonprofit agencies
of all denominations, city and federal properties, churches, set-
tlements, convents, libraries, museums and, of course, the Y
groups.

Actually 43,924 persons were placed in work, who by this
means were helped to support approximately 75,000 children.

Unemployment relentlessly increased the following year, and
suffering was acute; the problem became one of major proportions.
Harvey D. Gibson accepted chairmanship of the Emergency Un-

employment Relief Committee. Chairman of the Women's Division was my assignment; Mrs. Courtlandt D. Barnes, vice chairman. By this time we had secured able representatives from New York's five boroughs and a large corps of workers. The total goal that winter for the committee was $15,000,000, of which our Women's Division produced nearly $4,000,000.

Weekly report luncheons were held in the old Astor Hotel. One meeting of the Women's Division at which I was presiding had over thirty at the head table; borough chairmen, heads of special committees, and guests of honor. Suddenly, one of our officers took me aside in genuine distress. An able committee chairman, born in the Deep South, had heard that a representative from Harlem was to report for the first time and, representing her area, she was scheduled to sit somewhere at the head table. The flurry arose from the fact that the Southerner said she would not sit at table with a Negro. What was to be done? The chief guest speaker obviously had to be on my right; I placed the Negro representative on my left and next to her, a worker who realized, as I did, that this delegate from Harlem was doing an excellent job, and had as much right to be here as anyone else. When she made her report, it was greeted with generous applause from the more than 2,500 representatives present.

Fannie Hurst made numerous speeches and wrote an appealing leaflet, *There Is a City Under the City* (the city of workers out of employment). James Montgomery Flagg and other artists contributed message-carrying posters and illustrations of the problem. Newspapers, magazines, all forms of communication, supported the city-wide effort. It is not possible in limited space to mention the names of even a reasonable percentage of those who performed an outstanding service in this vast operation. Equally, it is impossible to mention important services rendered by individuals and organizations that worked independently or side by side with the Emergency Unemployment Relief Committee.

In addition to the financial cataclysm that had struck the nation, a severe drought plagued the farming areas during 1931–32.

Probably seven states, chiefly in the northwest, were in dire distress. Farmers reported their animals on the verge of starvation.

By act of Congress, the Federal Government made available to the National Red Cross for distribution some 85,000,000 bushels of wheat and 844,063 bales of cotton. This was a tremendous responsibility, a gigantic and complex operation. It involved a multiplicity of agencies in its handling, for the Red Cross had to administer the changing of these bales of raw cotton of various grades into cloth, sheeting, and other materials. The materials were transformed into articles of clothing by volunteers in Red Cross production departments or in relief supported "made-work" sewing rooms.

The bushels of wheat were turned into barrels of flour. The handling of this involved operators of grain-storage elevators, flour mills, railroads, steamship companies and, ultimately, the vast number of relief agencies servicing the families in all parts of the country.

"Through the Red Cross Chapters and other local agencies, nearly 6 million families received clothing relief. This clothing was distributed in all but 18 of the 3,098 counties in the United States and in Alaska, Hawaii, and Puerto Rico," the official report states. Judge Payne, National Chairman, took personal charge of the operation, which provides a splendid page in Red Cross history.

The five borough chapters of New York administered this city's share of cloth, and the wheat which had been provided by the National Red Cross. The chapters distributed the goods to their volunteer production workrooms, and also provided material for the Emergency Work Bureau sewing rooms. Our Bureau paid the wages of people assigned to those workrooms, and directed them. Then the clothing produced by the chapters and the relief sewing rooms was distributed to the many thousands of men, women, and children on relief rolls.

Mabel Boardman wrote from Red Cross headquarters in Washington:

Don't let the Gibson Committee take the place of the
Red Cross in your interest, and don't let it swamp the Red
Cross by doing its work. This is a marvelous opportunity
now to revive the interest of American women in giving
service to our organization and one we have not had since
the war. It is an opportunity it would be a pity to lose.

My work for the unemployed actually added to my usefulness
to the Red Cross; participating in the program-making of each,
I acted often as interpreter and at times as co-ordinator, thus
serving as a link between the two groups. To succeed with the
colossal task in hand, the utmost co-operation was necessary.

5

THE "MADE-WORK" IDEA probably originated in the old Association
for Improving the Condition of the Poor, under the leadership of
W. H. Matthews, Director of Relief. This type of assistance
had been a board policy for a number of years in this fine private
welfare organization, where they had found in times of depression or seasonal unemployment that self-respecting men and
women wanted work, not relief. My husband used to say, "It
takes the same fundamental principle to run a successful peanut
stand as a big business." From the peanut-sized experiment in
the A.I.C.P. the city-wide "made-work" program expanded to
a very big business and functioned extraordinarily well in spite
of its emergency growth. Later, this same "made-work" program
was bodily adopted by Harry Hopkins for the Federal program
during President Franklin D. Roosevelt's Administration.

The Association for Improving the Condition of the Poor led
the program, but all agencies in the city—big, little, and every
kind—helped in the struggle. President of the A.I.C.P., Cornelius N. Bliss, was the mastermind of the operation. A modest
man who never cared for personal credit, his only concern was to
get the job done. Alfred E. Smith became a warrior–co-ordinator who invariably helped at every turn, especially when co-
operation with the city was essential.

Lillian Wald, one of the great social workers, a woman of vast experience, said that in spite of the widespread unemployment and the extended period of the depression, it was the first time to her knowledge in similar emergencies that no one starved. Secretaries in large numbers were placed, while over 800 nurses were sent to hospitals and other institutions. The families ranged from wife and child to a wife and eleven children. There was a large number of Negro applicants, and four-fifths of all registrants were under fifty. The great majority had never applied for relief before, and were unknown to the Central Social Service Agency, through which all cases were cleared to avoid duplication.

In 1932, the third year, the Fund goal was $28,000,000, an Everest peak in those black days. Mr. Gibson's leadership had been brilliant, his well-laid organization fanning out in all directions over the Greater City. By this time, an army of volunteers with professional assistants was engaged in the struggle to save a greater army held in the cruel grip of public enemy number one—Unemployment. Our Women's Division alone had nearly 4,000 volunteers. The group captains were tireless. Mrs. Charles S. Payson, Mrs. Winthrop Aldrich, Mrs. George Baker, developed into marvelous gleaners of gold. In addition to the usual special gift list, Mrs. Barnes's responsibility, and lists of other agencies, we had block campaigns. Gertrude Robinson Smith was chairman of the block solicitors. These workers, some 3,000 strong, went from house to house, apartment to apartment—a difficult job for anyone—ringing doorbells. The Women's Division that year collected as its share approximately $9,000,000 of the total $28,000,000.

After prolonged unemployment and the tragic intensity of the depression, numerous cases became evident of white-collar workers who had been confronted with serious illness in addition to financial need. Surgical operations, foreclosure of mortgages on houses, and other problems had to be provided for. So once again the Women's Division set out to raise a special fund to rescue a *family in need*. For want of a better name, the new effort was called "The Adopt a Family Campaign." A private individual, or several, would pay all necessary expenses in each case, which might include rent, hospitalization, dental work, eyeglasses, clothes.

This time a few tired committee folk protested; but the need was so serious, we persisted. After a brief interval to organize, we soon found individuals who agreed to adopt families. They carried them for days, weeks, months—even years. The donor was kept informed as to every detail of his "family's" need, yet never came in contact with the actual case; and a recipient of assistance never knew the donor's name. The liaison was handled by professional social workers; these intermediaries formed the strong link between a chasm of desperate situations faced by helpless families and financial security provided by the committee. Bridge players turned over their winnings. In private schools, children earned and saved for their adopted "family." The program was popular. Our contributors were tenderly interested in every detail that concerned these families. That first year, 1932, we raised close to $400,000.

The project is still running in 1957 as a special committee affiliated with the Community Service Society of New York. Always the main purpose has been to assist those who are in need of temporary aid, "a tide-over" to put them back on the track where, once more on their own, they may earn an independent living without becoming regular city welfare dependents. Frequently the problem of re-education is involved; if the breadwinner is incapacitated or dies, the wife must learn a trade and be helped to find employment. Meanwhile, the family will be carried until she is able to assume responsibility. The committee proudly states that 74 per cent of cases handled through this service have again become self-supporting.

6

PEOPLE MEETING ME in the street often say, "Don't you remember me? I worked for you." At times it seems as if everyone in New York has worked with me in one campaign or another, and working together is a precious association. Throughout that prolonged crisis the women did a magnificent job. Many of them had never attempted to raise money before, yet, like myself, they became remarkably good beggars. No words can describe how generous of time, money, and ability the men of our city were during that terrible period. In three years under their leadership, the Emergency Work Bureau found employment for from 30,000 to 50,000 individuals a month. Approximately $55,000,000 in cash was raised and distributed, aside from attendant services, medical care, clothing, and feeding. We counted any gift as twice blessed. The gift created employment for men, women, and girls. Equally important, it helped many hospitals and other fine organizations to continue their services by freeing them from part of their budgetary burdens. They needed workers to carry on. The Bureau supplied workers in every category *and* the Emergency Unemployment Relief Committee paid the bills.

Those strenuous days of unemployment beat upon one's sympathy, but surmounting all the misery with which we came in contact, and the hard work involved, there were moments of genuine inspiration. William H. Matthews, director of work projects for the Emergency Committee, and Ollie Randall who administered the Women's Work Bureau with great skill and devotion, directed the placement of many thousands in work relief. Large committees of men and women begged, wrote letters, harangued meetings, and did everything possible to disturb the peace of the haves in behalf of the have-nots. How those committees did beg! Never in any financial crisis had we known such an outpouring of spontaneous generosity as was evident during those first miserably unhappy years of the great depression. The spirit of mutual helpfulness was thrilling—democracy at its best. A national need—a people and their government united in service.

The campaign emblem should have been the Prince of Wales' three feathers with the motto, "*Ich Dien.*" The number of hours committee members, volunteers, and paid staff alike spent daily in these offices would make any self-respecting union shudder. The popular song was "Brother, Can You Spare a Dime?"; the slogan on our banner and leaflets read: "I will share." By and large, people were wonderful—they gave and gave again, and *again* they gave.

We never could have pulled through those sad and tumultuously catastrophic days that lengthened into years, without the heart-warming generosity of the poor to the poor. We often hear quoted, "There is but one virtue, enthusiasm; but one vice, inertia." Unquestionably enthusiasm *is* a virtue. Be grateful if you have it, for when you must push forward for cause or principle, you feel as if you had swallowed radium. Inertia is not the only vice, but make no mistake, it is a big one. Who knows, it could prove to be the most serious vice that democracy has to face.

Leadership is essential in campaigning for philanthropic causes. The standard of success achieved depends upon the quality of that leadership. Years of experience with the Red Cross, Emergency Unemployment Relief Committee, and the Metropolitan Opera brought me in close association with businessmen of surpassing ability. Three of them, then and still in retrospect, appeared to be magnificent executives. Harry Davison, Red Cross; Harvey D. Gibson, Red Cross and Unemployment Relief; Cornelius N. Bliss, Red Cross, Unemployment Relief, and opera. Each man was a leader, and in each the conception of the problem which lay before him was large. Harry Davison should have died many years later and not in 1922, when he was only fifty-five.

Dragons, fire, flood, and famine torment the world, but thank heaven there still walk among us giants who arise to slay the dragons. New York may be wicked; New York frequently is dirty and in modern times abominably congested with traffic; but in the experiences of this citizen, New York is undoubtedly the most generous city in the world.

7

I SAID at the time—and it is still true, one problem—a very serious problem—which confronts us in voluntary giving, requires study and correction, namely, a distressing amount of duplication in appeals to the public—duplication which definitely limits, by waste of money and effort, our capacity to accomplish the best results. Furthermore, we find a dozen groups handling one phase of welfare, while another important phase may be left untouched. We need a central planning agency with authority, a citizens' clearing house, whose business it should be to study public needs and bring about a co-ordination of effort along many lines.

After three years or more of intensive, heartbreaking, and exhausting work fund raising, some of us came to the definite conclusion that voluntary giving was totally inadequate to meet this or any similar unemployment situation, in spite of the amazing generosity shown by givers among rich and poor alike. Private aid is uncertain, spasmodic, and frequently insufficient—particularly when unemployment is widespread and of long duration. England had an unemployment-insurance plan which was critically called "the dole" in the United States. Yet it provided a definite, although modest, relief for all; furthermore, it recognized government responsibility. Our "American way" of voluntary aid was increasingly difficult to maintain; also, it permitted the ungenerous to stand aside from the tragedy. We, too, had our untouchables. *Time* magazine of May, 1933 carried the following article:

"Penalize the Generous"

. . . These last two years graceful, white-haired Mrs. Belmont has been the most conspicuous Unemployment Relief woman in New York. On May 1 she will retire. Last week, at a meeting of Jewish women, she began her valedictory speech: "If you will permit me I will be absolutely frank."

Three thousand women, including Mrs. Franklin D. Roosevelt, hitched forward in their chairs.

Mrs. Belmont's point: private charity, keeping 13,000,000 idle alive, is haphazard, wasteful. Said she: "The major portion of the relief program should be assigned to the city, State or Federal Government, and the amount agreed upon .

. . . as necessary to carry out an adequate program, should be obtained by special taxation. . . . I do not believe it is a wise policy to carry on the work of serious emergency relief with voluntary contributions. The system is as wrong as that of voluntary enlistment in times of war. It simply means that you penalize the generous."

Thanking Paul N. Kellogg, then editor of *Survey Graphic* magazine, for a paper on unemployment insurance, I wrote:

I am deeply interested in that phase of the problem. At the moment it is quite impossible to do more than I am doing, and while this drive is on, it is of such importance to the relief problem in New York that I must give my entire attention to the work in hand. When it is over and I have had a chance to catch my breath, I want to swing any influence I may have in the direction of promoting unemployment insurance. We must, I feel sure, move carefully and wisely as to which form we endorse, but we must not be confronted another year with this inadequate machinery for meeting the situation.

8

APRIL 8, 1932, I sailed for England to study British, German, and other unemployment-insurance programs at first hand. With me was an old and dear friend, Mrs. Eliot Wadsworth. On the same ship traveled Norman H. Davis, returning from Washington to Geneva, where he had been stationed for some time as our chief delegate to the disarmament conference. Mrs. Davis was at home awaiting the arrival of a grandchild. Henry L. Stimson (at that time Secretary of State in President Hoover's cabinet, later Secretary of War under Franklin Roosevelt) and Mrs. Stimson were also en route to Geneva. Mr. Davis urged me to join this secretarial party, for in Geneva, he said, matters of world importance would be discussed. However, with unemployment firmly fixed in heart and mind, London was my goal.

Thanks to Lord and Lady Astor—she was still a Member of

Parliament—every facility was made available for me to study British insurance plans. Among other things, I learned a world survey was being prepared; that the man who had this study in hand was financed by the Rockefeller Foundation, and that his headquarters were in Geneva. With all haste, Mrs. Wadsworth and I proceeded to Switzerland, arriving in time for a farewell dinner which Mr. Davis was giving to Secretary and Mrs. Stimson.

Among those present on this occasion were Chancellor Brüning and Dr. B. W. von Bülow of Germany; Dino Grandi of Italy; Eduard Beneš of Czechoslovakia; Sir John Simon of Great Britain; Sir Eric Drummond, Secretary of the League of Nations (the only man whose name, by virtue of his office, permanent Secretary of the League, was mentioned in the Treaty of Versailles); Mary E. Woolley of the United States Disarmament Commission; Joseph Paul-Boncour; Hugh Gibson of our State Department; Senator Claude Swanson, later Secretary of the Navy under President Roosevelt; Allen Dulles; Mr. and Mrs. Norman Armour; Mrs. Wadsworth, and a number of others.

When seating the table, of course after all notables had been taken care of, Mr. Davis gave us, the late-comers, a choice of location. The Germans were strangers and, interested in their thinking, I requested that I be placed near them, and was seated between Chancellor Brüning and Dr. von Bülow. I found the latter a proud young man, deeply shocked by the results of the war, and miserably unhappy about the plight of his country. He talked of his ancestors and their part in German history. Chancellor Brüning's view of the future was seriously realistic. The sincerity of his approach to existing problems was reasonable. I thought then, and have continued to believe, that had he been given the half loaf for which he earnestly begged to aid his administration at that time, the world crisis which followed certainly would have been delayed; it might even have been avoided. After dinner, Sir John Simon claimed my attention. I was eager to learn his opinion about international affairs, but though he was playing an important part in the disarmament discussion, he talked as if the only subject he knew or cared about was William Shakespeare, which author, incidentally, he quoted extremely well.

Norman Davis with difficulty secured tickets for Mrs. Wadsworth and me to attend an assembly meeting of the League of Nations. The gallery was crowded. The delegates represented forty-two countries. The United States, of course, was officially barred from participating in those discussions by an act of Congress. But the group of Americans, headed by Mr. Davis, were officially in Geneva for disarmament talks. I can see Mr. Davis now, seated with his associates in one corner of the hall, behind a red velvet rope, and with them a group of other "unofficial observers."

Members of the Governing Board of the Assembly were seated behind a long bench on a raised dais, simple in appearance, yet judicial. Paul Hymans of Belgium presided, and the proceedings were in French. The delegates were seated at long tables in the hall. In front of them, directly under the dais with the presiding officers, was a pulpit-like stand. Here anyone called to address the conference took his place.

The Assembly was meeting to consider China's plea to be allowed to maintain her sovereignty, her administrative and territorial integrity which she considered indispensable to the maintenance of peace. The resolution presented to the Assembly in her behalf recommended that Japan's forces, already occupying Manchuria, should withdraw and that Japan and China, together with other League representatives, should discuss peace terms on neutral territory.

After several impassioned speeches, voting on the China Resolution began. Suspense was terrific. We could hardly breathe with anxiety; our world seemed to hang on the edge of a precipice. Japan abstained from voting. Every other nation seated in the Assembly, as the alphabetical roll was called, solemnly answered, "Yes," in approval of the resolution.

Shortly thereafter Japan gave notice of her intention to withdraw from the League of Nations. Mr. Stimson later wrote in *The Far Eastern Crisis:* "Her continuance of association with an international society whose principles and rules she had deliberately and flagrantly broken could have been nothing but an embarrassment and likelihood of future danger to the other members of that society as well as to the rest of the world."

9

WHEN I RETURNED, packed to overflowing with unemployment systems and recommendations, I was besieged by social workers whose conviction, like my own, that something must be done by the United States Government had grown rapidly. Paul Kellogg urged that I should present our cause to the President. Franklin Roosevelt was known to favor Federal legislation along these lines, yet to the disappointment of interested observers, no definite bill was before Congress. To my protest that a specialist in the field should assume responsibility for this interview, Mr. Kellogg urged that my close contact with the subject of unemployment relief through the past years, my recent investigations in Europe, plus my sincere conviction, made me the best person for the job. A fifteen-minute appointment was secured, and I journeyed to Washington for an interview with America's Chief Executive.

Franklin Roosevelt was at all times a gracious host. His cordial friendliness unconsciously put a visitor at ease, but there is a certain justifiable element of pomp and circumstance surrounding an appointment with any President that is in a measure awe-inspiring. He listened with earnest attention as I presented our case and appealed to him for Federal legislation that would provide insurance against a similar national disaster in the future. New York had social security, but to be forced to adopt a different plan for every state—state by state—would take long, long years; and then the national result would not be uniform. It was obvious that convinced espousal of unemployment insurance and leadership from the White House were essential for a Federal program.

From that moment, Mr. Roosevelt took over. He reviewed the immediate circumstances and the problems inherent in recurring depressions—as a skillful lawyer might present a convincing brief. Any dyed-in-the-wool advocate might have envied his approach to the subject. Then, as he developed his ideas as to the remedy, he used a phrase which I had never heard before in this connection, namely that workers should be insured "from the cradle to the grave."

A secretary appeared to signal that the allotted time was up; but it was the President who delayed my departure. The secretary withdrew. With increasing enthusiasm my host warmed to his subject. When the secretary returned again, I rose, thanked the President for his interest in the problem, and left. On my return to New York, Mr. Kellogg greeted me eagerly. After describing the interview, I expressed some discouragement—the President's conception of the program seemed too vast. In Shakespearian words my feeling was, "They are as sick that surfeit with too much, as they that starve with nothing."

To those who watched anxiously, legislative assistance seemed slow in coming. However, within two years the President had achieved a Federal social-security program and at least part of the extensive plan he envisaged.

10

THE RED CROSS once again had developed rapidly under the pressure of World War II and Korea. Over the years more and more professionals were employed, and the hazards involved in their work increased. The unemployment situation had emphasized the need for a pension program for those permanently employed. But there was no policy at national headquarters, nor in the chapters, for pensioning employees. A climax to the subject was brought vividly to my attention when I was approached to ask if assistance could be secured through the Emergency Unemployment Work Bureau for a needy Red Cross worker, a faithful secretary for twenty-five years, for whom there was no provision.

Following this episode a survey was started by national headquarters to discover the best plan, if any, for Red Cross personnel. Because of its volunteer status and the emergency nature of the program, a number of people were reluctant to enter into any comprehensive insurance plan for employees. As a member of the

Study Committee, I hounded the believers and needled the reluctant until it was finally agreed to provide insurance for Red Cross personnel. After studying innumerable group-insurance plans, our committee recommended that due to its unique character, the organization should create and control its own program. Today, the American Red Cross administers probably one of the soundest welfare and pension plans operating anywhere in the country, thanks in large measure to Eliot Wadsworth, for many years the wise chairman who guided the Pension and Retirement program, and an excellent committee with James K. McClintock from headquarters staff as secretary.

PART SIX

Say not the struggle nought availeth,
The labour and the sounds are vain,
The enemy faints not, nor faileth,
And as things have been, things remain.

If hopes were dupes, fears may be liars;
It may be, in yon smoke concealed,
Your comrades chase e'en now the fliers,
And, but for you, possess the field.

For while the tired waves, vainly breaking,
Seem here no painful inch to gain,
Far back through creeks and inlets making
Came silent, flooding in, the rain.

And not by eastern windows only,
When daylight comes, comes in the light;
In front the sun climbs slow, how slowly,
But westward, look, the land is bright.

—Arthur H. Clough

CLOUGH'S POEM was new to me when Sir Ronald Lindsay, the British Ambassador, quoted it one day while I was staying at the Embassy in Washington, and then, at my request, wrote out a copy. The poem sprang into American attention when Prime Minister Winston Churchill used the last verse in a letter to President Roosevelt at a critical moment during the Second World War.

Sir Ronald had been stationed as Ambassador to Turkey several months when, in the autumn of 1924, he took his new bride, Elizabeth Sherman Hoyt, to Constantinople. Drastic events important to that country had been taking place. The whole nation was still struggling with boundary adjustments due to war and the aftermath of a convulsive revolution. Changes in the architecture of government were frequent and the atmosphere at times was tense, but the Lindsays thoroughly enjoyed Turkey, and told many delightful stories of their interesting days there. The Ambassador, as a crowning achievement, had been able to negotiate an important treaty between Great Britain and the Ottoman Empire. The rich oil fields in the vilayet of Mosul had been under serious discussion between the two governments for several years when Sir Ronald procured a satisfactory agreement by means of the Mosul Treaty.

During their stay, the new ruler of Turkey, Kemal Pasha Atatürk, was building what he intended should be a new capital in Ankara. Only at this point there was practically nothing substantial in housing accommodations, no embassies, no reasonably comfortable hotels. Sir Ronald had left the Embassy in Constantinople to attend the conference called by Atatürk in Ankara, and forgot to tell his wife that the Feast of Ramadan was due that night. Late that evening, firing suddenly coming from all directions shattered the tense silence. At last, unable to control her anxiety, Lady Lindsay opened her shuttered window and called down to the kavass, the Embassy guard. The most serious reprimand she could think of was, "The Ambassador will be *very* displeased. What does all this shooting mean?"

"A mere little nothing, Your Excellency," he replied. "Retire, please. I assure you presently everything will pass into quiet." There being literally nothing else to do, Her Excellency shut the window, although she remained dressed throughout the long night—ready, she hoped, to meet any emergency. Next day she learned it was the custom for natives at the time of the lunar eclipse to shoot cannons skyward and let off a barrage of firecrackers, the intention being to frighten away the Great Bear and thus prevent him from stealing the moon. How simple a faith! Yet, surely we can sympathize. Haven't we all had moments when we, too, were reluctant to part with the moon?

After Turkey, the Lindsays spent nearly two years in Germany. This postwar assignment in a defeated country could not have been cheerful, but I remember they talked with warm enthusiasm about an outstanding diplomat, the papal nuncio Archbishop Pacelli. In March, 1930, Sir Ronald came as his government's representative to the United States. Lady Lindsay was, without doubt, the wittiest and one of the ablest women who ever came to Washington as wife of a foreign ambassador. American by birth, a great-niece of General William Tecumseh Sherman, she had served with distinction our Red Cross in America and France before her marriage. She had known Sir Ronald from girlhood, when she and her cousin, Martha Cameron, who became his first wife, met this younger son of the Earl of Crawford and Balcarres, one of the oldest Scottish titles in the British peerage.

Sir Ronald stood six feet four; when on state occasions he appeared resplendent in full-dress uniform, wearing his Scotch cap with a long, floating eagle feather, he was a fine sight to behold. This daughter of the United States looked up at him from her five feet four inches as the tourist might admire the Empire State Building or the Eiffel Tower. Diplomats said Ronald Lindsay knew the United States better than most American citizens; also, he had visited every state of the Union; not many can claim such a travelogue. The strengthening of Anglo-American relationship was a major objective with him. The Ambassador was a man of genuine reserve, on occasion, shy. Speechmaking, considered essential to an ambassador's position, was obnoxious to him; nevertheless, in matters of diplomatic importance, he rendered distinguished service to his country and to ours. The Ambassador told me that in his experience, visits of athletic teams did not help to cement friendship between nations, for all too frequently bitter jealousy entered into the contest. As good-will ambassadors, he gave the palm to the D'Oyly Carte Opera Company. He proudly asserted that their enchanting performances of Gilbert and Sullivan furnished joy to people of all ages; moreover, it is a joy that leaves no sting of rivalry behind.

Settling into the newly built British Embassy in Washington was a seriously difficult task. Sir Edward Lutyens, although a distinguished architect, apparently had a limited idea of what human beings need by way of closet space, entrances and exits, to exist in comfort. In the midst of the responsibility of readjusting this new embassy to meet the requirements, a coronary thrombosis struck Lady Lindsay down. Air conditioning did not exist, and Washington was steaming hot, hotter than usual that summer. The devoted Embassy staff arranged fans in her room that blew the air over pans filled with blocks of ice in an effort to reduce the temperature, which for two weeks never fell below 94 degrees, day or night.

When the doctors permitted, she was moved to Oakdale, to

the home of a dear friend, Mrs. Bayard Cutting of New York. Her heart continued to cause trouble; from then on, holidays free from Washington climate and Embassy responsibility became essential. Two or three times during the year, in an effort to rest the damaged heart muscle, she left the hubbub of embassy life, and one or another friend usually accompanied her on these "breathing spell" expeditions. Her most frequent companions were Olivia James, a daughter of Mrs. Cutting, Irene Boyle, her personal friend and official secretary, Aileen Tone, and myself.

June 21–1931

ON BOARD R.M.S. "OLYMPIC."

My dear, you ought to travel with me—really. I find that my passport is No. 13; the voyage has been ideal in the matter of weather, of comfort, of rest—and of companion. The sea has been as smooth as a French sauce, the ship is my favorite, and Irene the perfect fellow traveller.

I find I can think of nothing else, save our "country's cause"— While I lived in Germany I was terrified by the similarity of the history of that country, & my own. Within the lifetime of one generation Germany sprang into world power,—and all unprepared; she went down in a drunken orgy of power. Within 15 years, America has become the world power; and fate is now giving her the great chance to save herself from these unearned benefits, by treating her to a dose of adversity— Pray heaven that she sees it, and comes through. Unless we "lay hold on life," we sink— Why have we won before;—and why is England winning now? The more I think of it, the more convinced I become, that only one thing is the answer. Faith in *ourselves!* "These times strike worried worldlings with dismay." But there is something there, *really* there in the U.S.A. which this moment ought to call forth. There must be many Miltons whose voices should be heard—oh—reread Wordsworth's sonnets, & I will be still. But I am sick of hearing the wail for *a* leader. What army has ever been led to victory by a Commander in Chief alone? Unless the sergeants, the captains & majors, do their part the battle is lost. . . . I'm sorry.

I've had too much time for thought; and I rebel against the whimperings & criticism of my own kind, or shall I say friends, or "class." We are failing at every step, but there is a real back bone behind us that we stupidly overlook.

In the mean time a most unusual thing has happened to me. I have had a dream and *remembered* it! You, in your purple dressing gown were talking to me. I need hardly say that it was a very hot night and we both were more than conscious of that fact. You were wearing glass slippers which caught my attention. And when I commented on them, you said you had bought them from Victor Hugo. This seemed quite natural, but what really roused my interest, was that you told me that they were difficult to walk in because the soles did not bend with the foot. Now, how on earth did Cinderella ever dance in glass slippers? I had never thought of that before. Had you? . . .

I am glad that I do not live in the days when the change from one planet to the other will be made by air between breakfast & dinner. When we die, I think that we will hang between the two worlds as we do on a sea voyage. It gives one time to readjust,—and it gives my "twin hearts" a breathing spell. And one of them always remains in the country where I have left all my faith. The other one is much consoled by the recent discovery my dear that you were born in Wigan! Do you realize that that is the "home town" of the Lindsays? I feel more at home among them!

I am NOT quoting Ronnie, but my own heart, when I say: "Of thee I sing"

Yours
Elizabeth

2

THE THOMAS LAMONTS loaned Lady Lindsay and me their cottage at Yeamen's Hall, South Carolina, while they visited Italy. We gratefully accepted "Uncle Tom's Cabin" and slowly toured the beautiful gardens near by with particular appreciation of the perfect landscape planning of Middleton Gardens.

Another rest period found us in the Boca Grande, where the

magic of shell collecting cast its hypnotic spell over us. Being a perfectionist, Elizabeth Lindsay had sent for special books in order to know more of the subject. When I had to return to New York and problems of unemployment, she telegraphed:

> I FOUND YOUR SCOTCH BONNET WITH A WEE BLEMISH ON IT SO JOIN IN MY LONG LOUD HOORAY I AM LAME AND WEARY AND BOTH EYES ARE BLEARY BUT ITS BEEN A PERFECT DAY

When she returned to Washington, she exhibited in the Embassy a fine collection of shells, each bearing a caption with its scientific name.

Periodically, on the advice of doctors, she sought various cures in Europe. The one at Royat in France was taken with lovely Aileen Tone, a girlhood friend. They were both "adopted nieces" of Henry Adams, to them, "Uncle Henry." To most of his countrymen, he was the Henry Adams who gave Chartres to America, or was it America to Chartres?

August 30–'32–
Royat-Palace
Royat (*P.deD.*)

Never can I tell you what a delight the newspaper clippings were my dear! Nor what ideal reading they made for a "baigueuse." You cannot imagine the fun I had. A thousand, *thousand* thanks. On the whole I thought Mr Hoover's speech good, although a little royal in tone. I found myself waiting & looking for the "my people," if not "my subjects." There was so much of the first person singular. . . .

I am appalled at the recklessness of your nature. How can you ask me to tell you how I am when I am at a "Cure"? Do you not know that all of us talk of nothing else, but blood pressure, pulses, reactions etc etc–ad infinitum? . . . I am enormously pleased with myself at having chosen a malady which brings me to this place. The country side, the air, the archeological "richesses" *and* the natives are each one lovelier than the last.

Finding myself in an inland country, where conchology

could not be practised, I have taken madly to archeology,
& roam the hills (in a motor) in search of XIIth Century
sculptures & buildings. My collection of Virgins far surpasses
my shells. And my friends can not be bored by them, as I
carry them about in memories only. . . .

Yesterday we found our Junonia, both in Curés & Virgins.
Idly turning the pages of a French architectural book I had
seen a mention of a XIIth Century Virgin in a certain little
village in Auvergne. My map proved the village to be about
30 miles from here. No guide book mentioned the Virgin,
& all whom I asked expressed polite doubt. No one had
heard of her, & surely there was some mistake. But yesterday we set forth determinedly to see for ourselves. The
village consisted of about 10 cottages & a tiny church in one
of the loveliest of all the valleys, reached only by a rough
country lane. The church was a gem in itself, built after a
design all its own. The whole building would go into your
drawing room in N.Y., and has no choir, no side aisles, no
transepts;—but *two* naves! We found many things of interest
but no Virgin, and our explorations were interrupted by the
arrival of a cow who strolled through the door which we
had left open! We ejected her firmly & in so doing met the
rest of the herd, accompanied by two old peasant women.
We asked at once for Monsieur le Curé. He they said was
at home, well did they know it, for he was entertaining 3
gentlemen—*strangers!* His house was au fond et à gauche
& was unlike the other houses! We found it, & boldly opened
the door in the garden wall. An old woman, obviously the
Bonne & the Keeper of the Curé was mending his socks in
the garden. Was this the house of Monsieur le Curé? Yes
(*very* forbiddingly) this *was* the house of Mon. le Curé.
And was he in? Yes (threateningly) he was in. Could we
perhaps speak with him? At this moment most fortunately
the head & shoulders of Mon. le Curé appeared from an
upper window, and I cowered behind the irresistible Aileen.
Instant & great enthusiasm from the Curé. But not at all,
not at all; he regretted to begin by disagreeing with us; but
(with one chubby finger laid across his mouth) we were
not disarranging him. He hurled himself down the stairs &
ushered us in to his house. Yes, yes, yes,—he had a Virgin,

classée she was too by the Beaux Arts. And miraculeuse
obviously, since she had brought ces dames to his door &
hearth. But we would talk of her later, after we had been
refreshed. A little white wine and some biscuits would be
the first step. Again we protested on behalf of the 3 friends
whom he had left upstairs. No, no, no. They did not matter.
One was a brave friend who had just completed 20 years
missionary duty in China. They would wait. Wine was produced and Antoinette was prevailed upon to get glasses &
plates & the biscuits. And fruit,—fruit was the thing on a hot
summer afternoon. We sat ourselves down and Mon. le Curé
bouncing himself & his chair up to the table said beam-
ingly "And now mesdames who have I the honor of receiving?" I told him our names & our nationalities, and Aileen
who has a child like desire to take the world into her confidence, told him who I was. Ambassadrice! cried he, rising
& bowing again, Très honoré, madame, très honoré. Antoinette was given this bit of information & remarked with
great understanding "Oh! la Pauvre". I began to warm to-
wards Antoinette. The Curé then launched into international
affairs, with both knowledge & intelligence. From there he
leapt into literature & the representative poets of France &
England. Never, never must we think of Lamartine as representative of France; he was a sentimentalist, not to be
tolerated by this rugged son of Auvergne. La Fontaine &
Le Musset were representative of France; & Shakespeare
&—Kipling (!) of England. After this we examined his
bibelots, shown to us with great pride & excitement and
always with "oh c'est peu de chose madame." Eventually he
accompanied us back to the church, took the key to the
Sacristy down from the lintel over the door, & showed us
his Virgin. She had every beauty & charm, & was a treasure
of treasures; and as we gazed at her the Curé delivered a
most erudite & poetic lecture on moyen age art! After which
he posed in front of his tiny church, while I photographed
him in spite of his excited protestations that he was not "en
tenue." Many regrets that we would not return to his house
& partake of liqueurs (!), more dissertations on the influence
of Byzantian art on European art, terrific excitement on dis-

covering that I had lived in Constantinople & seen those things of which he had read; and with many promises to return next year, we parted. (Do I hear a sigh of relief from you?)

And here is my masseuse!

Yours,
E.

3

THE LINDSAYS and I talked of the poetic curé who admired the Bard of Avon in particular and all poets in general. We wished he might have been in America that winter. Wasn't it Goethe who said, "Mount Parnassus has two summits. Upon one dwell the nine muses; upon the other, William Shakespeare."

Thomas W. Lamont was the most active member of the American Committee which undertook to assist the English group engaged in raising funds to replace the old burned Shakespeare Theatre at Stratford-on-Avon. At about this time Mr. Lamont had drawn me into this campaign to join John W. Davis, Otto Kahn, and a few others. Believing the American theatre would wish to participate, I found myself on Sunday, January 29, 1928, chairman of a monster benefit at the Metropolitan Opera House. Winthrop Ames gave of his time and skill as director of the production. Next day the papers reported some $25,000 netted. Thomas van Dycke wrote in the New York *Telegraph:*

> The huge Metropolitan was filled to capacity . . . when Guiseppe Bamboschek waved his baton for the overture from "The Merry Wives of Windsor." Contrary to the rule which seems to prevail at this institution, the audience was on time, had no bronchial troubles (to speak of) and remained seated until the final curtain. . . .
>
> George Arliss and his supporting cast did a scene from "The Merchant of Venice". . . . After this fiery speech of invective, Elsie Janis came out and halted the proceedings with her parody of John Barrymore singing "Bananas," in the fashion of the gloomy Prince of Denmark. . . .

The result is that the American committee is nicely started in its attempt to raise the million needed from this side for so great a work as restoring to Avon a theatre in memory of the man who remains, to quote Ben Jonson, "Not of an age, but for all times."

Our list of patrons and patronesses was long. Among them were Elihu Root, Charles Evans Hughes, Robert Lansing, the British Ambassador and Lady Howard, Nicholas Murray Butler, Mrs. William K. Vanderbilt, and Mrs. Charles Dana Gibson.

Incidentally, one of the great thrills of my fund-raising career came at a dinner when the appeal for the Shakespeare Memorial Theatre was launched. Charles Evans Hughes set the keynote with a fine speech. John W. Davis, always distinguished, added an eloquent appeal for the cause. Seated between Mr. Davis and Edward S. Harkness, who had already subscribed $100,000 on condition that we raise $500,000 by November 15, 1927, I turned to Mr. Harkness and said, "Please accept my apology in advance if when you expect me to say *yes*, I say *no*. The fact is, I am overcome with fear to find myself scheduled to speak in such exalted company."

Mr. Harkness said, "Let me see if I can divert you." With that, in the most delightful way, he talked about seeing a play of mine, and quoted from *The Dawn of a Tomorrow*—lines which even I had almost forgotten. Any mere mortal would have been touched and diverted. "Are you finding fund raising for this cause difficult?" he asked.

"Of course," I replied, "with educational projects money does not spring lightly from people's pockets."

Then he said, "Would it help you if I added to my original gift?" And very simply he pledged another $50,000! Needless to say, the fact that my speech was bearing down upon me was forgotten. A few days later I wrote to express my gratitude and to request, on behalf of the Committee, an extension on his first pledge, with its fast-approaching time limit. The following message from his secretary was dated November 5, 1927:

In response to your letter of November 3rd to Mr.
Harkness, who is at present out of the City, he has asked
me to say that, in place of the $50,000. which he promised
informally at the dinner the other evening, he will be glad
to give the sum of . . . $100,000 . . . unconditionally towards
the $1,000,000. the American Shakespeare Foundation is en-
deavoring to raise.

In reference to his former conditional pledge of $100,000.
to this object, made June 6, 1927 and expiring November 15,
1927, I am authorized to say that Mr. Harkness will extend
the time limit to April 23, 1928, as you suggest.

I only hope Mr. Harkness enjoyed his gift as much as I did.

The American Shakespeare Committee not only raised the
$500,000 quota by April 23, but transmitted a total contribution
of $800,000 from our United States to the theatre at Stratford-
on-Avon.

The opening of the New Shakespeare Memorial Theatre was on
April 23, 1932. I was invited to attend with Mr. and Mrs. Thomas
W. Lamont. Mr. Lamont and I were to speak for America, the
allotted time three minutes each, and our speeches were to be
broadcast to America.

That morning, Andrew Mellon, then Ambassador to the Court
of St. James, raised the American flag beside the British flags.
At luncheon, Stanley Baldwin, lord president of The Privy
Counsel, spoke for his government. The greatest applause came
when he greeted the American delegates, saying, "Welcome
home." The guest list glittered with ambassadors (no women
held the post in those days); the elite of the literary world were
in attendance, Galsworthy and Masefield among them. The latter
wrote an ode for the occasion. The whole affair from early morning had been a thrilling succession of events, capped by the
presence of Edward, Prince of Wales, making his first visit to
Stratford. With graciously expressed congratulations, he handed
the golden key of the modern building, presented to him by
Elizabeth Scott, the architect, to Sir Archibald Flower, chair-

man of the board. With trumpeters of the Life Guards and fanfare from the local band the new theatre was declared open.

Inside, seated on stage with the official party, I was conscious
of one person only. Bernard Shaw had been pointed out to me,
in the front row of the balcony, a choice spot in that small house.
He never lowered his opera glasses as he listened to the proceedings. My thoughts were on the great author in the balcony,
for whom my admiration had grown with the years. Nonetheless,
when my turn came, the core of my speech was the Stratford
Bard, and it came from the heart.

I wish that every friend of the theatre, every admirer
of Shakespeare, every lover of poetry might be here today
in Stratford. It has been a rare treat to share in these ceremonies, to see this brilliant gathering made up of distinguished representatives from all parts of the world, assembled
with distinguished representatives of "this blessed plot, this
earth, this realm, this England, this happy breed of men"
who are the direct heirs of Shakespeare.

It is a privilege to be a representative of those other
English-speaking people who form, shall we say, "the sisters
and cousins and the aunts"—those who proudly claim their
share of this inheritance at the same time that they humbly
acknowledge their debt to the man who has so greatly enriched our joint literature.

At the present moment we are living in a world of changing material values. This celebration is of the spirit! It could
not have come at a better time. For there is a thrill in the
thought that we are gathered here from all parts of the
earth to do honor to a poet-dramatist who, as we thought-
lessly say, has been *dead* for 316 years. Yet, death had no
dominion over him.

As we have watched this fine performance [*Henry IV*]
in a lovely setting, there has come to us a poignant realization that true beauty is the most stable, inspiring—the
most *permanent* thing in the world, and that the conception
of a poet's dream is, after all, magnificent reality. [In conclusion I quoted Shakespeare's sonnet which begins:]

"Not marble, nor the gilded monuments
Of princes, shall outlive this powerful rime;
But you shall shine more bright in these contents
Than unswept stone, besmear'd with sluttish time."

and ends,

"So, till the judgment that yourself arise,
You live in *this,* and dwell in lovers' eyes."

Lady Lindsay's account of what took place at the receiving end of the broadcast follows:

April 24—1932

BRITISH EMBASSY
WASHINGTON, D.C.

Well, well, well. You may have had a busy day yesterday opening the Stratford Theatre; but it wasn't a patch on ours. Your letter arrived in the morning, saying you were to talk over the radio. A rush for the Washington papers & a scramble to find the Radio programs, which none of us had ever looked for before. Yes, there it was: 5.15 P.M. But horrors, the Prince of Wales had talked at 8.15 A.M. & we had *missed* it! Never mind, we would hear you. Of course, we *were* having a tennis party at 4.30—but mine is a portable radio & could be taken to the court side. My rest after lunch was abandoned while I got out my radio, dusted it off & prepared to find out how to tune in on you. The Arnold Whitridges & the Parker Gilberts who are staying with us retired to rest, & dress for tennis. In a frenzy I discovered that my radio had died. Keep [the chauffeur] was sent for & pronounced it fatal. Nothing could be done in under 8 hours, & we had only 2. Never mind Keep had a radio which he would lend us, & the rest of the afternoon was spent in running wires from the garage out into the garden where the radio was set up. Guests came, & were ignored. Ronald had gone to the opening of the Folger Library where he was reading a message from the King. But we had got your station, & dared not switch to Ronald's. Loyally, we clung to the alphabetic omen which would bring us your voice

& painfully we bore with a terrible voice which assured us that this was a great day in "'Lizabettan litterachure", and that something was happening at a place called Stratford on "Wan." The mystic moment arrived. . . . Someone mentioned your name, & we all held our breath. Only to have a local voice inform us that the program was cancelled due to atmospheric conditions! ! ! So, like the King of France, we marched down the hill again, feeling *thoroughly* sold. I only tell you all this to prove to you that wherever two or three are gathered together, all hearts beat with yours. . . .

Bless you my dear.

Elizabeth

The colorful pageantry of England always appealed to her.

July 18—1932—

CLARIDGE'S
BROOK STREET W. 1

Although we seem to occupy separate planets, & you will send no signals from yours, to mine; I persist in waving from time to time. . . .

Yesterday morning at 10.30 I nearly cried aloud to you. For suddenly I came upon a scene which was quite unique. I found myself at Hyde Park Corner in a motor. Traffic from *five* directions was held up, & stood quivering silently & respectfully while a solitary London Bobby with one arm majestically raised escorted a mother duck & her 9 ducklings up Constitution Hill, across Hyde Park Corner, & into Hyde Park! No one of us moved, or showed the faintest sign of impatience. The Royal Guards in their scarlet coats, stood marking time, for the only moments that they have ever been held up on the London streets as they proceed to Buckingham Palace to relieve the sentries on duty. The fifes played softly and the feet rose & fell silently, and we all sat quietly while the family made its way across London's busiest corner. Here was a mother duck who prefers (every year it seems) that her offspring be born in St. James' Park but be taken to Hyde Park for their education. That, this year she chose a moment when the Royal Guards were

waiting to be relieved, & when all of London was rushing
to its business, mattered not one whit. Above all things do
we bow to the sanctity of family life. These are a *great*
people!

In the mean time, they greet with enthusiasm the opportunity to "convert" their War Loan, & sacrifice another 20%
of their income. No one murmurs, no one complains; & yet
I have the impression when I lunch or dine with them that
there is barely enough food to go round— But they are
nourished in other ways, & more & more do I believe in
Pitt's words—"England has saved herself by her efforts; and
will save Europe by her example."

In the mean time I, like all crocks, spend all my time in
the pursuit of health . . . and I *may* return, a decent human
being. Provided always that I return! For dreadful rumours
are afloat here of our being moved *again*. I dare not even
let myself think of it, and only mention it to you in the
greatest confidence. I pin all my hopes to Ronald's lack of
self importance. And to his one & only international interest,—the U.S.A.

Rumor, as frequently happens, was a false messenger. The
Lindsays returned to Washington and the Ambassador struggled
valiantly with the complex and disagreeable subject of war
debts between the United States and Great Britain. My own
definite feeling has been that the United States put unfair pressure upon our chief ally in this connection.

4

AMERICAN-BORN WOMEN who marry foreigners and foreigners
who marry Americans frequently face the problem of divided
loyalties. As Elizabeth Lindsay saw the matter it meant having
"twin hearts." During the strenuous debates on war debts and
other controversial subjects between Britain and the United
States, she wrote from the Embassy, November 9, 1932:

My "twin hearts" are rocking. From this moment on I
shall not say what I think or feel; but I would give much

to have my individual rights restored to me & my freedom
of speech. I am shocked beyond words. Perhaps partially by
my own idiotic optimism, over this my country. What in the
name of heaven are they headed for? The English twin is
comforted and grateful beyond measure, for the kindly sympathy and silent understanding of my feelings. No one has
even hinted at what an utter fool I am, nor how entirely
wrong I have been in my estimation of what my countrymen would do in a crisis.

And again on June 14, 1933, she wrote:

    . . . We have been through gruelling days & nights.
The tension has never let up for more than an hour, & yesterday just as we thought everything was calm & settled
came the Senate jam & we spent our last ounce of strength
trying to persuade Chamberlain to tell the House of Com-
mons nothing. R. has done nothing but urge his own people
to give in on various points, & they have each time agreed.
The Pres. has behaved like a man & a gentleman, and some
day I will tell you of his greatest gesture. R. has just received the thanks & praise of H.M. Government, which is a
very rare prize. Also the thanks of these people for one great
victory on their behalf. I only wish Mr Roosevelt might get
the same from his own public. But the whole thing will be
out by the time you get this, & the Senate who is only waiting for the opportunity, will sling mud & stones. *We* don't
care whether it is now, or next January. But its p. d. hard
on their own President who is trying to keep the ship afloat.
The next few days are crucial. . . .
    What with the crises, the heat, a continuous stream of
guests and a domestic upheaval, I am about ready for the
lunatic asylum. But I am proud again of two men. In December it was Stimson & Ronnie & now it is Roosevelt &
Ronnie. Their fair mindedness, their patience & their infinite
toil fills me with admiration. . . .

The arguments continued in Congress and Britain made concession after concession. December 15, 1932, came a note which
contained the following:

... Golly, what days! But all is not lost, & we have our brighter moments. Two days ago R. concluded a treaty with the U.S. Gov. which assures the Island of Bum-bum to the British Empire. We have our compensations.

... I am far too bewildered by what I may think of anything to write coherently at the moment. I can only conclude that human beings, like trees, die in the head first. I rather wish it were the heart, which seems to remain the cause of all one's troubles. Surely we would all be better off if we did not feel, & only thought.

When confronted by the foibles of her friends Elizabeth had a light yet perceptive touch.

British Embassy
Washington, D. C.

April 18–1934

In the watches of the night I opened the copy of "Whither Bound" which you left with me, & out of it fell the enclosed papers. You always do open new avenues of thought for me, & this time has been no exception. First I said to myself: "When is a Book not a Book?", and immediately answered: "When it is a Filing Cabinet." "What," said I, "becomes of lost papers?"—and the answer came: "They are put into a Book, & become Loose Leaves."

5

ONE SUMMER Elizabeth Lindsay and I set off to discover the delights of Scandinavia. Sir Ronald had to remain on duty in Washington. The ultimate goal was a cure in Marienbad, and a famous doctor. Paul Cravath, an experienced traveler, gave us his excellent itinerary. John Mason Brown provided me with advice and a list of restaurants to seek on the trip, adding, "Don't for any reason miss the Royal Theatre in Drottningholm."

We had a marvelous few weeks, from the moment Lady Lindsay's convertible was unloaded from the ship until we left those northern isles of legend and beauty, refreshed and enthusiastic. En route to Munich where we expected much of the opera, we paused at Konigssee to make a trip around that justly famous waterway. As our boat returned from the hour journey, we saw a crowd assembled on shore. Their excitement, their cheers, led to the question, "What's the matter? Who is it?" We were not surprised at the answer: Hitler. Afraid to be late in Munich, we hurried away just as he embarked on a sightseeing tour in the boat we had vacated. Along the route as we passed, individuals and small groups extended their arms in salute, saying, "Heil Hitler."

At the opera shortly afterward, we noticed a man some five rows forward, apparently alone. He looked like Hitler, only this was a relaxed human being. Besides, we had left Hitler at Konigssee. Furthermore, there had been no applause as he entered the house. During the next entr'acte we asked a friend who could this man be. It was Hitler. There was no demonstration because orders were that there should be none. The Führer insisted he came to enjoy the music, and that applause and cheers in an opera house belong to the artists. I mention this in passing, as one hears so little good of this mad dictator.

Occasionally my companion said her diplomatic conscience was troubled, for I carried with me the Treaty of Versailles, given to me by Henry White, seeking in each country the signatures of those who had been party to the peace conferences and had signed the original document. Elizabeth shook her head, "What a scandal this would create if we had an accident to the car, and it should be found that the wife of the British Ambassador was traveling in Germany or in neutral countries with a copy of the Treaty of Versailles in the luggage!"

Doctoring at Marienbad necessitated an after cure. Forced thus to stay abroad, and lonely, Lady Lindsay urged me to extend my holiday two weeks, as my work for the unemployment committee had come virtually to an end. "Absolutely nothing seems to require your attention in America," she said. Yet an imperative instinct, an unexplainable magnet, drew me home. At the dock on my arrival in New York, my faithful maid Nora greeted me with word that Mother had had a slight heart attack so could not meet the steamer as expected. The news was startling; it was Mother's first failure to come to me on any count. Within two weeks she died, the most tolerant, the most generous, the most unselfish human being I have ever known. Had my sailing been delayed, I could not have been with her those last days.

The going of elders is normal, it is accepted as the way of human life; yet when the parting comes, we, their children, seem unprepared. Standing suddenly alone, as the dear one passes over the horizon, one feels so old and yet, so bewilderingly young. Thinking of her over the years, I keep saying to myself, "Through such souls alone God stooping shows sufficient of His light for us to rise by."

6

THE FOLLOWING SUMMER, when I returned via England from a League of Red Cross Societies Conference in Brussels, the Lady Flower invited me to spend a weekend in their comfortable old house at Stratford with a rarely interesting company—Sir Austen and Lady Chamberlain, Sir Ronald Storrs, the Frederick Whites, and the Flower family.

The new Shakespeare Theatre, in spite of its much-criticized modern design, was proving a genuine success. The productions were good, although be it said the performances were still not first class. London theatre folk were slow to give the project their personal co-operation. Some refused the sacrifice of leaving London; some regarded it as partly a promotion plan for the town of Stratford; others, when they thought at all, considered it as a training school for the young who were interested in theatre classics.

Sir Archibald had a one-track mind. The dream, to which he zealously dedicated most waking hours, was to build the quiet village of Stratford-on-Avon into a national shrine; to see, in addition to the swans gliding up and down the winding river—boats, trains, motor buses bringing visitors by the thousands to this old Warwickshire town.

He drove me that weekend to a large property for sale, perhaps a mile away, with a huge, well-built house on it, in really good order. The burning question was, Should the Theatre Corporation take up its option and use this roomy building with modern plumbing (yet to be installed) as a hotel to house the hoped-for tourists? The land was beautiful; Welcombe Hall itself ideally situated. Knowing the almost emotional emphasis my compatriots place on plumbing, as opposed to quaint buildings with charm minus modern facilities, I enthusiastically tossed my pebble of influence in favor of prompt purchase. Sir Archibald needed little encouragement. Today the Welcombe Hotel is a comfortable refuge in Stratford for visitors on Shakespeare bent.

Although my personal acquaintance with British generals has been limited, those I have met impressed me with their wide scholarship, aside from brilliant military accomplishments. Viscount Allenby, Sir Ronald Storrs, Field-Marshal Sir Archibald Wavell, whose anthology *Other Men's Flowers* is delightful, were men out of the ordinary; each accepted with almost filial appreciation what Latin, Greek, and Arabian scholars have offered the world. They read and spoke in several tongues, and with British tolerance, offered wise interpretations of foreign people, their religions, and the traditions they follow. Such men keep the centuries together and culture alive in the minds of human beings instead of crumbling to dust on a book shelf.

Sir Ronald Storrs, a fine soldier, and they say a brilliant administrator, understood the East and loved to tell stories about that old world. We had met several times in New York and London. That weekend at the Flowers', there had been general conversation at dinner, mostly on the Stratford performances, and, due to the company present, politics. When we left the dining room, Sir Ronald led me to a quiet corner and confided that in his bag he had brought a home-made anthology of poetry, prepared for T. E. Lawrence by Maurice Baring, poet and author. This book Lawrence had been reading, and it was found open on his desk after the motorcycle trip when he had sped to his death. The brother of T. E. Lawrence loaned it to

Sir Ronald, a close friend. This soldier expressed with emotion his admiration for Lawrence's accomplishments, none of which was really lessened by the arrogance of this complex man of genius when confronted by what he felt was false in spirit or purpose. Apparently he could be rude, as only a brilliant intellectual can be, when confronted by pretense or incompetence. Responding to my interest, Sir Ronald went to his room, and in a few moments placed the book in my hands. It was about two inches deep and approximately six inches long by four in width. The vellum cover bore the title, *Gepäck*. When our party disbanded for the night, I most gratefully took the volume with me and read far into the night.

Maurice Baring, poet and friend of poets, made several of these anthologies for intimate friends. They contained selections from anthologies including French, German, Italian—and, of course, many fascinating and unusual poems in the English language. Cut from their moorings they were pasted back to back with poems of Greek, Russian, Persian origin—occasionally a rare item was typewritten.

People said Baring must have mutilated many copies of the *Oxford Book of Verse* during this labor of love. Sir Ronald told me this was not so, the paper of the *Oxford Book* being too thin for such pasting; but in the making, he had "probably slaughtered hundreds of books." To hold this original work in my hands, with all its associations like an aura round it, was a precious experience.

In a speech, I once said:

> Where in history are there more picturesque figures than Amundsen and Captain Robert Scott, Cardinal Mercier and Lawrence of Arabia? These are men that poets will write legends about. Surely Arthur's Knights never imagined deeds more heroic than were performed on the British ship *Vindictive* at Zeebrugge, or by the French during the gallant defense of Verdun. Perhaps the crowning romance, and adventure of modern times is the redemption of the Holy Land by the British Army under the leadership of General Allenby.

The fact that Palestine was delivered from the Turks after four centuries of domination is profoundly moving to the hearts of millions of people. This conquest represents brilliant strategy and deeds of superlative courage. Courage is the most important word in any language, but it takes more than courage to inspire this blasé old world. Sometimes while conquering land or sea or air, men reveal qualities finer than courage; qualities that make our hope seem justified that we mortals have a kinship with eternal things.

"A chance fragment of a great star is our planet, and man as far as his physical framework is concerned, being of the earth, earthy, is therefore of the stars, starry." It wasn't only what General Allenby did, but the way he did it that will forever stir the imagination of mankind. The manner of his entry into Jerusalem, his modesty as he walked, not rode at the head of his troops; the deeds of mercy performed for the poor civilian population, have been described as "the civilizing march of the British Army." This modern crusader more than redeemed the Holy Land. He is one of those who have redeemed our period in world history from the slurring title of the materialistic age, as he modestly refrained from playing the conqueror during a great triumph.

7

THE GARDEN PARTY given June 9, 1939, by the British Ambassador and Lady Lindsay in Washington during the visit of King George VI and Queen Elizabeth was a lovely sight to behold. The Embassy garden, entirely the product of Lady Lindsay's horticultural knowledge and her devoted care, was at its peak of flowering beauty. The ladies wore elegantly graceful gowns; the gentlemen, dressed with attention to regulations as to what the well-dressed man must wear at a garden fete, royalty being present, looked smart but oh, *so* uncomfortable, for Washington weather registered the warmth of its welcome with 97 degrees Fahrenheit in the shade, and 87 per cent humidity.

The Queen moved among the throng of guests in a beguiling white muslin gown, carrying a dainty parasol, and looked positively ravishing. As we were presented, the men bowed low and the ladies dipped and dripped, but the King and his beautiful Queen were apparently untouched by the tropical jungle atmosphere of our capital city.

Lady Lindsay and her staff spent many hours studying the guest lists objectively in the endeavor to give as much pleasure to as many people as space would permit. Diplomatic requirement had to be considered, but the whole event was to be part of a public-relations demonstration. She and the Ambassador regretted that only 1,700 could possibly be present, and for months afterward, they felt the crushing burden of reproach of the uninvited, who, by force of circumstance, were legion. A friend sent me a Cleveland newspaper clipping of May 25:

UNCLE HAD IT SOFT

Lady Lindsay, wife of the British Ambassador in Washington, is American born. She is, in fact, a grandniece of General William Tecumseh Sherman, he of the famous three-word essay on the nature of war.

As she hears the shrill and tactless outcries from some of those who aren't invited to the embassy garden party for the King and Queen, Lady Lindsay must feel like whispering to the shade of her illustrious kinsman:

"Uncle Tecumseh, if war is hell, please think up a word to describe this job of mine."

Lady Lindsay told me a delightful incident connected with the royal visit. Mrs. Franklin Roosevelt, an old friend, telephoned to inquire if there would be any objection if she arranged to have little Diana Hopkins, whose mother had died not very long before, stand in line next morning to see the Queen before she started on her sight-seeing rounds. The Queen immediately replied, Could the child come a few minutes before eight that evening, when she would be leaving the White House dressed in full regalia, tiara, and the Order of the Bath, to attend the Embassy Dinner for President and Mrs. Roosevelt and the royal visitors? Her Majesty told Lady Lindsay, "In the morning, I shall have on a simple daytime suit. It would be much better if she can come at night. Any child expects to see a queen wearing a crown; the jewels and tiara are things she will like to remember."

The vitally important foreign policy of Anglo-American friendship never reached a higher peak than during the visit of this royal couple, who impressed everyone by their simplicity and their genuinely warm understanding of the average human family. They formed a perfect link between the people of Britain and the people of the United States.

PART SEVEN

Of all the noises known to men, opera is the most expensive.

—MOLIÈRE

Music is the universal language of mankind.

—HENRY WADSWORTH LONGFELLOW, *Outre-mer*

What is music, as the lifeless notes exhibit it? An outline to be filled, indefiniteness to be defined, dust to be breathed upon, clay to be made flesh, inertness to be made flame, the sleep-bound to be awakened.

—LAWRENCE GILMAN, *Toscanini and Great Music*

"Manhattan Island contained all the official 1,164,673 residents of New York City on 30 April 1880, when George H. Warren journeyed downtown to keep an appointment with August Belmont and three other gentlemen. The Brooklyn Bridge had not yet been completed; Madison Square was the centre of the city's social activities; and most of the area beyond Fifty-ninth Street was populated by 'squatters,' their children, and large numbers of goats. . . . the engagement was with Mr. Belmont in his official capacity as president of the Academy of Music's directorate, and with three fellow-members of that Board. . . ." *

The discussion centered on the proposal to build a larger opera house farther uptown with enough boxes to meet the fashionable demand which the Academy, largely for reasons of size, could not satisfy.

Among copies of August Belmont Sr.'s letters written to Colonel James Mapleson three or four years later, we find him urging the Academy of Music's impresario to secure the Musical Miracle Adelina Patti for the following New York season. Colonel Mapleson answered it would be impossible, as Madame Patti

* Irving Kolodin, *The Metropolitan Opera*, New York University Press, 1936.

insisted she already had signed a contract to sing before the sovereign Czar. Mr. Belmont replied, "Tell Madame it is better to sing before a sovereign people than one Czar."

In the heart of the theatre district of Manhattan stands, one might say without fear of contradiction, an ugly, dingy yellow brick building. Once inside the auditorium, we see a transformation take place. There, dignity and beauty reign. The warm red walls, the proscenium arch, gilt trimmed, induce memories. Memories, too, seem to float from folds of the gold curtain, the curtain that so often in rising and falling has revealed, then concealed greatness from view.

Since the opening of the Metropolitan Opera House in 1883, and its rebuilding after a fire in 1892, this unromantic-looking edifice has encompassed more beauty of sound than any other theatre in the United States. For accomplishment, it ranks with the top operatic theatres of the world. James Roosevelt, the first president, said: "We never expected that it would pay. No opera house in the world has ever paid as an investment, and none ever will."

My initial grand opera experience was as a standee. It had never been possible to hear a Metropolitan performance because of my own theatrical engagements. During the run of *Merely Mary Ann* at Madison Square Theatre, I met, at the home of an intimate friend, Mrs. Charles Robinson Smith, the dramatic soprano Milka Ternina. One night when she was singing Brünnhilde in *Götterdämmerung*, I almost telescoped the intermissions of *Mary Ann*, and after a hurried change, rushed to the Opera House. The curtain was going up on the last act. No seat was available so I stood throughout and heard Ternina interpret that glorious final immolation scene. The impression made upon me was profound, but no premonition warned me of the significant part opera would play in my future life.

In 1933 the Metropolitan Opera House was governed by two groups of directors: the Real Estate Board, which represented the stockholders who owned the building and the boxes; and the Opera Board, which controlled production. Signor Gatti-Casazza, general manager, for many years had directed the selection of artists and opera performances. Following World War I and the depression of the early thirties, maintaining grand opera was extremely difficult, to say the least. A splendid reserve fund accumulated from previous profits had melted away. Special contributions from stockholders were provided with more and more reluctance. Proceeds from brilliant benefit balls given several years in succession produced diminishing returns. In this predicament the board of directors was prepared to accept help from any source.

Cornelius N. Bliss, an officer of both boards, remembering unemployment fund-raising, suggested bringing a woman into the conservative circle and put my name in nomination. When I accepted the invitation to join the board, I felt an impulse to help avert unemployment, with which I was all too familiar, rather than any lofty idea of preserving an art. The Metropolitan Opera Company employs approximately six hundred people regularly, aside from occasional specialists. It is a fact that in war or depression the first to be affected are the artists, those of the opera, and to a lesser degree, the theatre. At such times, like jewelry and furs, the arts are listed as luxuries and are not considered essential.

My first meeting in May, 1933, was almost as difficult as an opening night in the theatre. It is not possible to say who was more perturbed, I or these formal gentlemen, several of whom were friends or had been cordial dinner partners. But mixed company on boards was far from a familiar sight at that time, and when I slipped into a chair, several of the directors looked solemnly uncomfortable. Missouri might have been their home state. As for me, I felt like misplaced matter.

Paul Cravath, board chairman, appointed me to the Executive Committee early in 1934. At the following meeting, he announced that unless real money were found within a month, a notice would be placed backstage indicating the Metropolitan Opera must end its career: a gloomy initiation! In a taxi with me on the way uptown, Mr. Bliss and Allen Wardwell vowed that the Metropolitan must not close. True to this pledge, Mr. Wardwell secured a gift of $100,000 from The Juilliard Foundation, and Mr. Bliss quarried $200,000 from other foundations and individual givers. These two musketeers saved the day which was, *that* day, a crucial moment in opera history.

Familiarity with danger may have given us a new perspective. What with war, union disputes and financial problems, opera has been perilously close to a shutdown on several occasions, but since that 1934 meeting, no brink on which we teetered has ever seemed quite so near to tragic finality. With solemn foreboding, every board member knew, and we always have realized, that should this opera close definitely, the loss to artists and the national community would be incalculable. To those who cared, the question then was, What must opera do to be saved?

Difficulties were accumulating, but one golden ray of light fell across our opera that next season as Kirsten Flagstad made her triumphant entrance upon the scene. When he retired, Gatti-Casazza said the contract he had negotiated with her was comparable to a $25,000 legacy left to the opera company—surely an understatement.

Nevertheless, the opera situation was more than serious; it was grim. As we studied the various problems, zealously seeking ways and means of assistance, we felt it important to broaden the base of responsibility for the future; to share in some measure privileges that had hitherto belonged to a small group of directors and stockholders. We thought of closer association with glamorous artists of the company; also, attendance at rehearsal, which had been one of my own delights as a box holder, and a channel through which tickets might be obtained. So, early in 1935, putting together piece by piece a mosaic of various ingredients, I presented to Mr. Bliss, chairman of the Executive Committee, a plan for a membership organization with specified privileges and services, in exchange for dues scaled from $10 to $100. It was agreed that a portion of each membership would go toward maintaining the opera.

My spine was stiff with fright when in April the Executive Committee approved this plan for an opera guild, and authorized me to take such steps as might be necessary to put it into operation. Democratization of the opera had begun! The nightmare-like imminence of the opera closing necessitated speed and faith. I kept reminding myself of the White Queen in Alice who practiced believing six impossible things before breakfast. The responsibility ahead gave me what an old friend described as "goose-pimples of pineappular shape and dimensions."

Robert Brewster, chairman of the Real Estate Board, asked, "Just how do you expect to get these members for your guild?" Mr. Bliss came to my rescue. "Probably Mrs. Belmont doesn't yet know exactly how, but if anyone can do it, she can." We had worked together in Red Cross and unemployment relief, so he knew the attempt might fail, but not for lack of effort by the newly appointed chairman of a Guild in embryo, a plan on a few sheets of paper, no more.

Cathedrals are built with pennies of the faithful. A great opera house also is a spiritual center, a temple of sorts, where many gather together for recreation, education, and inspiration—a blessed trinity worthy of public support. From this belief, the Metropolitan Opera Guild took form.

It was agreed money would be needed to finance the initial undertaking. The Opera Board approved an appropriation of $5,000. Feeling that the sky should be the limit in calling attention to the importance of this operatic cultural institution, by the first of August, I decided to invite a national group of sponsors, before presenting the plan to the public.

President Franklin Roosevelt, with a generous letter of endorsement, headed our list, and governors of nine states joined two hundred citizens of nation-wide distinction, including, of course, Fiorello La Guardia, Mayor of New York City. Mrs. Myron C. Taylor consented to be vice chairman.

Herbert Witherspoon, a distinguished American singer, had been appointed general manager in May, 1935, a few weeks before he died, and I invited his widow, Blanche Witherspoon, an extremely capable woman, to become Secretary. Evelyn Ploger, who had served with me through unemployment drives, was executive secretary. Supported by a fine board of directors, we were off into the wild blue yonder. Many searching questions were presented to us—the crop that usually arises with any change in the *status quo*. At last I went to place these puzzlers before the chairman of the Real Estate Board, Robert Brewster. One important question was, what is the position of the Opera House owners? Following my visit, he wrote:

R. S. BREWSTER
52 VANDERBILT AVENUE
NEW YORK

December 3, 1935

Dear Mrs. Belmont,

Here are some figures summarized from the books of the Metropolitan Opera and Real Estate Company, which you may wish to use, and I am sure that we would welcome your making use of them in any way you see fit. Of course I can give figures in greater detail, but at this short notice I imagine a summary is all that you can make use of now.

Since the present company was organized in 1893, the Stockholders have put the following amounts into the enterprise of enabling New York City and this country generally to have opera presented.

(1) Original subscription for stock $1,050,000.
(2) Mortgage on the building paid of $1,000,000.
(3) Annual assessments from 1893 to 1935 inclusive, for the payment of taxes, insurance and the like $4,994,500.
(4) Additional mortgage on the property $500,000., making a total supplied by Stockholders of $7,544,-500.

We have not definite figures of the costs to the old company which built the original house in 1883 and continued it until the fire in 1892, but we are satisfied that the capital loss was $1,459,867. What the old company paid in the nature of assessments during those ten years we do not know, but presumably they were assessed in those days just as the present Stockholders have been assessed since. Without allowing for any annual payments the total of the payments given above amounts to $9,004,367., which I think you will agree with me is a substantial contribution by a comparatively small group for the cultural advantages enjoyed by the people of this country and especially New York City.

> Yours very truly,
> Robt S. Brewster

A postscript pointed out that "none of the stockholders ever got anything in the way of dividends or interest on their investment." Of course they had the exclusive use of their boxes, which they occasionally rented or gave away.

2

SEASON NUMBER ONE for the Guild, 1935–36, saw Edward Johnson, the popular tenor, reluctantly assume the role of general manager of the Metropolitan Opera. A Guild "At Home" launched our first function in the Opera House and brought the new manager and his artists together with their devoted public. Nearly 2,000 members were recorded that year. From dues received, our Guild provided a much-needed cyclorama, upon the plain unpainted surface of which the chief electrician, with a skillful play of lights, presented sunrise, sunset, and moonlight to the delight of the new-found opera patrons. A cash surplus sent us on our way rejoicing, while more and more opera fans joined the Guild. Like the Peers in *Iolanthe*, we found wings.

Within a few months it became obvious that a medium of communication was needed to inform eager members of the ever-increasing activity of their organization as it entwined itself into every opera department. By a stroke of luck, we secured the services of Mary Ellis Peltz to help us with magazine articles and other means of promotion. The Guild gained immeasurably by the ability of this gifted walking encyclopedia on opera, and her missionary devotion to opera the world over has been a national and an international asset. After a trial issue of a Guild Bulletin in May, 1936, on recommendation of C. D. Jackson, a board member, the *MET Bulletin* was transformed to *Opera News*, the only magazine in America devoted exclusively to opera. Thanks to Mary Peltz, its dedicated editor for twenty-one years, it still brings information and delight to 60,000 avid readers, who in turn share their magazine with many others. The second year, Mrs. Witherspoon was engaged as director of the Guild. Again we were lucky to secure the services of this dynamic and resourceful businesswoman.

Earle R. Lewis, box-office wizard and assistant manager, suggested that schools should be encouraged to bring youth to the Metropolitan. So in the spring of the 1936–37 season, our first student performance of *Aïda* was given, and voices of teen-age enthusiasts rang through opera corridors. After that experimental matinee, opera house attendants collected a bushel basket of chewing gum from under the crimson plush seats! The next winter two operas were selected, and public, parochial, and private schools responded eagerly. Building opera audiences for the future has many compensations. Most important is the fact that teenagers from various backgrounds, who now-a-days have too many demands upon their interest, find opera first-class entertainment.

The Guild now sponsors six, occasionally seven, such performances annually. The music department in each school prepares the students. Tickets range from 75 cents to $4.00; and more than 21,000 high-school students attend. They come by bus, train, and subway from nearly 500 schools in New Jersey, Long Island, Connecticut, Westchester, and Greater New York. It is a thrilling sight to see the beautiful old opera house filled to overflowing with young people and their chaperons, who listen with rapt attention and ever-increasing appreciation to each matinee performance. Gum collections have decreased to the vanishing point!

Year by year, the Guild grew steadily. Meanwhile, support from the old stockholders' regime was crumbling. It became more and more evident that to maintain a permanent opera for New York and the nation, a complete change of policy was required. After lengthy negotiation in 1940, The Metropolitan Opera Association, under the leadership of Cornelius N. Bliss, launched a drive for $1,000,000 to purchase the theatre from the Metropolitan Opera and Real Estate Company, which had held title to the property since 1891. George A. Sloan was chairman. I was vice chairman.

Opera is an art to which talent and genius have contributed. Here was a cause to stir one's imagination and loyalty without tearing one's heart to shreds as war and unemployment had done. Association and Guild board members, artists, David Sarnoff and his splendid Radio Corporation of America, and the NBC network, which broadcast opera in those days, worked shoulder to shoulder with us to assure the Metropolitan's future in a home of its own. Final figures revealed that the Campaign Committee, the Opera Guild members, and the radio listeners through R.C.A. each had provided approximately one-third of the million-dollar goal; a total of nearly $1,300,000 was received. The following season, as the freshly made successor to the famous gold curtain gracefully parted, a new era dawned for our Metropolitan Opera.

Edward Ziegler thought he had made a good bargain and was preparing to sell the original gold curtain to a motion picture house for $100 when I snatched (figuratively speaking) the ten-ton antique from his hands, and had the dust of ages cleansed from its folds. The Guild sold it piecemeal for souvenirs: the result—almost $11,000. With this gradually assembled income we launched a student ticket service. Each year since then a given number of opera seats are sold at a 30 per cent discount to students and schoolteachers. The Guild compensates the box office for the difference in price. Long ago we sought and found other sources of income to replace that received from the curtain.

3

EDWARD JOHNSON (or Edoardo di Giovanni, as he was known in Italy during his operatic salad days) accepted the post of general manager at a critical time. Through the painfully lean years of closely rationed budgets that followed, he valiantly endeavored to keep costs under control and gave the board the complete co-operation essential to opera's survival. From time to time his artistic soul must have blushed. Several productions emerged from uptown storehouses literally dropping to pieces. The patchwork necessary to hold them together, plus a fresh coat of paint and some new costumes, he called "refurbishing." The Guild helped secure funds to provide this new look; but such a stopgap was far from satisfactory. The association's Executive Committee approved my recommendation that a production fund should be established and gifts sought for this purpose.

Shortly thereafter Lauritz Melchior, distinguished Danish tenor, broke his toe during a performance of *Die Walküre* when a stump crumpled under him. Even the usually uncomplaining Flagstad protested the appalling condition of *The Ring* cycle scenery. By sympathetic acclamation new sets were agreed upon. Lee Simonson was chosen by Management to design them and our adventuresome Guild undertook to raise the money for these four Wagnerian operas. "Gold for *The Ring*" we urged. The goal stated originally was $125,000; later it was increased to $150,000; we raised $165,000 but it took two years to do it. Lauritz Melchior and Helen Traubel were the first contributors. Walter Damrosch made speeches for the cause and aided by his family, a fine clan, helped us considerably.

These new productions were received with mixed emotions. Strangely enough, artistic originality, cleanliness, and sturdiness held little charm for our audience. The fact that gods of Valhalla had to move up and down long steps cut from rocks troubled the faithful Wagnerites even more than it did the singers. "Why did the Valkyries wear red cloaks instead of the old blue ones?" A giant tree in Hunding's hut "took up too much room." Where was the tree that since childhood they had seen on the right in the last act? et cetera, et cetera. I asked a Guild member who had twice given a generous gift, "How do you like your new sets?"

A shrug of the shoulder signified "so-so," and she added mournfully, "You know, I *loved* those old rags." Tradition is deeply embedded in the hearts of opera-goers at the Metropolitan.

In twenty-two years, through special fund drives and annual contributions, over and above opera tickets sold to members or many other services, the Guild has given the Metropolitan nearly

$2,000,000. Incidentally, it is pleasant to think that the original underwriting allowed by the Board remains untouched. Lawyers might say that commitment would be outlawed today by the statute of limitations.

Frequently people ask, To what do you attribute the Guild's success? Our answer must be, First, an idea; then, a hard-working, music-loving board of directors and a devoted staff. Extraordinary co-operation was forthcoming on the part of Edward Johnson and his associates, Edward Ziegler and Earle Lewis. Above all, we had hitched our wagon to The Metropolitan Opera Company, a galaxy of glamorous people. Then, too, our members have followed with particular pride the young American artists who today, by their individual performances, and through their recordings, command admiration in every country where grand opera is known.

4

THE SATURDAY MATINEE BROADCASTS opened a glorious new world to people far removed from any opera center. Due to a ruling of the Federal Communications Commission in 1940, the National Broadcasting Company, which controlled both the Blue and the Red Networks, was compelled to surrender the network over which Metropolitan Opera was broadcast. Ultimately the Blue Network was transformed into the American Broadcasting Company. During the season of 1940–41, the Texas Company became a sponsor for the Saturday opera broadcasts, and a more co-operative sponsor could not be found. The company pronounces the radio listeners to the opera broadcasts the most loyal audience of any program it now sponsors. The gratitude the letters convey, the appreciation of the beautiful performances, have made daily office work, even begging for funds, worth while. Broadcasting for me resembled an "Experiment in Time," because hundreds of people writing about the Metropolitan Opera have added their remembrance of *Mary Ann, The Dawn of a Tomorrow,* and *Salomy Jane.* Linking present with the distant past in this friendly way has been a happy experience.

Speaking of a new era, in the spring of 1941, Edward Johnson served as master of ceremonies at the first television opera to be presented by the Metropolitan Company. An act of *Pagliacci* was sung in the National Broadcasting studios under the baton of Frank St. Leger.

5

WE USE IMPORTANT WORDS too frequently and they lose value; for instance, *charm* and *great*. An actor or musician often is proclaimed *great* when we really mean he is *outstanding*. Consequently, on those rare occasions when the miracle of greatness shows its amazing head, to say he or she is a great artist seems understatement.

Fiorello La Guardia, when he first met Kirsten Flagstad, is reported to have said, "A hundred years from now I shall be remembered because I was Mayor of New York City when Flagstad sang here." A compliment does not need to be 100 per cent true to be a gracious tribute. The Mayor found a charming way to salute a great artist.

One morning following a performance of *Die Walküre*, I met Flagstad in the auditorium. She had been rehearsing Isolde. We talked of the ecstatic enthusiasm of the audience the previous night. I said, "Madame, you outdid yourself. What happened? Your Sieglinde was inspired."

A radiant smile flashed across her happy face, and she answered, "My husband arrived yesterday from Europe."

Perhaps this gave me understanding when she left for Norway via Lisbon in April, 1941, disregarding warnings from George Sloan and others that she might find it impossible to get back to this country during the war. The United States was still neutral and we clung to a slender hope that, being the world-renowned Flagstad, she might get through; such artists are privileged people. In any case, she had purchased a return ticket from Portugal in September.

December found our country plunged in war following the Pearl Harbor tragedy. Occasionally through the turmoil and anxiety of the following years rumors floated about, but little definite news of Flagstad was available. Years later, after many misunderstandings had been cleared away, a visa was granted for her re-entry into the United States. From her concerts so courageously presented, we realized that she still had a voice, and what a voice!

Steadily the conviction grew with some of us that the greatest woman singer of our century should be heard again in the Opera House. The question was how to bring it about. Lauder Greenway, an officer of the Metropolitan Opera Guild, agreed with me and arranged that we three should lunch together in order to find out her wishes. A peak of accomplishment seemed within reach when Madame declared that she "loved the Metropolitan Opera," as well she might: it had provided an opportunity for her magnificent musical contribution to America. This was, of course, coupled with the prestige that comes of being a Metropolitan artist. Flagstad was leaving in a few days for Europe, but we discovered that she had sixteen free dates next season that could be made available. I asked, given her choice, which role would she prefer to sing at her opening performance. The answer was prompt, "Elisabeth." This conjured up a thrilling vision of her entrance to the Hall of Song in *Tannhäuser*, singing *Dich, teure Halle.*

We were thrilled by the prospect of her return and I hurried to Edward Johnson to report the interview. He agreed that the time had come to secure the consent of the Metropolitan Executive Committee and to discuss return dates with Madame's manager. The majority of the committee approved; it looked like clear sailing ahead. At this moment, Walter Gieseking was scheduled to appear at concerts in Chicago and New York. When he landed in America, protests were immediate; in the midst of violent controversy, his concerts were canceled and this artist returned to Europe. The situation with Madame Flagstad, politically or otherwise, was not comparable, but aroused war emotions threatened again to divide both board and audience. The tide of public opinion was too strong. Two years later Rudolf Bing announced for his first season as General Manager in 1950–51, the return of

Madame to the opera she had adorned so gloriously before the war.

Her interpretation of *Alcestis,* in which role she decided to make her farewell appearance, was a triumphant creation. Her final performance at the Metropolitan in April, 1952, was an artistic achievement. Olin Downes said, "No artist could take a nobler farewell of her public." The effect upon the audience ranged from cheers to tears. Flagstad has left memories that some day may be equaled, but certainly they will not be surpassed. After her last performance on the Metropolitan stage, she wrote:

Chicago, April 12ᵗʰ 52

Dear Mrs. Belmont,

It is difficult, if not impossible, for me to put into words my thanks to you for your wonderful loyalty through the difficult as well as the good years of my life here in America. I have always known how you have stood by me.

It was a very touching ceremony at the Metropolitan on April first and I was glad to have Mr. Sloan announce from the stage that you had written the beautiful tribute engraved on the cup.

Now that I have come to the end of my "professional" road in America I must tell you that happily for me the good memories so far out-shadow those of unspeakable sorrow, that the latter need never be thought of.

Thank you again for your friendship through the years and for your efforts to make life pleasant for me here in this grand country, which I love dearly.

With warm greetings.
Sincerely yours
Kirsten Flagstad

I was haunted by memories of an unforgettable performance of *Walküre* given in the early days of Flagstad's connection with the Metropolitan (February 16, 1939), when Friedrich Schorr was Wotan; Lauritz Melchior, Siegmund; Elisabeth Rethberg,

Sieglinde; Risë Stevens, Fricka. In his review in the New York *Herald Tribune,* Lawrence Gilman wrote: "Even a respectable performance of the final scene of 'Die Walküre' is affecting. A good one is irresistible. A great one is unbearable." Although the *Alcestis* performance was beautiful, I had visions of seeing Flagstad make her farewell as Brünnhilde, and after the great scene of pleading and farewell, being put to sleep by Wotan with protective flames mounting around her.

6

THE SAME SEASON of the *Walküre* performance to which I refer, a handsome dramatic Australian, Marjorie Lawrence, sang Richard Strauss's *Salome,* and waited for an opportunity to be heard more often in Wagnerian roles. She had been called the most adventurous of Brünnhildes because she rode the horse Grani off stage in the last act, instead of leading him away to the funeral pyre. Miss Lawrence had been chosen as next in line to catch the torch from the hand of Flagstad when the Norwegian star left America in 1941. While on a concert tour in Mexico, she had been cruelly stricken with polio, and was unable to fulfill her promised destiny as Flagstad's successor.

"The Guild," to quote *Opera News,* "has formed a bridge between the public and the opera company." The loyalty of our members has been valuable to the artists; the artists, in turn, have been unendingly generous, by their art and mere presence, making our luncheons, receptions, and the like memorable affairs. The most poignant occasion I remember, when the Guild demonstrated its strength as a span of communication, was the luncheon marking the return of Marjorie Lawrence. After a long and brave fight against the crippling polio, she came back to sing for us—seated on the hotel stage. Bruno Walter, a poet conductor, recently returned from war-tortured Europe, had accepted our invitation to be an honored guest and to speak. As a souvenir of an eventful day marked by emotion, he gave me a page of his handwritten notes:

Men and events stand in the glaring light of historic glory today and disappear tomorrow, and we may ask: What has remained of all this danse macabre? What has proved durable in those dust storms of history? A question of problematic meaning. Certain is one thing: Survival of Mozart's *Nozze di Figaro*, of Beethoven's *Fidelio*, Gluck's *Orfeo*. This we may call a sort of survival of the fittest. The good genius of mankind seems to condemn to oblivion so-called great historical events and to grant duration and immortality to creative works of the human spirit. On a former occasion I tried to express this thought in a drastic way by the words: "Napoleon is dead, but Beethoven lives." But, of course, Beethoven, Bach and Mozart are not yet fully alive by their works alone. This is the case in other arts, with Michelangelo, Rembrandt, and Van Dyck. But our great composers have to be performed in order to survive. They live on the efforts of the interpreting artist; their survival depends on the work of institutes like the Metropolitan Opera, the Philharmonic-Symphony Society.

Here then lies the responsibility of the Metropolitan Opera, here is our task, and so we will continue in our artistic activities, consoled and satisfied that for the sensitive ear the song of the little bird in the medieval poem had perhaps a deeper sense than the thunders of destruction. And you, the Metropolitan Opera Guild, you have chosen to assist the great old Institute in its task and to do whatever you can to serve in this valuable way your country. And everyone who has a comprehension for the values here at stake must feel deeply indebted to you and wish you all success in your noble endeavor.

7

IT HAS ALWAYS BEEN a matter of regret that our opera had no endowment and perforce has led a hand-to-mouth existence. During the Guild's early years, we made an effort to impress upon our friends that the time was ripe to take the first step. Inspired by a statement that the great Harvard University was founded on a gift of 800 books and $1,000, the Guild started a fund for an opera reserve. A modest beginning of $35,000 was the result, but the ever-present need to keep the curtain up was paramount, so no further effort has been made along this line.

Early in the Guild's history, *Time* magazine stated in its own inimitable style that we had "put the tin cup on the shelf." The figure is appropriate in that the tin cup was not presented as the immediate obligation of our membership. They were offered privileges with more in actual cash value than the dues paid. Money, although an important objective, was a by-product. So were the increased subscriptions, the various funds and gifts to the Metropolitan. To create general public interest came first; then, to get people into the opera house was our aim.

Today the situation has changed. More people wish to attend opera than the house can hold. Production costs have risen, yet with rising taxes few private funds are available to meet them. The tin cup cannot be consigned to the shelf, and ways and means for further revenue continue to face us as a major concern.

The awareness and responsibility of the vast radio, television and recording audiences must be further developed to keep opera alive. Such is the challenge of the future.

When Mr. Johnson definitely decided to retire after twenty-eight years with the Metropolitan—thirteen as a leading tenor and fifteen in the high office of general manager—we arranged a gala performance in his honor. It was a memorable occasion in which every one concerned wholeheartedly gave their services. Advance prices for tickets brought net profits that night to $51,000. Following the example of his predecessor, Giulio Gatti-Casazza, Edward Johnson generously agreed that this fund should become part of a reserve for the Metropolitan.

Following a performance of *Tosca* with Ljuba Welitch in the title role, the stage was set for the last act of *Nozze di Figaro*. For a grand finale, the principals in famous operas during Johnson's regime moved forward in appropriate costumes down the beautiful stairway, while chorus and ballet surged on from the wings and our fine orchestra played familiar music from each opera. When beloved Lucrezia Bori appeared in the *Traviata* group, the audience applauded wildly. Finally all departments of the company crowded around as Edward Johnson walked on stage to receive a standing ovation, in which gratitude mingled with admiration and affection. The gala came to a close as we, the company and audience, sang "Auld Lang Syne."

8

THE QUESTION of new productions was accorded first place on the agenda when Rudolf Bing accepted the post of general manager. As he saw the future, productions were of pivotal importance, and with courageous determination he pushed the point by every means at his skillful command. In his first five years he has presented three completely new productions each season, made possible by generous special gifts for this purpose. In a season's repertory which provides twenty to twenty-five operas, refurbishing of necessity continues its undistinguished way, but these days it plays a minor, not a major, role.

Mr. Bing and his associate managers, Max Rudolf, Reginald Allen, John Gutman and Francis Robinson, deserve great credit for many outstanding accomplishments. Today public interest surges around the old house, drawing visitors from all parts of the globe. Metropolitan performances are a major attraction, and each year of this regime has seen a steady advance in season subscriptions, the life blood of our opera. Best of all, it is a comforting realization that if grand opera is your quest, you might travel many thousands of miles today and not find better casts or more beautiful performances.

Opera troubles are not all financial. To paraphrase Joyce Kilmer and his tree, only God can make a tenor, and the supply is never large. Moreover, the best training in the world cannot produce great singers; they are born, not made, although hard work is always essential, with the result that opera occasionally suffers from underproduction of its most necessary commodity. War is definitely responsible for part of the shortage.

"Auditions of the Air" annually bring to the Metropolitan talented young singers with excellent voices, but little or no acting experience. Mr. Johnson, ever-mindful of the opera's poverty, sighed for dollars necessary to engage an instructor, and our sympathetic Guild enabled him to start a training program that every year has been increasingly useful.

A Guild vice chairman, Mrs. Joseph B. Long, who became keenly interested in this joint experiment, bequeathed funds amounting to $435,000 for similar training. As one of three trustees she appointed, I gratefully participate in services performed by the Kathryn Long School, which we established in her name. The faculty is drawn from the Metropolitan roster of producers and conductors, under the skillful direction of Max Rudolf. These specialists are supplemented by teachers of language, stage deportment, fencing. The Long classes, without fees, serve young members of the opera company; also a few finalists on the audition broadcasts are accepted. All participants will not achieve the Metropolitan stage, but students acclaim the training they receive, which will be beneficial in any musical field.

9

THERE IS a vital force in rumor. Though crushed to earth, to all intents and purposes buried, it can rise again without apparent effort. Rumor has it that men do not care for opera. Women frequently say, "I love it, and would come often, but my husband won't stand for it." Our experience reveals that almost as many men as women revel in opera. Of course frequently they are not married to opera-minded women.

It was a man who took over when, after thirteen years of Guild leadership, I refused to stand for re-election and we persuaded Lauder Greenway to accept the post of president. His administration was outstandingly successful, resulting in an exceptional growth of friends for the Guild. He resigned to become chairman of the Metropolitan Opera Association. Langdon Van Norden, with zeal and ability, now heads the Board. Richard Leach succeeded Mrs. Witherspoon as director, and the Guild marches on.

10

BECAUSE OF MY experience in the cruel years of unemployment, the Guild started early in its career a retirement fund for employees. The Metropolitan, due, alas, to its hand-to-mouth existence, has no such compensation to offer but tries to meet each case as it comes along. Yet steadily its operations have improved. Voluntarily the board adopted Social Security before it became law, and an expanding severance fund program was started in 1946.

At times it is difficult to believe that singers are mortals, but automobile accidents, heart attacks, strokes, and the like descend without discrimination. Unfortunately, the Metropolitan never possessed a reserve to meet such emergencies. The custom was that after the blow fell, a collection was hastily taken up—a slow, haphazard method of assistance. When Richard Strauss's charming *Arabella* was presented for the first time in New York, George Sloan and I used the occasion for a benefit to establish an employees' welfare fund. The present reserve is modest in size, around $45,000, but a start has been made, and means are at hand to provide prompt assistance when need arises.

George Sloan's effort to develop national support was unceasing. Letters and gifts that flooded the office in response to radio and other appeals during opera fund drives were encouraging. Continually we discussed ways to strengthen interest in this unique institution. One day I proposed that we form a National Council for the Association. It should be advisory in nature, with roughly two hundred representatives, drawn from every state. We hoped we might expand the artistic usefulness of the company, and at the same time foster interest in its survival. The board approved the idea, set up a committee, and off we went! Contributors from east to west who were civic-minded, even if not opera conscious, were listed, and included many known to us only through generous campaign letters.

The first season, 110 members were reported from 23 states. From National Council membership funds totaling $70,000,

$50,000 were contributed toward a new production of *Bohème*. Our committee recommended that the National Council should be led by a chairman selected from a state other than New York, with several vice chairmen representing different areas of the country.

The Metropolitan Opera Guild and the National Council in the season 1956–57 contributed in money alone—aside from educational and many other important services—$180,000; a modest but definite evidence of a people's appreciation of a great art.

Opera unquestionably is on a forward march in the United States. Through its editor, *Opera News* has kept a maternal eye on the steadily increasing enthusiasm for opera in civic companies, university workshops, grass-roots experiments; their efforts, their accomplishments for years were faithfully highlighted.

In the spring of 1954, Mary Peltz returned from a visit to several such out-of-town productions. Impressed by their evident devotion, she was also distressed by the multiple problems that confront the majority of little opera groups in America. At the moment when she reached out to report her findings to me, I telephoned her to discuss a contemplated National Council development for an opera service with these groups. We pooled our ideas and forthwith agreed to urge the National Council to form an information bureau for opera-producing companies. We believed that through the council, with its representatives, useful information could be made readily available in a multiplicity of ways to any opera unit that desired professional assistance. Obviously, the service would be strengthened by leadership and the essential know-how of the great Metropolitan Opera.

In spite of a fantastically heavy work schedule during the opera season, Mr. Bing and his associates co-operated splendidly. The National Council president, Mrs. Frederick Weyerhaeuser, and her Executive Committee called a conference of opera-producing groups; 60 representatives from the North, South, East and West attended. With their assistance, the plan to form a Central Opera Service was born.

Boris Goldovsky, Director of the New England Opera Theatre, and Mrs. Norris Darrell for the National Council, were ap·

pointed co-chairmen of the project. In the two years the Central Opera Service has attracted over 200 opera units in 28 states, including settlement-house and television experiments. Information is exchanged daily about questions of repertory, translations, musical scores, casting, scenery, and costumes. Through meetings and correspondence, mutual problems are presented and the best solutions possible are found to the tantalizing question of how to produce opera in any community with reasonable financing or with the all-too-familiar and fragile shoestring support. Once again the fact has been made apparent that "union gives strength."

Like a will-o'-the-wisp, the idea of a new house for the Metropolitan Opera has flitted before the eyes of New Yorkers for the past thirty years at least. Not so long ago a Federal bill was drafted proposing that Congress should establish a site and approve the building of a National Opera House in Washington. In 1936, someone had sent me a plan which seemed to propose the creation of an American Stratford-on-Avon in Washington. Knowing Winthrop Ames's unfailing interest in theatre affairs in spite of his retirement, I forwarded the plan for his comment. By return mail came the following:

TEL. EASTON 7

WINTHROP AMES
NORTH EASTON, MASS.
26 Oct. 36

Dear Eleanor,

. . . It seems to me a *perfectly swell* idea IF (1) there would be an adequate sustaining audience; IF (2) enough actors of sufficient genius could be found and kept; IF (3) genius producers were available; IF (4) sufficient money could be raised.

I don't like the role of Doubting Thomas, but I must confess little nasty doubts on all four of these trivial minor points do keep creeping into my mind.

By the way, I wonder if you've ever thought of starting an entirely new Metropolitan Opera? *My* idea would be that (1) you should first build another, and perfect, Opera

House. (2) Engage better stars, chorus and conductors (3) Make only perfectly directed and staged productions (4) Give an entirely new set of operas—all works of genius (5) Play at cheap prices & so ensure popular support. I confess I don't know anything about running Grand Opera, but the above seems to me a perfectly swell scheme, too. Aren't you enthusiastic? !

Lucy sends her love, as I do mine. . . .

Yours always,
Winthrop

Many bemoan the fact that ours is the only great nation that does not provide a subsidy for opera. George A. Sloan frankly stated his fear that government subsidy might be accompanied by interference with artistic administration. After the war ended, with untiring determination he marshaled effective aid to remove the tax on opera tickets, realizing that this tax threatened to make the Association's fund-raising burden too heavy to carry.

Those who have struggled to maintain opera have dared courageously to face heavy deficits to insure its survival. Is it not true that with religion, art, a child, or a cause, what you believe in and defend becomes doubly precious? Humans are proverbially careless about things they get for nothing. During the past twenty years we haven't merely "maintained" the Metropolitan. Constructive steps have been taken that will make for a more efficient institution when the company goes into its new home in Lincoln Square, sustained by a constantly mounting public faith in opera. Let us admit that opera which continues to inspire devotion while it fights for existence has some sweet compensations. Nevertheless, it is hazardous living, especially for hard-working artists.

Personally, I dream of a time when our country will realize the value of Old World cultures, some of which require, but cannot afford to experiment with, opera in modern dress. I firmly believe the United States government should recognize an obligation to the questing spirit as well as to the physical body of its citizens. If only the bare bones of a subsidy were provided, then interested public effort could be expended on embellishments rather than on the eternal struggle for existence.

The British Arts Council offers an excellent pattern—to be adjusted, of course, to American conditions and requirements. Meanwhile, the nation grows increasingly opera conscious, and step by step, our Metropolitan Opera forges ahead, adding to its world stature as a unique center of musical art, expanding its service to the nation. The Metropolitan is more than a noble house; it is a noble institution. We love it well. My belief is that for this—our national opera—the best is yet to come.

PART EIGHT

I am of the opinion that my life belongs to the whole community, and as long as I live it is my privilege to do for it whatsoever I can.

I want to be thoroughly used up when I die, for the harder I work, the more I live. I rejoice in life for its own sake. Life is no "brief candle" to me. It is a sort of splendid torch which I have got hold of for the moment; and I want to make it burn as brightly as possible before handing it on to future generations.*

—G. B. Shaw

* Archibald Henderson, *George Bernard Shaw: Man of the Century* (New York: Appleton-Century-Crofts, 1956), p. 710.

I HAVE NOT ATTEMPTED to place events in chronological order, but have allowed memory to roam over the years. When one starts reading old letters, diaries, and such, memories surge forward like traffic in a crowded thoroughfare. Any attempt to record them involves selection. Why some events, trivial perhaps, are etched upon the memory while others, more important, are vague is a mystery.

This story began with the theatre and now, after covering a span of many years, it comes back to the theatre, always a subject of interest in spite of the variety of other things that have filled my life.

An offer to return to the theatre that I have not mentioned came in 1928 from St. John Ervine, an ever-delightful author and friendly companion. He sent by messenger a manuscript he had discussed with me, *The First Mrs. Fraser,* and this note:

Heaven tells me that you are intended to take the part of Mrs. Fraser. Can you confirm Heaven?

For better or worse, I could not and did not, but the invitation was appreciated.

The evening before he had come to take me to dinner and

the theatre. We stood at the window of my apartment watching the spring sunset and a beautiful new moon reflected in the reservoir outside.

"How lovely that view is; like the Lake of Como," he said wistfully.

"Yes," I murmured, not wishing to break the spell. After a pause I added truthfully, "I have never seen the Lake of Como."

"Neither have I," said St. John Ervine.

In 1957 when I finally was engaged in writing my memoirs, it became essential to receive permission to quote the letters to be included. Among others I wrote this author mentioning that in case he had forgotten me, we had met under such and such circumstances, to which he replied:

Honey ditches,
Seaton, Devon.
Tel. 154.

MONDAY,
4th March, 1957

Dear Eleanor Robson,
    For you will always be Eleanor Robson to me, who remember vividly the first time I saw you, so charming and attractive as Zangwill's Mary Ann, that even now I have no need, 53 years later, I have no need to shut my eyes so that I may more easily visualise you in that pleasant comedy. I can see you as plainly with my open eyes as I can with them shut. How often have I seen you? That time, then two or three times in New York, and then, the last time, in London when you stayed in a quiet hotel off Picadilly—six or seven tiimes altogether—and yet I feel as if I had known you intimately all my life. (You will observe that I am the world's worst typist. This is the second attempt I have made to write a flawless letter to you—and look at it! If I had to earn my living as a typist, I should die of hunger) Give up this raw misapprehension you have that anybody who ever saw you act, is capable of forgetting that enchanting fact. I was a youth of 21 when I saw your Mary Ann. I'm now 73, but I remember your performance as clearly and with as much pleasure as if I had seen it only yesterday.

Actors sometimes complain that their time is short, but is
that complaint justified? I'm sure that more people have
heard of Mrs Siddons than have ever heard of Voltaire.
The player does not die when all who saw him act have
been buried. David Garrick is better known than the philosopher, Hume. Don't you feel a glow of pride when I tell
you that you fulfilled the imagination of a youth of 21 so
brilliantly that now, more than half a century later, I can
still see you standing at the foot of a staircase listening for
the footsteps of the character played by Henry Ainley?
Multitudes remember Henry Irving and Ellen Terry who
cannot tell you the name of any of the Prime Ministers of
their generation. Out, out brief candle is stuff and nonsense
so far as players are concerned; and anybody who tells me
that you are capable of being out-outed by anybody who
saw you act, will cop a clout on the snoot from me.

The single complaint I have to make about you is that
you *didn't* play Mrs Fraser. God may forgive you for that
failure, but I shan't, though the tears will be running down
my cheeks when I withold my pardon.

Yes, of course, you may quote the line. You may quote
anything from me that you like, provided that you add a
footnote to say that the quotation fails to fulfill my intention
by acclaiming you as one of the most enchanting actresses I
have ever seen.

Will I call on you if ever I go to New York again? My
dear Eleanor, the ship will not have been berthed securely
before I am leaping off its deck to get ashore before anybody else, I shall be in such haste to speed up Fifth Aeve-
nue. . . . (Oh God, who can do anything, why didn't you
make me fairly efficient as a typist! But I doubt me much if
I shall ever travel anywhere again. Even a trip to London
makes me feel despondent. If I had been told in my youth
that a time would come when I could write *that*, I should
have derided the prophet as the ass of asses. Yet such is the
fact. I love my home and have no wish to leave it. Luckily
for me, everything in my life these days is full of delight. I
hear moans of alarm around me, but I do not believe a word
of them, and I remain certain that this nation is still a great
country, still full of good sense, still able to tell the younger

nations something that is good for them. Between the buoyant ardour of America and the despondent lethargy of Russia, there stands, unshakeable and essential to the good conduct of the world, the wisdom of this old nation which somehow contrives to retain the impulses of intelligent youth.

I sometimes wish I could return to the world once every century, so that I might see what the world has done with itself since I last saw it. A condition, of course, is that I should retain an exact memory of all I had ever seen on previous visits. On the whole, I think I should feel pleased; and I'm sure I should feel certain that the first fifty years of this century were one of the most impressive periods of history. Think, Eleanor, of the changes in general conditions we have all seen in that short time. In two respects alone, the status of women and the circumstances of the working class, the improvement in this country anyhow, is astounding. I never see ragged, barefooted children now, but they were plentiful in my childhood. If I see a boy in this small town without boots and stockings, it is because, having first taken himself out of his mother's sight, he has removed them, as I often did myself when I was a child, and tied the laces together so that he could sling them round his neck and go about the world like a confident, barefooted man who doesn't care too hoots what anybody thinks. Oh, dear, my typing is steadily deteriotating while I write, and I must stop or you'll send for the police and have me arrested as an incurable illiterate.

I look forward to reading your memoirs. Hurry up, time is not as long at it looks.

Yours affectionately,
St. John Ervine

2

BERNARD SHAW meant much to me in early days, and there is no more stimulating figure in the literary world of our day, so perhaps these pages should close with our last meeting.

I had not seen Shaw since the *Mary Ann* days until we met one summer at Glyndebourne. We were guests at a private operatic performance held in the large drawing room of John Christie's house. (Later Mr. Christie built a gem of a little theatre when he started the Glyndebourne Festival.) As Shaw and I strolled through the beautiful gardens during an intermission, I recalled *Major Barbara* and his letters to me at that time. He laughingly said, "They were probably love letters. Well, if you have any love letters of mine, better sell them. They would bring a lot of money today." In a way his advice was followed, for the letters were read to a large New York audience when we were using every means to raise money for the relief of the unemployed in 1931. John W. Davis, a true master of the English language, introduced me to the audience. The reading netted close to $7,000, and Shaw's letters remained in my possession.

In the spring of 1949, eleven years after my last visit to England as an American delegate to the League of Red Cross Societies meeting, I returned to London to see old friends, but primarily with the hope that G.B.S. would see me. However, so many years had passed since our last meeting that I hesitated to approach him directly. Therefore I asked our mutual friend, Lady Astor, if she would arrange an appointment and perhaps go with me. With unfailing generosity, she telephoned Ayot St. Lawrence to Mrs. Alice Laden, the housekeeper, asking an appointment for herself. Later she informed me that Shaw had been fractious lately, so no mention was made of my name on the chance that should the great man be in a bad mood and put her off, this would leave me free to find another avenue of approach. Eventually, it turned out to be a wise precaution, as G.B.S. declared that he was too busy to arrange an appointment. She telephoned once more, insisting that she was anxious to find out how he really was feeling. He sent word that he couldn't see her, but that he was "well and *very* busy." Again she telephoned that she must see him as she had promised Charlotte she would look after him. Back came the message immediately, "I absolve you of that promise to Charlotte."

Time was slipping by, and my visit to London was rapidly drawing to a close. Finally deciding to take matters in my own hands, I telegraphed asking if he remembered the young American for whom he had written *Major Barbara*, that I was in London but was leaving England in five days. I would go to Ayot St. Lawrence any time during that period if he would arrange an appointment.

Promptly, very promptly, a telephone message came from his secretary. He stated that Mr. Shaw would gladly see me the following Sunday any time after four o'clock, and that he was writing. Without delay I engaged a car for the trip. The next day a note postmarked June 1, 1949, arrived, mostly a printed form of instructions for reaching Shaw's Corner. There was also a generous space for a personal message in which he had written in the same delicate, but not quite so firm, handwriting of more than forty years ago. *After this turn avoid all roads signposted to Welwyn, which is 5 miles out of the way.*

FROM LONDON TO AYOT ST. LAWRENCE BY ROAD

1. Go out to Finchley Road through Swiss Cottage. Shortly before reaching the cross roads at Golders Green Station turn left along No. A 5092, signposted as leading to Mill Hill, Welwyn, and the North. About twenty miles further on, this joins the main north road A.1. beyond Hatfield. Keep on northward, avoiding a fork to the left at the Bull Inn, and another to the right to Welwyn Garden City. At the highest point in the road at the top of the long hill which follows, Ayot Green is on the left. Turn left across it at the signpost *marked to Wheathampstead, Harpenden, and Luton;* and presently bear right. After passing Ayot Station turn right under the railway bridge up a steep pitch. Bear left at the top; and at the church further on bear left again. Follow the lane as it winds about until you come out on a main road. Turn left along it for a short bit; and then turn out of it to the right at a signpost marked Ayot St. Lawrence. The lane twists about and rises and dips and rises again. At the top of the second rise, at a signpost marked to Welwyn, bear left into the village of Ayot St. Lawrence. Drive through it past the ruined church; and at

the end, where the road divides, Bernard Shaw's gate is facing you in the angle.

Time from London about an hour and a quarter.

2. To reach Ayot St. Lawrence from St. Albans, leave the town at the north end of the main thoroughfare by a road to the right signposted to Sandridge and Wheathampstead. After passing under the railway bridge in Wheathampstead turn to the right. About a mile further turn to the left up a lane signposted to Bride Hall. At the top of the lane, after passing a cottage, turn to the right and follow the windings of the lane past a block of two cottages on the right, then through a widened corner and up a short pitch. The hedge on the left of this pitch is Barnard Shaw's hedge; and his gate is at the joining of two roads at the top.

218 TELEPHONE:

CODICOTE (through Toll from London.)

Postal Address:

AYOT ST. LAWRENCE, WELWYN, HERTS.

Nearest Station:

WHEATHAMPSTEAD, L. & N.E., 2 Miles.

My dear Eleanor

Of course I remember, and am, it seems, remembered. But it will shock you to see a very old man instead of the brilliant author of Major Barbara. I cannot honestly advise you to come: I am no longer worth the journey.

However, if you are bent on it, you must come by car from door to door, as this is an otherwise inaccessible village. Without the above directions you will lose your way; but if you hire the car from Fred Day, Telephone Kensington 5257, you will have no trouble; he knows the way.

I shall be free after 4 o'clock on Sunday.

G.B.S.

This was too good an opportunity to miss. I cancelled the previous order for a hotel car and engaged the chauffeur mentioned. He turned out to be an exceptional man who told me he had taken Jawaharlal Nehru, Gertrude Lawrence, Vincent

Sheean, and many other distinguished callers to Shaw's Corner. Due to understandable impatience on my part, we set out from London well in advance of the time required to reach our destination, which was approximately thirty miles northeast of London.

The sky was gray, the air chilly, but the trip was, beyond belief, interesting, thanks to Fred Day; he out-stripped all acclaimed taxi drivers as a conversationalist. To begin with, he was an exceptionally good driver, a vitally important asset when driving along English country roads leading into or out of London any Sunday in June. He talked easily and with appreciation of the many visitors he had transported to Ayot St. Lawrence; also, he imparted choice tidbits of information about the great man who was at the end of the pilgrimage. As to Mr. Shaw's friends, it is safe to say that Prime Minister Nehru impressed him more than any other passenger, but undoubtedly the visitor whom he thoroughly enjoyed driving to Shaw's Corner on various occasions was Gertrude Lawrence.

As we moved through narrow lanes, he confided his aspiration to write a book about G.B.S. and his experiences with the various celebrities whom he had conducted in this connection. He talked knowingly about the United States and asked my advice about coming to America to live. In 1949, austerity was still the rule for everyone in England, and he yearned for an easier life and the comfort American dollars might bring. My personal opinion is that Fred Day would be worth meeting either as a chauffeur, author, or fellow-citizen.

In spite of the fascinating conversation and the traffic, we arrived within a few miles of Ayot St. Lawrence a full hour before the designated time for the interview. Therefore, Day suggested we should make a detour to see the noted Cathedral at St. Albans, which is well worth a visit—not just to pass the time, but for its own sake.

A rumor vouched for by his secretary tells us that when Mr. and Mrs. Shaw were looking for a country home, they came upon a gravestone at Ayot St. Lawrence which bore this inscription: *Jane Eversley, Born 1815—Died 1895. Her time was short.* Promptly Shaw decided that Ayot St. Lawrence was the place for him.

3

THE WINDING LANES of England, ribbon-narrow, lined with tall hedges, over which thrushes and other trusting birds vault grace-fully, were never built with a provision for automobiles, or with the machine age in mind. Progress is slow, and should be, as the roads are winding and hazardous. Finally, we reached the gate, nine minutes before four o'clock. Fred Day descended from the car, and with a sweeping gesture, slowly opened the double gate with "Shaw's Corner" woven in an arch across the iron pattern. He closed the gate behind us and delivered at the front door an eager visitor, literally trembling with anticipation.

The small sitting room into which the maid ushered me was simply furnished. A bay window at one end revealed an expanse of green lawn with a small summerhouse beyond, where Shaw did so much of his work. On the walls were various framed pictures of G.B.S.—one was even resting on a chair. The desk and the bookcase held a bas-relief, a bust, and a statuette of the author.

Opposite the window was a fireplace with gas logs, ready to offer occasional warmth for brief periods in chilly weather, and alongside was obviously the great man's chair, while directly in front of the fire, a couch offered both a cozy approach to the master of the house and the fireplace.

I had brought with me a basket of fruit, including uniquely flavored raspberries and half a dozen precious English peaches, some vegetable or other, and crowning the basket were two or three bunches of well-groomed tiny young carrots. Their fresh green tops made a lacy drapery around the edge of the basket. As the fruitful tribute to a vegetarian was assembled, I remem-bered a childhood episode when, for some sin of omission, the punishment had been to write in a copybook one hundred times, "Carrots are for horses." This remembrance was followed by the later recollection of the well-known critic, James Huneker, who years ago had written in an article on Shaw, "If he writes like this on vegetables, think what he could do on meat."

My fear had been that my host would arrive leaning on the arm of a nurse or secretary. Not at all! Punctually at four o'clock the door opened, and he stepped quickly into the room. He was dressed in a grayish-tan tweed suit. Plus fours suggested that he might be outward bound. Over his shoulder was slung a leather strap from which hung a small pair of field glasses.

Surprisingly erect, slender, keen of eye (as stage directions might indicate). Enter at door, left, G.B.S. Of course, he had changed. Even in a miracle man, twenty or more years must register at least a minor transformation. Yet in no outward way, appearance, or later in conversation, did he even suggest his ninety-three years.

A delicious tea was put before me. He took nothing. With interest he asked why the call of the theatre had never been strong enough to bring me back. We talked of wars; Red Cross; the problems of unemployment—and opera—opera in America. Finally we came to *Major Barbara* and his letters to me, one of which seemed important as revealing Shaw himself. "It is a frank outpouring of disappointment after the opening night; it is a good letter," I told him. "Everyone puts something of himself into his work, and this letter is a revelation of you at work."

He nodded thoughtfully; then with a puckish smile he asked, "Do you know Augustus John?"

Surprised, I said that my last sight of him had been two weeks earlier in Oxford. "I suppose you know that occasionally he . . ." Shaw crooked his elbow and lifted his hand to his mouth. After a nod from me, he continued, "In line with what you were saying about a man's putting something of himself into his work, John has painted me several times, but his portraits always make me look as if I were a heavy drinker." He chuckled at the thought of the drinks he had never had, except as they might be reflected in the work of Augustus John.

A portrait of Mrs. Shaw hung over the mantelpiece. To the comment that it was a charming likeness, he replied, "That was done several years before I knew her."

The drift of our conversation led quite naturally to Charlotte Shaw and the illness that ultimately caused her death.

Looking at me with a piercing and serious expression, he said, "The disease from which she suffered was arthritis. Her face was so disfigured that you would not have recognized her. Distortion is the principal effect of the special form of arthritis with which she was afflicted." He mentioned the medical term, *osteitis deformans*, I think. "It was not the extremely painful type, only as the disease progressed, her features changed; they became different beyond belief from the woman you knew. The night before she died, no—it must have been two nights—she came downstairs to dinner. Her appearance amazed me. Again she had changed, but remarkably. She looked almost as she had when we were married. I gave her my arm and we went into the dining room. Throughout the meal I talked gaily, entertaining her with news, gossip, jokes—anything that came to my mind. I reminded her of people and events we had not talked of for years. My idea was to charm her thoughts away from illness." He smiled. "I paid her compliments—I made love to her. After dinner, when I gave her my arm and we left the dining room, she looked incredibly younger. It was very strange, this transformation.

"The next day the nurse told me that she had had a bad night and was seriously ill. All during that day I went in and out of her room, cheerfully keeping up a gay chatter, telling her stories. I am not sure that she understood; probably not, most of the time. She was, as a matter of fact, slightly delirious. If she understood, I knew she would be glad to have me there. When I said 'Good night' and left her, she looked like that picture, even younger than when I had first met her. During the night, she died. They never called me. About 8:30 in the morning the nurse shook me by the arm and said in a cheerful voice, 'Mr. Shaw, wake up; your wife is dead.' I often wonder why people, nurses in particular, always tell you bad news in a cheerful tone of voice.

"After her death, messages poured in from all parts of the world. Everyone was very kind. They all said about the same thing; people sympathized with my grief; they were sorry for my loneliness. But—I did not grieve. Why, I did not grieve when my mother died. I was *not* lonely. I am *never* lonely.

"Over the years," he said impressively, "many people, a number of them artists, especially actors, have come and talked to me of their troubles, their losses. At times they have cried, even sobbed out their grief. Yet, in a short time—a year, two years at most, they have forgotten."

After a pause he repeated firmly, "I do not grieve; no, I am not lonely, but—I remember."

Altogether we talked for fifty minutes or more, reminiscing about the theatre in general, his Joan of Arc, about life as it had touched us both during the intervening years. Then I questioned, "How did you happen to write *St. Joan?*"

He answered quickly, "It was Charlotte. I seemed to have come to an end. I had no new idea, and one day I said, 'What shall I do now?'

"She answered, 'Joan of Arc.'"

"Oh no, dear friend," I said, "it couldn't have been as simple as that. Remember, you wrote in 1905 that you hoped Rostand was writing a Joan of Arc for me. You had been thinking about Joan a long time."

"For several years," he said, "I had read everything on the subject that I could lay hands on, both in English and French."

"So," I replied, "the fire was laid; your wife applied the match. The time was ripe."

He nodded. "I suppose so."

"Had you written Joan of Arc for me instead of Barbara, just think how totally different my life might have been."

"What have you been doing?" he asked. "I always thought you *had* to come back to the theatre."

He listened attentively as I told him of Red Cross and the other interests that had held me. Then he said, "Now I know why you didn't come back. You used your dramatic energy in other directions."

He told me that publishers were keeping him busy; hounding him, in fact, for a new book; magazine articles were underway;

also, that he was working on a play. The housekeeping problem was troublesome. At long last, he was moving from the London apartment he had lived in for so many years to a smaller flat. He remarked, "I should have moved from Whitehall Court after Charlotte died, but somehow—somehow, I didn't."

When I got up to go, he asked if I would care to go up-stairs while he went to see if the chauffeur was inside the gate. He had just returned to the front door, cane in hand, as I came down. When I commented enthusiastically on a remarkably fine set of bird pictures that lined the stair wall, his face lighted with pleasure, and he told me how much he valued his collection. We shook hands warmly. He said he was glad that I had taken the trouble to make the journey. As I entered the motor he said, "Wait a moment." Then walking with an incredibly firm, almost youthful, step along the gravel path to the gate, he went once more to see if the road were clear, for that corner is truly dangerous. A small crowd had gathered outside; evidently the sight of the broad iron gate, wide open, and an automobile at the door, suggested that the great man of Ayot St. Lawrence might be entertaining. The unknown has a mysterious fascination, and certainly Shaw's visitors were a mixed group—sometimes strange, yet frequently interesting, gifted people from the fields of art and politics, who came from all parts of the world.

His tall figure was silhouetted at the entrance, framed by the gateposts. He completely ignored, as if they were not there, the silent assembled villagers, some of whom had gotten off their bicycles and were patiently awaiting developments. After look-ing carefully to the right and left, G.B.S. waved his cane, beckoning Fred Day to follow. As we passed slowly through the gate and along the road, he waved a gay good-by to me. Looking back through the rear window, I saw him stand for a moment, cane raised high—a gesture of hail and farewell. Then he turned and walked briskly in the opposite direction along the lane. A bend in the road, and the high hedge hid him from view—or was it a mist that clouded my vision, as it does now, when memory once more reveals the most unforgettable character I have ever known.

> . . . I have heard of an eastern monarch who once charged his wise men to invent him a sentence which should be true and appropriate in all times and situations. They presented him the words, "And this too shall pass away." That is a comforting thought in time of affliction—"And this too shall pass away." And yet—let us believe that it is not true! Let us live to prove that we can cultivate the natural world that is about us, and the intellectual and moral world that is within us, so that we may secure an individual, social and political prosperity, whose course shall be forward, and which, while the earth endures, shall not pass away. . . . I commend you to the care of the Almighty, as I hope that in your prayers you will remember me. . . . Good-bye, my friends and neighbors.*

---

* *Abe Lincoln in Illinois,* Robert Sherwood. (New York; Charles Scribner's Sons, 1939.)

INDEX

White, Henry, 165, 254
White, Mr. and Mrs. Lawrence, 202-03
White Sister, The, 66
Whitney, Harry P., 86, 91, 103
Wilson, Woodrow, 116, 117, 122, 130, 131, 157, 165
Windsor, Duke of, 104, 105, 247
Wise, Stephen S., 145
Witherspoon, Blanche, 267, 270, 281
Witherspoon, Herbert, 267
Wolcott, Mrs. Frances, 78, 79, 80, 109, 111, 112
Women's Organization for National Prohibition Reform, 214-15, 216
Woodward, William, 83

Woollcott, Alexander, 111, 112
Woolley, C. Leonard, 205-06
Woolley, Katharine, 205-06
Woolley, Mary E., 229
Wylie, Elinor, 198, 200, 202
Wylie, Dr. W. Gill, 95, 96
Wylie, Mrs. W. Gill, 96

Yeats, William Butler, 17, 206
Yorke, Oswald, 49, 50
You Never Can Tell, 31, 34, 51

Zangwill, Israel, 23-24, 25, 26, 29, 34, 56; letters by, 26-27, 28-29, 53-54
Ziegler, Edward, 271, 273